MORMONISM AND WHITE SUPREMACY

MORMONISM AND WHITE SUPREMACY

AMERICAN RELIGION AND THE PROBLEM OF RACIAL INNOCENCE

JOANNA BROOKS

OXFORD
UNIVERSITY PRESS

OXFORD
UNIVERSITY PRESS

Oxford University Press is a department of the University of Oxford. It furthers
the University's objective of excellence in research, scholarship, and education
by publishing worldwide. Oxford is a registered trade mark of Oxford University
Press in the UK and certain other countries.

Published in the United States of America by Oxford University Press
198 Madison Avenue, New York, NY 10016, United States of America.

CIP data is on file at the Library of Congress
ISBN 978–0–19–008176–8

3 5 7 9 8 6 4

Printed by Integrated Books International, United States of America

In memory of my teacher Eugene England,
who opened freshman orientation at Brigham Young University
by writing out 2 Nephi 26: 33 on the chalkboard.

CONTENTS

Contents

CHAPTER 1

AMERICAN CHRISTIANITY, WHITE SUPREMACY, AND RACIAL INNOCENCE

This book seeks to instigate soul-searching—academic, institutional, and personal—on the matter of how American Christianity has contributed to white supremacy. When I use the term "white supremacy," I refer not only to the grossest forms of racist terrorism but also to the entire system of ideas, beliefs, and practices that give white people better chances based on perceived skin color and ancestry.[1] Racism is not a character flaw or extremist conduct; racism is the centuries-old construct that marked people with dark skin as available for exploitation—for advantage-taking of their lands, labor, bodies, cultures, and so forth. White supremacy is not just torches at Charlottesville. It is the fact that a Black woman in New York City is far more likely to die in connection with pregnancy and childbirth than a white woman—even if she has comparable access to health care, insurance, and education. It is the fact that the average Black family holds a small fraction of the wealth—assets, not income—the average white family holds, due in large part to slavery and past discrimination in education, employment, housing, and banking. It is the fact that African American men are disfranchised and incarcerated at astonishingly disproportionate rates, due in large part to laws that effectively continued the racial domination of slavery beyond its abolition. It is the fact that African and Latinx refugees are being held in indefinite detention or returned summarily to death threats in countries destabilized to the point of low-level civil war by American foreign policy. It is the fact that minoritized people must do additional spiritual

Mormonism and white supremacy. Joanna brooks, Oxford University Press (2020). © Oxford University Press.
DOI: 10.1093/oso/9780190081768.001.0001

and emotional work every day to safeguard their wholeness and the wholeness of their children. And it is the fact that these and so many other systematic inequities persist while white people sit in church and call it good. It is easy to see torches at Charlottesville and resort to our Sunday meetings to pray; it is not easy to look at our Sunday meetings and see how over time they have conditioned us to accept Black death and suffering by other peoples of color.

As a person of faith and as a scholar of religion, race, gender, and culture in America, I see a role for scholarship and teaching in unsettling and interjecting urgency into conversations around religion and race in America. When I look back, I can see that historical scholarship has focused on the clearest examples of good and evil: on the ways religion has been mobilized in the service of anti-racist activism, especially by Black churches, or, conversely, in the service of explicit forms of white racism, especially among white evangelicals in the American South.[2] But given that the definition of white supremacy has evolved to incorporate the quotidian systems of white privilege that structure American life everywhere, it seems to me that we need to evolve our discussion of the role American Christianity has played in securing and sustaining racial privilege more broadly.[3] The Reverend Martin Luther King Jr. famously called eleven o'clock Sunday morning "the most segregated hour in Christian America."[4] Fifty years later, the Pew Foundation's American Religious Landscape survey found that Protestant denominations like Presbyterianism, Episcopalianism, Congregationalism, Methodism, Lutheranism, and Mormonism still made up the bottom ranks of American religions in terms of racial and ethnic diversity.[5] While American Catholics were 59% white and American Muslims were 38% white, Pew found, mainline Protestants were 86% white and Mormons were 85% white. How do we understand this pervasive racial segregation of American Christianity? Is it an accident? I would like us to press deeper to investigate American Christianity as a mass culture that (even when it has not appeared explicitly concerned with "race" as such) has in fact contributed essentially to the establishment and maintenance of white supremacy broadly defined: the entire system of legal, social, cultural, and economic advantage that has benefited white lives at the expense of Black and brown ones. Progressive leaders and scholars of white American Christianity like Jim Wallis and Jennifer Harvey have urged white Christians to recognize racism as a national "original sin" that must be repented of through not only "reconciliation" but also "reparation."[6] My goal is to move the conversation yet another step by exploring how the predominantly white venues and denominations through which we have pursued the sacred and hope to pursue mercy and justice have themselves contributed—if unknowingly—to white supremacy.

We can start with the way American Christianity teaches its white practitioners about what it means to be "good" or "moral" and how it rewards that "goodness." Christianity takes as its central theological concern sin and redemption. Consequently, how American churches teach their adherents about sin—through instruction and through ritual—exerts tremendous influence on our individual and collective capacities for moral reasoning and problem solving. As the legacy majority religion in the United States, American Christianity has effectively furnished our national language for judging value, worthiness, guilt, and innocence and for establishing moral priorities to guide the allocation of resources and the application of power. It has instilled in white American imaginations notions of the good, the holy, and the evil that are permeated with racial privilege and fear. Predominantly white American churches have also fostered identity-based social networks among whites that have generated opportunity and advantage for white people. For these reasons, racial segregation of American Christianity must be understood not only as a testament to the powerful role of Black churches in creating domains for the experience of sovereignty, freer self-expression, and collective and individual care but also as a reflection of the role church spaces have played for whites to comfortably experience the same, often in the service of white privilege—which is to say, white supremacy.

I am particularly interested in white American Christianity as a technology for the production of what scholars describe as "racial innocence." The option to believe that one is "innocent"—morally exempt—of systematic and pervasive anti-Black racism is a privilege cultivated among, by, and for the benefit of American whites. James Baldwin observed the "willed innocence" of white America in his 1962 letter to his nephew "My Dungeon Shook," published first in *Progressive* magazine and then in 1963 in *The Fire Next Time*:

> They have destroyed and are destroying hundreds of thousands of lives and do not know it and do not want to know it. One can be—indeed, one must strive to become—tough and philosophical concerning destruction and death, for this is what most of mankind has been best at since we have heard of war; remember, I said most of mankind, but it is not permissible that the authors of devastation should also be innocent. It is the innocence which constitutes the crime. . . . There is no reason for you to try to become like white men and there is no basis whatever for their impertinent assumption that they must accept you. The really terrible thing, old buddy, is that you must accept them, and I mean that very seriously. You must accept them and accept them with love, for these innocent people have no other hope. They are in effect still trapped in a history which they do not understand and until they understand it, they cannot be released from it.[7]

White American Christianity has done a great deal to reassure white people and maintain us in our misunderstanding. It has sown into our imaginations a deep association of whiteness—as color, as symbol, as identity—with innocence and blackness with guilt. It has engaged Americans in performances and rituals designed to convey a sense of absolution or transcendence without moral responsibility. White American Christianity has also advanced one of the constituting mechanisms of whiteness by creating spaces that do not require white people to name their whiteness and acknowledge their privilege. According to American studies scholars like George Lipsitz and Anne DuCille, whiteness derives power from the fact that it does not name or acknowledge itself but rather assumes an unnamed role as an organizing principle of social relations and a driver of value.[8] Whiteness thus serves as its own alibi. It excuses itself; it refuses to speak its own name to make itself invisible and exculpate itself from agency and responsibility.[9]

Moreover, Christian concepts of innocence, sin, and retribution or redemption have been essential to legal reasoning around racial issues in the United States. There was a time early in the Christian movement when sin was broadly understood as a collective condition to be redeemed as gathered-in communities transacted with God and each other through the medium of Jesus Christ. Over time, and especially with the coming of Enlightenment rationalism, prevailing concepts of sin in American Christianity shifted dramatically so that it became somewhat normal to think of sin as an individual act to be expiated through transaction with the church. This greatly diminished understanding of sin was useful to a white American nationalism predicated on the belief that God had put white people on this land in a state of innocence to fulfill a divinely appointed mission. It allowed mainstream white American Christians to simplify morality, to associate it with the unknowing blamelessness of children rather than the hard-won wisdom of adults who make difficult choices.

Indeed, as critical race theorists have shown, the Protestantism-influenced formulation of moral wrong as individual "sin" requiring remedy provided the framework for the US Supreme Court's deliberation of cases involving school desegregation and affirmative action remedies to past wrongs. Unfortunately, this simplistic, incidental view of sin is totally insufficient and inappropriate, not only to capturing the systematic and collective dimensions of racism but also to the fullness of Christian theology as well. A more robust Christian conceptualization of sin would hold that it is a deadly but structuring condition of mortality, just as racism is a deadly but structuring condition of life in the United States. This more robust view of racism as sin would require individuals and institutions to conduct a moral accounting not only of their own conscious acts of harm or injustice but also of the way they have participated in and benefited from the entire system of harm and injustice that has meant death and suffering to others. As legal scholar Thomas Ross asks, "What white person is 'innocent,' if innocence is defined as the absence of advantage at the expense of others?"[10] By refusing a more complicated understanding of racism as a perpetuated and transhistorical system, judges and US Supreme Court justices have created the conditions for treating individual instances of segregation or discrimination as disconnected from earlier historical instances. This is a pattern legal scholar Neil Gotanda identified in Chief Justice Earl Warren's opinion in *Brown v. Board of Education* (1955), which treated *Brown* as though it were entirely unrelated to the issues raised in *Plessy* (1896). "Cut[ting] off the moral, social, economic and political ties to the past," the court thus affords whites, according to Gotanda, "the innocence of a new beginning."[11] The logic of the court allows each petitioner to present themselves as individuals outside of history, not as citizens whose standing obtains and takes shape in relation to fellow citizens with a shared history. Adopting a more responsible notion of innocence may also have prevented the court from barring even limited legal remedies like affirmative action on the grounds that they harm white "innocents" who bear no direct responsibility for racism, as the US Supreme Court found in several high-profile cases in the 1990s.[12] A simplistic version of white Protestantism has supplied US institutions with a limited moral reasoning that stands in place of and prevents the kind of collective work that would be required to consciously dismantle the legal, economic, and social infrastructure of white supremacy.

White American Christian churches have provided spaces where without acknowledging white racism white people can take refuge and experience belonging in shared white identity, build relationships and develop intimacies with people like themselves, cultivate opportunities from these relationships, and do so in the name of God. They have offered rites, performances, and salvific formulas that in exchange for a specific individual performance of piety (typically defined by heteronormatively married sexual monogamy, polite manners, and deference to authority) promise moral exculpation from the wrongs of history.[13] They have also through the auspices of missionary work sustained white supremacy by directing the energies of well-meaning white people into efforts to "save" darker-skinned peoples, whether by evangelism or by charity, without recognizing their own role in creating global inequities and conditions of deprivation. And in its construction of "morality" as a matter of being "good," white American Protestantism has played a role in the maintenance of white supremacy and structural racism by appealing to what Barbara Applebaum identifies as "white desires for moral goodness and innocence."[14] A more robust form of morality might recenter, Applebaum suggests, around values of uncertainty, carefulness, reflection, humility, openness to criticality, willingness to defer validation, listening, tolerance for discomfort, and gratitude for experiences that radically surprise, disrupt or "ambush," and transform consciousness.[15] In its mainstream institutional variants, white American Christianity has largely failed to cultivate in its adherents the sobriety and capacity for tolerating and learning from disruption and discomfort essential to dismantling structures of power. It has, in fact, stood in the way of and crowded out that more developed moral sense, like a cowbird in a robin's nest.

Asking what role religion has played in advancing white supremacy will require an interrogation of white silences in the effort to sound out the individual choices and tacit agreements that undergird white privilege. The work of interrogating white silences to understand how they work has been a matter of survival for people of color in the United States. As W. E. B. Dubois wrote in 1920:

> I know many souls that toss and whirl and pass, but none there are that intrigue me more than the Souls of White Folk. . . . I see these souls undressed and from the back and side. I see the working of their entrails. I know their thoughts and they know that I know. This knowledge makes them now embarrassed, now furious.[16]

This work entered the realm of academic scholarship with books like Winthrop Jordan's landmark study *White Over Black* (1968) and Toni Morrison's *Playing in the Dark: Whiteness and the Literary Imagination* (1992).[17] Calling out what Martin Luther King Jr. described in his "Letter from Birmingham Jail" the "appalling silences of good people," especially white people who frame their "goodness" in moral and religious terms, has been the work of Black theologians like the late James Cone, who in 2004 asked very directly why white theologians too committed the "sin" of "silence":

> Few American theologians have even bothered to address White supremacy as a moral evil and as a radical contradiction of our humanity and religious identities. White theologians and philosophers write numerous articles and books on theodicy, asking why God permits massive suffering, but they hardly ever mention the horrendous crimes Whites have committed against people of color in the modern world. Why do White theologians ignore racism? This is a haunting question—especially since a few White scholars in other disciplines (such as sociology, literature, history and anthropology) do engage with the phenomenon of racism. Why not theologians? Shouldn't they be the first to attack this evil?[18]

Cone extended this line of questioning in his landmark book *The Cross and the Lynching Tree,* which included an indictment of the arrogance of white Christians who pretended piety while steadfastly refusing to take on moral reckoning with the suffering of their African American neighbors, and even the limited moral vision and exasperatingly safe take on Christian morality offered by white theologians like the esteemed Reinhold Neibuhr.[19] If Neibuhr, according to Cone, held his privileged place as a globally recognized theologian in his office at Union Theological Seminary without seriously reckoning with the death and damage incurred by white supremacy, perhaps it falls to thinkers and writers outside religious institutions to do this hard, searching work. Given the historic role of universities as seminaries for the unorthodox and dissenting, American studies and religious studies can and I hope will take up this work of understanding how mainstream American Christian traditions have contributed to the maintenance of white supremacy. I hope that others working in different domains of white American Christian tradition will ask how rituals like confession, baptism, and worship produce public spectacles of innocence and redemption, construct moral responsibility, and promise a way out of the deeply complex and coimbricated histories of racialization and discrimination. Many of these rites have been marked as "outside" the domain of "politics" and hence race, but to what extent must we read this referral elsewhere as the consequence of a mutually negotiated agreement between religion's providers and its adherents to produce a form of comfort that leaves privilege undisturbed and structures unchanged? In the United States, is it possible to speak of religion as such, on its own terms, as innocent, a given fact, an antecedent condition, and racism as its sequel, or has religion in the United States been developed as a set of practices in the service of racial hegemony—either its resistance, its promotion, or its quiet maintenance? Research on the Black Church leaves little question that the Black Church was the product of American racialization and racism. Does it not reinscribe narratives of ahistoricity and white innocence to assume that white churches are not to a great extent the same?

In this book, I will pursue these questions through the medium of Mormon history and culture. I grew up a true-believing white-identified Mormon girl in a religion and a region carved up by anti-Black racial segregation. I was born a fourth-generation *Angeleno* with Mormon pioneer and mixed-race Okie ancestry, in Lynwood, California, a predominantly Black municipality of Los Angeles, and raised in white-flight Southern California suburbs. I was taught to see Los Angeles and its surrounding environs street by street, freeway by freeway, as "safe" and "unsafe" zones, so inscribed with red lines drawn by mortgage lenders and insurance companies marking out neighborhoods too Black to merit investment. But I was not taught to see the Black and white dividing lines within the warm and loving Mormon community (including Native Americans, Latinos, and Pacific Islanders) that defined my life—though those lines were most assuredly in place. I was not taught to see the near-total absence of African Americans in the pews at my local congregation on Sundays. I was not taught to see the near-total absence of men of color from the leadership ranks of the Church of Jesus Christ of Latter-day Saints, even though I studied the pictures of these prophets, seers, revelators, apostles, and seventies as published semiannually in the *LDS Church News*. And I was most certainly not taught the history that stood behind the Church's century-long exclusion of people of Black African descent from priesthood ordination and sacred temple rites, which ended on June 8, 1978, when I was six years old.

In the decades after its end, I would hear many rationalizations for the ban: an allegedly canonized mish-mash of Old Testament genealogies, names like Cain, Ham, and Egyptus, and speculations about the quality of spirits destined to come to this earth with melanated skin. At some point—I can't pinpoint it now, but assuredly it was an embarrassingly belated one—these stories started feeling wrong. But I had nothing to replace them with. Through four years of 6 a.m. "seminary" classes in high school, even through four years of study as a scholarship student at Church-owned Brigham Young University, I did not encounter a more realistic accounting of how Mormonism absorbed anti-Black racism into its very marrow at great cost to itself. Despite focusing my own doctoral and professional research on race and religion in the United States, it has taken me many years and a lot of searching to begin to get a grip on the dynamics of white racism and white supremacy in the Mormon context.[20]

First, I had to develop an understanding of racism not just as an individual character flaw but as a system of ideas, beliefs, and practices that divides people and gives some people better life chances— opportunities to live a happy, healthy life—based on their skin color and ancestry. I had to realize that individuals are born into these systems, absorb them, learn to operate within them, and make choices over time that will build them or dismantle them. My initial education in this took about a decade; it continues every day.

Then, I had to teach myself the history of Mormonism's specifically anti-Black racism, studying an archive of independent scholarship published largely in venues unsupported by the LDS Church and unfamiliar to if not openly disregarded by virtually everyone in the conservative Southern California Mormon communities where I grew up. Reading historiographic scholarship by Newell Bringhurst, Lester Bush, Dennis Lythgoe, Eugene England, Armand Mauss, Ronald Coleman, Edward Kimball, and Mark Grover; then through the public writing and activism of Darius Gray, Margaret Young, Zandra

Vranes, Tamu Smith, Darron Smith, and Janan Graham Russell; and finally through a new generation of scholars including Paul Reeve, Max Mueller, and Amy Tanner Thiriot, I pieced together for myself a history. The basic outlines of that history are these: from the 1850s until 1978, the Church did not permit men of Black African descent to be ordained to the lay priesthood available to all other religiously observant LDS males over the age of twelve (including men of color of indigenous American, Latino, Asian, Polynesian, and Fijian descent), and it did not permit men and women of Black African descent full access to marriage and other sacred rites performed in LDS temples. (The ban did not extend to other peoples of color, including indigenous peoples of North and South America and the Pacific, Latinos, or Asians.) LDS Church founder Joseph Smith Jr. had permitted ordination of Black men—Elijah Abel or Ables, Kwaku Walker Lewis—to the priesthood in the 1830s and 1840s. But the Church's second president, Brigham Young, announced in 1852 that such ordinations would no longer take place. Through the end of the nineteenth and the beginning of the twentieth century, LDS Church leaders rebuffed appeals from individual Black members for priesthood and temple access and reconstructed Young's policy as the timeless will of God, despite documentation of Black ordination in the 1830s and 1840s. In the face of public protests and, more saliently, under internal pressure driven by Church growth in Brazil where concepts of "Black" identity diverged from those held by the white North American Church leadership, the ban was finally rescinded in June 1978 by LDS Church President Spencer W. Kimball. But the array of official and folk defenses of the ban as the will of God revealed to inerrant Mormon prophets was not addressed until 2013, when the Church quietly published on its website a professionally researched essay on "Race and the Priesthood." The core ideas of this essay have never been presented in essential venues like the Church's worldwide semiannual General Conference, and no institutional effort has been made to address let alone dismantle persistent structures of white privilege and complicity that initiated and sustained the ban. African American Mormons over time have organized fellowship groups like Genesis to provide support and spiritual refuge against the anti-Black racism they have encountered on a day-to-day basis from white Mormons, even in the faith's most sacred settings. But the problem of anti-Black racism as a system that degraded the faith and its adherents has not been systematically addressed.

To this day, church-attending Mormons report that they continue to hear from their fellow congregants in Sunday meetings that African Americans were the accursed descendants of Cain whose spirits due to their lack of spiritual mettle in a premortal existence were destined to come to earth with a "curse" of Black skin. One can make this claim in many Mormon Sunday schools without fearing an adverse comment. In some congregations, people are more likely to encounter pushback if they argue that the ban was a product of human racism, that it was *wrong*, and that it had always been wrong. Like most difficult subjects in Mormon history and practice, the anti-Black priesthood and temple ban has been managed carefully in LDS institutional settings with a combination of avoidance, denial, selective truth telling, determined silence, and opportunistic redirection. Most white Mormons have believed and hoped that by looking forward and doing better, the ban and its legacy would take care of themselves. We told ourselves that new, more cosmopolitan (albeit white) Church leaders would endorse tolerance, love, and compassion; newly sensitized Church media would begin to feature images of Mormonism's growing diversity; and old doctrinal folklore would fade out with the passing generations. The past did not have to be reckoned with, undone, or confronted. It could simply be outlived if we turned our faces toward Zion.

But what this theory of change did not account for was the way that the institutional preference for silence (or near silence) on difficult issues like white racism created a context that placed the burden on members of color for raising consciousness and making themselves feel at home in sometimes discouraging spiritual environments. It freed white Mormons of responsibility for self-education, searching reflection, and personal and institutional change. Most distressingly, it allowed openly racist white Mormons to feel comfortable if not emboldened in Mormon religious contexts. This fact became strikingly clear after the election of President Donald J. Trump in November 2016. Trump's unabashed alliance making with white supremacist or "alt-right" partisans combined with the affordances of digital media created opportunities for extremist white supremacist Mormons to reach significant audiences. A small group of extremist white supremacist Mormon media personalities took to blogs, Facebook, YouTube, and Twitter, creating racist memes enlisting LDS scriptures and statements and images from LDS Church leaders past and present in the service of a radical white nationalism. In May 2017, Mormons who identified with the "alt-right" convened a #TrueBlueMormon conference featuring bloggers such as "A Thoughtful Wife," and in June 2017 LDS alt-right bloggers organized to attack and demean via Twitter Black LDS anti-racism advocates. In August 2017, the LDS white supremacist social media figure Ayla Stewart, who writes as "A Thoughtful Wife," was invited and scheduled to speak at the "Unite the Right" rally in Charlottesville, Virginia.[21] She ultimately withdrew from the event but in the days after the rally's deadly violence "A Thoughtful Wife" continued to misappropriate official LDS Church statements to claim divine sanction for white nationalism. This extremism is not representative of mainstream American Mormonism, but it does reflect the extent to which mainstream American Mormonism is a comfortable habitat for white supremacy—from its everyday expressions in white privilege to the extremist expressions of figures like Stewart.

This book seeks to use the tools of historical research and critical analysis to identify how anti-Black racism took hold in Mormonism. I want to state at the outset that I recognize that Mormonism's handling of race, gender, and sexuality are deeply intertwined and that there are also histories specific to Mormonism's indigenous communities and non-Black communities of color. This book focuses on the history of anti-Black racism in Mormonism because the LDS Church's specifically anti-Black segregation of its priesthood and temple rites from the 1850s through the 1970s constitutes a specific archive through which we can begin to understand these interlocked systems in greater depth and detail. I will seek wherever possible to highlight the intersections. I should also state that at times I will write as a person of faith who loves her community and is grateful for its many strengths even as she feels deeply its shortcomings and stumbling blocks; this may be unsettling to academic readers who prefer the traditional detachment of scholarly writing. At times, I will write as a scholar with an incisive, critical analysis of words and actions by LDS Church leaders and members; this may be unsettling to Mormon readers who feel protective of the faith and revere its leaders. I am both a scholar and a person of faith, and I strive to use the time-proven tools of my profession like · historiography and critical textual analysis to inform and advance understanding in my community.

What role has anti-Black racism and white supremacy played in the growth of the Mormon movement and key institutions of the Church of Jesus Christ of Latter-day Saints? In asking this question, I hope to develop insights that can be used to further anti-racist work in the faith community I consider my original home. I hope also to contribute to a critical and intersectional turn in Mormon studies. From its foundations in biography and regional history, Mormon studies has in the last two decades entered broader scholarly conversations about American society and culture, particularly the role Mormons have played in the American imagination. Scholars like Kathleen Flake, Terryl Givens, Spencer Fluhman, and Patrick Mason have examined the role Mormonism as a white religious minority played in the service of majoritarian ideological purposes: as a limit case for marking the social boundaries of whiteness, the legal status of churches, the idea of consent, and the intellectual value of credibility.[22] To some extent, Mormonism's minority positioning has allowed Mormon studies scholars to benefit from academic multiculturalism on the claim that American experience in general cannot be understood without accounting for the peculiar minority Harold Bloom once heralded as "the American religion."[23] But Mormonism's claim to multicultural minority status requires a more nuanced approach. Scholars like Paul Reeve, Max Mueller, Hokulani Aikau, Gina Colvin, and Amanda Hendrix-Komoto have more recently examined how Mormonism benefited from its host majoritarian cultures of white supremacy and American imperialism and established as well its own internal logics of white supremacy and American imperialism through its own theological and social mechanisms.[24] And still within these domains Mormon people of color have appropriated and redirected the facilities and resources of the faith in the pursuit of their own wholeness, happiness, and well-being, as scholarship by Aikau, Colvin, Elise Boxer, and Melissa Inouye has shown.[25] A critical and intersectional Mormon studies must account for all of these dynamics— at the faith's historic geographical center in the Intermountain West and at its global peripheries—because the relationship between center and margin is never arbitrary, and when we recenter our focus on the margins, as bell hooks has shown, we revolutionize our understanding of the whole.[26]

My goal is to offer the history and experience of my own home faith tradition as a case study in how white American Christianity has been constructed in and through white supremacy. My goal is to understand how it was that so egregious a policy as total exclusion of Black men and women from priesthood ordination and its ritual correlates took hold. Not all white American Christian denominations had so explicit a policy, but most mainline Protestant denominations were, effectually, as exclusive of Black participation as my home faith. In its history, I see the following contributory dynamics:

- In the absence of a defining commitment to racial equity and solidarity, white people in early Mormonism preferred relationships with other whites over the lives and well-being of fellow Mormons or prospective Mormons who happened to be Black.

- As Mormonism institutionalized in church and state, whites extended their preferential relationships with each other to formally exclude Blacks from religious and political power, thus discouraging a Black presence in Mormonism and rendering Black experience abstract and unimportant.

- As the church consolidated its theology and history in print, institutional histories abandoned facts in favor of coordinated storytelling that presented Black exclusion as the will of God from time immemorial revealed to infallible Mormon prophets.

- In the service of normalization, assimilation, and growth, LDS Church members entered into silent agreements among themselves and with the American public to coaffirm the innocence and moral goodness of the white majority.

- To maintain control over the narrative, the institutional LDS Church and Mormon culture repressed internal critique and dissent.

- In place of critical self-examination, the LDS Church has used multiculturalism, rhetorical evasion, and duplicity to manage the legacy of Mormon anti-Black racism without taking responsibility for it.

These dynamics may be in their particulars specific to Mormonism, but similar or parallel dynamics can be found across the history of white American Christianity. There is no predominantly white American Christian denomination that is innocent of white privilege and white supremacy. At some moment in the histories of predominantly white denominations, preference for white comfort over Black lives took hold. It gained systematicity as denominations institutionalized, through formal and informal rules and regulations, bureaucratic organization, and acquisition of real property. Systematic theologies, catechisms, study materials, devotionals, and other religious texts generated out of these contexts by white American Christian theologians demonstrate—with few exceptions—a moral indifference to the specific problem of Black death and suffering benefiting whites as a collective moral liability. This indifference was reaffirmed and replicated through silent agreements among white Christians who did not hold themselves or each other accountable within or across denominations. White American Christians did risk and give their lives for Black emancipatory struggles, but these were acts of individual conscience, often carried out in extra-institutional spaces. What institutional concessions and adjustments have come have been largely symbolic or occasional—the passing of resolutions, the promotion of people of color to visible leadership positions, multicultural theming—and have focused on enabling the institution to preserve its own sense of recti-tude. While the more progressive mainline Protestant denominations have attempted a move toward "reconciliation," as religion scholar Jennifer Harvey has noted, this effort has foundered, reinscribing again and again the recursivity of white segregation. Harvey argues persua-sively that a substantial commitment to righting the wrongs of white supremacy at the expense of Black lives would entail reparations. And reparations have not come.[27] In none of this or the chapters that follow do I wish to impugn the character of individuals. Rather, my goal is to assess how systems of inequality take shape through everyday conduct and choices, policies, laws, and theologies, so that we have a better sense of how to dismantle them. No one individually opts into the system of racial privilege that structures everyday life in the United States. But it is up to each of us who want to dismantle racism to begin the work of choosing *out*.

NOTES

1. This formulation reflects a consensus view of racism as a social system and also more specifically the influence of geographer Ruth Wilson Gilmore, who defined racism as "the state-sanctioned and/or legal production and exploitation of group-differentiated vulnerabilities to premature death, in distinct yet densely intercon-nected political geographies" in her essay "Race and Globalization," in *Geographies of Global Change*, 2nd ed., ed. P. J. Taylor, R. L. Johnstone, and M. J. Watts (Oxford: Blackwell, 2002), 261.

2. G. T. Marx, "Religion: Opiate or Inspiration of Civil Rights Militancy Among Negroes?" *American Sociological Review* 32.1 (1967): 64–72; J. F. Findlay, "Religion and Politics in the Sixties: The Churches and the Civil Rights Act of 1964," *Journal of American History* 77.1 (1990): 66–92; F. C. Harris, "Something Within: Religion as a Mobilizer of African-American Political Activism," *Journal of Politics* 56.1 (1994): 42–68; A. Morris, "The Black Church in the Civil Rights Movement: The SCLC as the Decentralized, Radical arm of the Black Church," in *Disruptive*

Religion: The Force of Faith in Social Movement Activism, ed. Christian Smith (New York: Routledge, 1996), 29–46; R. E. Ross, *Witnessing and Testifying: Black Women, Religion, and Civil Rights* (New York: Fortress Press, 2003); J. E. Williams, *African American Religion and the Civil Rights Movement in Arkansas* (Oxford: University Press of Mississippi, 2003); D. W. Houck and D. E. Dixon, *Rhetoric, Religion and the Civil Rights Movement, 1954–1965* (Waco, TX: Baylor University Press, 2006). On Christianity and white supremacy, see A. Burlein, *Lift High the Cross: Where White Supremacy and the Christian Right Converge* (Durham, NC: Duke University Press, 2002) and J. Dailey, "Sex, Segregation, and the Sacred After Brown," *Journal of American History* 91.1 (2006): 119–144. On Christian evangelicalism, see Michael Emerson and Christian Smith, *Divided by Faith: Evangelical Religion and the Problem of Race in America* (New York: Oxford University Press, 2000); Darren Dochuk, *From the Bible Belt to the Sun Belt: Plain-Folk Religion, Grassroots Politics, and the Rise of Evangelical Conservatism* (New York: Norton, 2012); Stephen Haynes, *The Last Segregated Hour: The Memphis Kneel-Ins and the Campaign for Southern Church Desegregation* (New York: Oxford University Press, 2012); J. Russell Hawkins and Phillip Luke Sinitiere, *Christians and the Color Line: Race and Religion After Divided by Faith* (New York: Oxford University Press, 2013); Carolyn Renee Dupont, *Mississippi Praying: Southern White Evangelicals and the Civil Rights Movement* (New York: New York University Press, 2015).

3. Newer works beginning to make this connection include Elizabeth Gillespie McRae, *Mothers of Massive Resistance: White Women and the Politics of White Supremacy* (New York: Oxford University Press, 2018).

4. Martin Luther King Jr., Interview on "Meet the Press," April 17, 1960, https://www.youtube.com/watch?v=1q881g1L_d8, last accessed July 15, 2018.

5. Pew Research Center, "Religious Landscape Study: Racial and Ethnic Composition," 2014, http://www.pewforum.org/religious-landscape-study/racial-and-ethnic-composition/, last accessed January 31, 2018.

6. Jennifer Harvey, *Dear White Christians: For Those Still Longing for Racial Reconciliation* (Grand Rapids, MI: Eerdmans Publishing, 2014); Jim Wallis, *America's Original Sin: Racism, White Privilege, and the Bridge to a New America* (Grand Rapids, MI: Brazos Press, 2016).

7. James Baldwin, *The Fire Next Time* (New York: Dial Press, 1963), 21.

8. Anne duCille, "The Occult of True Black Womanhood: Critical Demeanor and Black Feminist Studies," in Ruth Ellen Joeres and Barbara Laslett, *The Second Signs Reader: Feminist Scholarship, 1983–1996* (Chicago: University of Chicago Press, 1996), 70–108; George Lipsitz, *The Possessive Investment in Whiteness: How White People Profit From Identity Politics* (Philadelphia: Temple University Press, 1998).

9. Eva Mackey, "As Good as It Gets?: Apology, Colonialism and White Innocence," *Bulletin (Olive Pink Society)* 11.1–2 (1999): 34.

10. Thomas Ross, "Innocence and Affirmative Action," *Vanderbilt Law Review* 43.297 (1990): 297–315.

11. Neil Gotanda, "Reflections on Korematsu, Brown and White Innocence," *Temple Political and Civil Rights Law Review* 13 (2003), 673–674.

12. Kathleen M. Sullivan, "Sins of Discrimination: Last Term's Affirmative Action Cases," *Harvard Law Review* 100 (1986): 78.

13. K. D. Guitterrez, "White Innocence," *International Journal of Learning* 12.10 (2005): 223–229; Dalia Rodriguez, "Investing in White Innocence: Colorblind Racism, White Privilege, and the New White Racist Fantasy," in *Teaching Race in the 21st Century: College Teachers Talk About Their Fears, Risks, and Rewards* (New York: Palgrave, 2008), 123–124; Jennifer Seibel Trainor, "'My Ancestors Didn't Own Slaves': Understanding White Talk About Race," *Research in the Teaching of English* 40.2 (2005): 140–167.

14. For more on "white innocence," see Timothy J. Lensmire, "Ambivalent White Racial Identities: Fear and an Elusive Innocence," *Race, Ethnicity, and Education* 13.2 (2010): 159–172; Paula Ioanide, "The Alchemy of Race and Affect: 'White Innocence' and Public Secrets in the Post–Civil Rights Era," *Kalfou* 1.1 (2014),

https://tupjournals.temple.edu/index.php/kalfou/article/view/14/ 51; Bree Picower, "The Unexamined Whiteness of Teaching: How White Teachers Maintain and Enact Dominant Racial Ideologies," *Race, Ethnicity, and Education* 12.2 (2009): 203–204; Michael G. Lacy, "White Innocence Myths in Citizen Discourse, the Progressive Era (1974–1988)," *Howard Journal of Communications* 21.1 (2010): 20–39; Jennifer L. Pierce, *Racing for Innocence: Whiteness, Gender, and the Backlash Against Affirmative Action* (Palo Alto, CA: Stanford University Press, 2014), 9, 44.

15. Barbara Applebaum, *Being White, Being Good: White Complicity, White Moral Responsibility, and Social Justice Pedagogy* (New York: Lexington Books, 2010).

16. W. E. B. DuBois, *Darkwater: Voices from Within the Veil* (New York: Harcourt, Brace, Jovanovich, 1920), https://www.gutenberg.org/ files/15210/15210-h/15210-h.htm.

17. Toni Morrison, *Playing in the Dark: Whiteness and the Literary Imagination* (New York: Vintage, 1992); for a review of American studies scholarship on whiteness, see Shelley Fisher Fishkin, "Interrogating 'Whiteness,' Complicating 'Blackness': Remapping American Culture," *American Quarterly* 47.3 (September 1995): 428–466, and AnnLouise Keating, "Interrogating 'Whiteness,' (De) Constructing 'Race,'" *College English* 57 (1995): 901–918.

18. James Cone, "Theology's Great Sin: Silence in the Face of White Supremacy," *Black Theology* 2.2 (2004): 142.

19. James Cone, *The Cross and the Lynching Tree* (Maryknoll, NY: Orbis Books, 2011).

20. A note on terminology: I use the term "Mormonism" to denote the broad religious movement that originated with Joseph Smith in the 1820s, a movement that has encompassed more than a dozen organized forms of Mormon identity and expression, including institutional churches like the Church of Jesus Christ of Latter-day Saints and the Community of Christ, fundamentalist communities, and unchurched Mormon web-based communities. This book focuses on histories of white supremacy in that sector of the movement identified with the Church of Jesus Christ of Latter-day Saints, the largest of Mormonism's many branches. Because these various branches stem from common origins, the issues I engage in this book will

have relevance to other forms of Mormon identity and expression as well. I will use the terms "Mormonism" or "Mormon" in connection with the dynamic religious, social, and cultural aspects of the broader Mormon movement and I will use the terms "LDS," "LDS Church," or "Church" to refer specifically to the organizational and theological workings of the Church of Jesus Christ of Latter-day Saints. At times, I will group Mormonism with other American Christian religions. Eminent scholars of Mormonism have argued that Mormonism is not in fact Protestantism but an entirely distinctive religion that has taken on the appearance of Protestantism with its institutionalization as the LDS Church in the United States. I hold the differing view that Mormonism is a heretical elaboration of American Protestant Christianity. Scholarship incorporating this view includes Christopher C. Jones, "'We Latter-day Saints Are Methodists': The Influence of Methodism on Early Mormon Religiosity" (MA thesis, Brigham Young University, 2009).

21. Mary Ann, "Wife With a Purpose: Mormonism's Alt-Right Representative," *Wheat and Tares blog,* August 15, 2017, https://wheatandtares.org/2017/08/15/wife-with-a-purpose-mormonisms-alt-right-representative/.

22. Kathleen Flake, *The Politics of American Religious Identity: The Seating of Senator Reed Smoot, Mormon Apostle* (Chapel Hill: University of North Carolina Press, 2005); J. Spencer Fluhman, *"A Peculiar People": Anti-Mormonism and the Making of Religion in Nineteenth-Century America* (Chapel Hill: University of North Carolina Press Books, 2012); Terryl Givens, *The Viper on the Hearth: Mormons, Myths, and the Construction of Heresy* (New York: Oxford University Press, 1997); Patrick Mason, *The Mormon Menace: Violence and Anti-Mormonism in the Postbellum South* (New York: Oxford University Press, 2011).

23. Harold Bloom, *The American Religion: The Emergence of the Post-Christian Nation* (New York: Simon & Schuster, 1992).

24. Hokulani K. Aikau, *A Chosen People, a Promised Land: Mormonism and Race in Hawai'I* (Minneapolis: University of Minnesota Press, 2012); W. Paul Reeve, *Religion of a Different Color: Race and the Mormon Struggle for Whiteness* (New York: Oxford University Press, 2015); Max Perry Mueller, *Race and the Making of the*

Mormon People (Chapel Hill: University of North Carolina Press Books, 2017); Gina Colvin and Joanna Brooks, eds., *Decolonizing Mormonism: Approaching a Postcolonial Zion* (Salt Lake City: University of Utah Press, 2018); Amanda Hendrix-Komoto, *Imperial Zions* (Lincoln: University of Nebraska Press, forthcoming).

25. See essays by Boxer and Inouye in Gina Colvin and Joanna Brooks, eds., *Decolonizing Mormonism: Approaching a Postcolonial Zion* (Salt Lake City: University of Utah Press, 2018).

26. bell hooks, *Feminist Theory: From Margin to Center* (1984) (Boston: South End Press, 2000).

27. Jennifer Harvey, *Dear White Christians: For Those Still Longing for Racial Reconciliation* (Grand Rapids, MI: William B. Eerdmans, 2014).

CHAPTER 2

THE RELIGIOUS MICROPOLITICS OF WHITE OVER BLACK

EARLY MORMONISM

White supremacy gains power through millions upon millions of micropolitical decisions that people who believe they are "white" make every day. I say "people who believe they are 'white' " because historians have shown us that whiteness has not always existed. It is not a "natural" category of being. It is a modern invention. The idea that being "white" was good and valuable took shape over time as people who believed they were "white" preferred one another's interests over the interests of those who were non-"white" and so began to consolidate group power. Noel Ignatiev, Karen Brodkin Sacks, and many others have observed that, if their skin color allowed and if their conduct did not contest white supremacy, minority groups in the United States, even new immigrants like Irish and Jews who were the objects of deep prejudice, could "become" white and enjoy at least some measure of its privileges.[1] Thus developed what George Lipsitz has called a "possessive investment in whiteness." He explains:

> Whiteness has a cash value: it accounts for advantages that come to individuals through profits made from housing secured in discriminatory markets, through the unequal educations allocated to children of different races, through insider networks that channel employment opportunities to the relatives and friends of those who have profited most from present and past racial discrimination, and especially through intergenerational transfers of inherited wealth that pass on the spoils

Mormonism and white supremacy. Joanna brooks, Oxford University Press (2020). © Oxford University Press.
DOI: 10.1093/oso/9780190081768.001.0001

of discrimination to succeeding generations. . . . White Americans are encouraged to invest in whiteness, to remain true to an identity that provides them with resources, power, and opportunity. White supremacy is usually less a matter of direct, referential, and snarling contempt than a system for protecting the privileges of whites by denying communities of color opportunities for asset accumulation and upward mobility.[2]

American Christianity as practiced in predominantly white churches has played a role in cultivating the possessive investment in whiteness. It has delivered powerful symbolic and rhetorical validation of "white" as "holy" and "pure," instituted and advanced segregation, and fostered the "insider networks" and "intergenerational transfers of inherited wealth"—how many people have been disowned for leaving the faith?—essential to white privilege. This is true even in churches with moderate and progressive political dispositions. In the late eighteenth century, St. George's United Methodist Church of Philadelphia was among the most progressive in America. Methodist leaders opposed slavery, and the church ordained lay Black preachers and helped foster a Black worship community. But it also maintained a segregated seating policy restricting Black worshippers to the upper gallery. One morning during services in 1794, white ushers attempted to forcibly remove Black worshippers including lay clergy member Absalom Jones from their knees in prayer to enforce seating segregation, leading to a mass walkout of Black members and the foundation of Mother Bethel African Methodist Episcopal Church. Any room where white-identified people cultivate preference for one another over the unsettling and discomforting presence of the "stranger" or the darker-skinned "neighbor" is a room where white supremacy is being forged.

There are moments that flash up throughout the history of American Christianity that remind us that it was always possible to choose otherwise. We see these possibilities often in the originary moments of new religious movements, when faith is chaotic, charismatic, and capable of expansive and emancipatory possibilities. Over time, through millions upon millions of micropolitical decisions, movements settle into institutions. Almost without exception, when predominantly white American Christianities have institutionalized, because institutionalization often requires the physical and social capital that whiteness can confer access to, emancipatory possibilities have constricted. This chapter traces constituting micropolitical decisions through which the Mormon movement institutionalized and, in the words of historian Max Mueller, "contracted"[3] its own emancipatory possibilities, decisions that consistently privileged white over Black.

* * *

It didn't have to be this way. There were, it seemed at the beginning, emancipatory possibilities in Mormonism. These must have registered with Kwaku Walker Lewis, who joined the faith in 1843. Born free in Barre, Massachusetts, in 1798, his parents, Peter, a free yeoman farmer, and Minor, an emancipated slave, gave him an Akan name after his maternal uncle "Kwaku." "Kwaku" had mounted two successful legal suits to win his freedom in 1781 and 1783, setting legal precedent for other freedom-seeking African Americans in the state of Massachusetts. By the age of twenty-eight, Kwaku's namesake Walker Lewis had established a place for himself among the Black politically progressive professionals of the Boston area. A barber by trade, Lewis joined with David Walker and other noted early Black activists to form the Massachusetts General Colored Association, which in 1829 published David Walker's famed *Appeal to the Colored Citizens of the World*, a ground-shaking radical rhetorical strike against white supremacy. David Walker served from 1829 to 1831 as grandmaster of the Prince Hall African Lodge of Freemasons, long the center of Black political organization and activism in the city, and in 1831, he assumed the presidency of the African Humane Society, a mutual aid organization that later sponsored Black emigration to Liberia; during the 1840s, he used his barbershop and his son's used clothing store to outfit and disguise Black slaves heading north on the Underground Railroad. This was the kind of company Walker Lewis kept. In 1843, Lewis heard the Mormon message and chose to become a baptized member of the Church of Jesus Christ of Latter-day Saints. He was ordained to the LDS Church lay priesthood by Church founder Joseph Smith's older brother William, the third known African American Church member so ordained. The year was 1844: the same year Joseph Smith mounted a campaign for the US presidency, proposing in his platform that the United States sell public lands to purchase slaves and pursue their gradual emancipation, education, and emigration to places where they could be a free and self-determining people.[4]

Walker Lewis was held up in 1847 by Brigham Young as "one of the best elders" in the Church and as an exemplar of noble character. In March 1851, Lewis stepped away from his strong, deep ties to Boston's storied free Black community and turned his face toward a different Zion, the one being attempted by his fellow Mormons in the American West. Lewis arrived in Salt Lake City in October 1851. He received his patriarchal blessing and proposed marriage to another prominent Black Mormon named Jane Manning James, who declined; she would have been his second (and hence polygamous) wife. But Walker Lewis did not stay in Utah territory for long. Within six months, he emigrated back to Lowell, Massachusetts, where he lived until he succumbed to tuberculosis in 1856.[5]

Surviving records provide no direct evidence as to why Walker Lewis left Mormon Utah in March or April 1852. But it does bear notice that in January and February 1852 the Utah Territorial Legislature under the leadership of Brigham Young had passed measures permitting a form of African American slavery in the territory and denying African American citizens in some municipalities the right to vote. Walker Lewis had education, experience, resources, and options, and he knew his own mind on matters of slavery and freedom. Who could blame him if his spirit could not accede to the politics of a slaveholding Zion?

And it was not the first time that white Mormons had for tactical and political reasons sacrificed the interests of their Black coreligionists. At no time in its founding decades had Mormonism established a clear theological or social commitment to inclusion and equality. The early Mormon movement (1830–1845) emerged solidly from within the context of mainstream American Protestantism in its disposition on matters of race. Its leaders and founding figures including Joseph Smith carried forward a mix of unexceptional attitudes on slavery—ranging from support for slavery to support for gradualist emancipation. Early statements and actions by Church leaders on matters of race reflect an incoherence and instability inflected less by Christian ethics than by licentious theological speculation and pragmatic adaptation to sometimes hostile political contexts.[6] Under pressure from their host communities in the border and frontier states, early Mormon settlements did not throw in with the cause of Black emancipation.

The most famous example is W. W. Phelps's printing in the *Evening and Morning Star* of July 1833 a notice to "Free People of Color" who might join the Mormon movement or its settlements warning them that Missouri was a slaveholding state:[7]

> To prevent any misunderstanding among the churches abroad, respecting free people of color, who may think of coming to the western boundaries of Missouri, as members of the church, we quote the following clauses from the laws of Missouri:
>
> "Section 4.—Be it further enacted, that hereafter no free negro or mulatto, other than a citizen of someone of the United States, shall come into or settle in this state under any pretext whatever; and upon complaint made to any justice of the peace, that such person is in his county, contrary to the provisions of this section, if it shall appear that such person is a free negro or mulatto, and that he hath come into this state after the passage of this act, and such person shall not produce a certificate, attested by the seal of some court of record in someone of the United States, evidencing that he is a citizen of such state, the justice shall command him forthwith to depart from this state; and in case such negro or mulatto shall not depart from the state within thirty days after being commanded so to do as aforesaid, any justice of the peace, upon complaint thereof to him made may cause such person to be brought before him and may commit him to the common goal of the county in which he may be found, until the next term of the circuit court to be held in such county. And the said court shall cause such person to be brought before them and examine into the cause of commitment; and if it shall appear that such person came into the state contrary to the

provisions of this act, and continued therein after being commanded to depart as aforesaid, such court may sentence such person to receive ten lashes on his or her bare back, and order him to depart the state; and if he or she shall not depart, the same proceedings shall be had and punishment inflicted, as often as may be necessary, until such person shall depart the state.

"Sec. 5.—Be it further enacted, that if any person shall, after the taking effect of this act, bring into this state any free negro or mulatto, not having in his possession a certificate of citizenship as required by this act, (he or she) shall forfeit any pay, for every person so brought, the sum of five hundred dollars, to be recovered by action of debt in the name of the state, to the use of the university, in any court having competent jurisdiction; in which action the defendant may be held to bail, of right and without affidavit; and it shall be the duty of the attorney-general or circuit attorney of the district in which any person so offending may be found, immediately upon information given of such offenses to commence and prosecute an action as aforesaid."

Slaves are real estate in this and other states, and wisdom would dictate great care among the branches of the Church of Christ on this subject. So long as we have no special rule in the Church, as to people of color, let prudence guide, and while they, as well as we, are in the hands of a merciful God, we say: Shun every appearance of evil.

The article is little more than a cautionary reprinting of Missouri statutes requiring African Americans to bring legal documents attesting to their citizenship. But it reflects the fact that the LDS Church had in the 1830s no specific commitment—"no special rule"—to the welfare of Black converts, slave or free. Moreover, its language—"they, as well as we, are in the hands of a merciful God"—indicates that the writer assumed that the readers of the *Evening and Morning Star* were not African American but white and would see African Americans as a differentiated group. Were African American converts to seek to join the community at Independence, the article seems to make clear, they would do so at their own risk. Empathy they could count on, perhaps, but not solidarity—not even from their own coreligionists. In the matter of slavery and emancipation, the message was clear: Black Mormons could not count on white Mormons in Missouri to bear their burdens. But even this discouragement was not enough to satisfy vigilantes who persisted in seeing the Mormons as an insurrectionary threat. Two days later Phelps printed an "extra" broadside to clarify and amplify the fact that he did in fact intend the article to discourage Black conversion. Still, townspeople organized to destroy the Phelps press, office, and home, and tarred and feathered two local LDS leaders.

What flashes up at this early moment in Mormon history is a dynamic that would take hold as Mormonism institutionalized: when predominantly white Mormon communities found themselves under pressure, at key decision-making nodes, they would elect, as had W. W. Phelps in Independence, to choose their relationships with other whites in positions of power over loyalty to or solidarity with Black people. If there was a logic in these decisions, it was that Mormonism had more to gain through collaboration with whites, even if that came at the expense of Black lives, Black equality, and white integrity. This meant that from its early decades, even when the Church had no official position on slavery and emancipation and comfortably accommodated a range of individual perspectives, it created an environment of conditional welcome that put the burden on Black people like Walker Lewis of making themselves feel at home in "Zion." Even in settlements like Nauvoo, located in the nominally "free" state of Illinois, Mormon communities were by no means utopian spaces for African Americans. Especially after the death of Joseph Smith in 1844, African American men especially experienced increasingly tenuous circumstances.[8] These facts are especially jarring given the early Mormon movement's professed commitment to establishing community.

Nor did the Black Mormon pioneers, free and unfree, who crossed the plains to Utah in 1847 and years following, find their situation there substantially improved. Utah took up the question of African American citizenship soon after it obtained territorial status in September 1850. On January 5, 1852, Brigham Young said in a prepared speech to the territorial legislature, later published in the *Deseret News*: "No property can or should be recognized as existing in slaves."[9] Just two weeks later, though, Young declared himself a "firm believer in slavery" and urged passage of "An Act in Relation to Service," which legalized a form of slavery in Utah that would persist until at least 1862, if not longer. After some debate, the measure was signed into law on February 4, 1852.[10] Historians Chris Rich, Nathaniel Ricks, Newell Bringhurst, and Matthew Harris have agreed that one significant factor in the passage of the act was regard for slaveowners and proslavery men who held positions of power in early Utah and desire to protect their interests by establishing what was at least on paper an ameliorated form of slavery to be called "servitude." Orson Hyde stated so much in the *Millennial Star* on February 15, 1851:

> We feel it to be our duty to define our position in relation to the subject of slavery. There are several in the Valley of the Salt Lake from the Southern States, who have their slaves with them. There is no law in Utah to authorize slavery, neither any to prohibit it. If the slave is disposed to leave his master, no power exists there, either legal or moral, that will prevent him. But if the slave chooses to remain with his master, none are allowed to interfere between the master and the slave. All the slaves that are there appear to be perfectly contented and satisfied. When a man in the Southern states embraces our faith, the Church says to him, if your slaves wish to remain with you, and to go with you, put them not away; but if they choose to leave you, or are not satisfied to remain with you, it is for you to sell them, or let them go free, as your own conscience may direct you. The Church, on this point, assumes not the responsibility to direct. The laws of the land recognize slavery, we do not wish to oppose the laws of the country. If there is sin in selling a slave, let the individual who sells him bear that sin, and not the Church. Wisdom and prudence dictate to us, this position, and we trust our position will henceforth be understood.[11]

First among the rationale provided by Hyde was consideration for white LDS Church members who brought their slaves with them to

Utah. The number of slaves brought to Utah was not large—the 1850 census counted twenty-six and the 1860 census counted thirty, though this number is largely regarded as an undercount. Newell Bringhurst estimated that twelve Mormon migrants to Utah brought a total of "sixty to seventy" slaves, and that early Utah's slaveholders held positions of influence: Charles C. Rich was one of the Twelve Apostles; William Hooper became Utah's representative to Congress; Abraham Smoot became mayor of Salt Lake City and Provo. Slaveholders' investment—economic, political, and social—was noted and regarded by Young, who pledged not to contest it.[12] In addition to consideration for the property interests of influential slaveholders, historians have identified other factors as well that made the act something of a "practical compromise," as Chris Rich described it, that would help Utah avoid becoming embroiled in national controversy, limit large-scale slaveholding in the territory, and signal that white Mormons belonged in the mainstream of American society.[13] "Young was not simply negatively situating blacks within Mormon theology," Paul Reeve explains, "he was attempting to situate whites more positively within American society."[14]

Documentary evidence supports an even stronger reading of Brigham Young's switch on slavery. Young's own writing reveals that it was his goal as territorial governor and LDS Church president to use territorial laws and LDS Church policies to build a domain where white men would "rule." I use this word deliberately, as did Brigham Young. It derives in Young's usage from Genesis 4:7, wherein God tells Abel that he will "rule over" his brother Cain as a consequence of Cain's faulty sacrificial offering. Young uses this language repeatedly in his private writings and public speeches in early 1852. His manuscript history (a record compiled by clerks from extant papers) entry for January 5, 1852, reads:

> The negro . . . should serve the seed of Abraham; he should not be a *ruler*, nor vote for men to *rule* over me nor my brethren. The Constitution of Deseret is silent upon this, we meant it should be so. The seed of Canaan cannot hold any office, civil or ecclesiastical. . . . The decree of God that Canaan should be a servant of servants unto

31

his brethren (i.e. Shem and Japhet [*sic*]) is in full force. The day will come when the seed of Canaan will be redeemed and have all the blessings their brethren enjoy. Any person that mingles his seed with the seed of Canaan forfeits the right to *rule* and all the blessings of the Priesthood of God; and unless his blood were spilled and that of his offspring he nor they could not be saved until the posterity of Canaan are redeemed.[15]

He had presented a similar argument, as Jonathan Stapley has shown, as early as February 1849 in Nauvoo. At that time, Young instructed LDS Church leaders that Cain's attempt to cut off Abel and his posterity from the family of mankind was to be answered by exclusion of Cain and his posterity from the cosmological family of God. "Black Mormon men and women," historian Jonathan Stapley explains, were according to Young "not to be integrated into the material family of God."[16] Establishment of a territorial theocracy allowed Young to institutionalize this perspective in both governmental and ecclesiastical affairs. In no matter, political or religious, were African Americans as the "posterity" of Cain to "bear rule" over others.

His sentiment was shared widely. Days later, Eliza R. Snow, who was a spouse of Brigham Young, published "The New Year, 1852" on the front page of the *Deseret News* on January 10, 1852. The poem celebrates the establishment of a theocratic Utah territory and defines Utah in opposition to political currents in the United States, particularly its reform movements:

> On, on
>   Still moves the billowy tide of change, that in
>   Its destination will o'erwhelm the mass
>   Of the degen'rate governments of earth,
>   And introduce Messiah's peaceful reign.
>   There is "a fearful looking for," a vague
>   Presentiment of something near at hand—
>   A feeling of portentousness that steals

Upon the hearts of multitudes, who see
Disorder reigning through all ranks of life.
Reformers and reforms now in our own
United States, clashing tornado-like,
Are threat'ning dissolution all around.

Snow wrote disparagingly of anti-slavery reform, holding to Young's vision of African Americans as "cursed" to "servitude", as shown in Figure 2.1:

Slavery and anti-slavery! What a strife!
"Japhet shall dwell within the tents of Shem,
And Ham shall be his servant"; long ago
The prophet said: 'Tis being now fulfill'd.
The curse of the Almighty rests upon
The colored race: In his own time, by his
Own means, not yours, that curse will be remov'd.

Reformers and reforms now in our own
United States, clashing tornado-like,
Are threat'ning dissolution all around.
Slavery and anti-slavery!   What a strife!

"Japhet shall dwell within the tents of Shem,
And Ham shall be his servant;" long ago
The prophet said: 'tis being now fulfill'd.
The curse of the Almighty rests upon
The colored race: In his own time, by his
Own means, not yours, that curse will be remov'd.

Figure 2.1. Excerpt from Eliza R. Snow, "The New Year," published page 1, *Deseret News*, January 10, 1852.

Image courtesy of Marriott Special Collections Library, University of Utah.

Similarly, she dismissed the quest for suffrage:

> And woman too aspires for something, and
> She knows not what; which if attain'd would prove,
> Her very wishes would not be her wish.
> Sun, moon, and stars, and vagrant comets too,
> Leaving their orbits, ranging side by side,
> Contending for prerogatives, as well
> Might seek to change the laws that govern them,
> As woman to transcend the sphere which God
> Thro' disobedience has assigned to her;
> And seek and claim equality with man.

Snow argued that political reform efforts were pointless because the only true government, the "perfect government," was priesthood:

> Can ships at sea be guided without helm?
> Boats without oars? steam-engines without steam?
> The mason work without a trowel? Can
> The painter work without a brush, or the
> Shoe-maker without awls? The hatter work
> Without a block? The blacksmith without sledge
> Or anvil? *Just as well as men reform*
> *And regulate society without*
> *The Holy Priesthood's pow'r.* Who can describe
> The heav'nly order who have not the right,
> Like Abra'm, Moses, and Elijah, to
> Converse with God, and be instructed thro'
> The Urim and the Thummim as of old?
> Hearken, all ye inhabitants of earth!
> *All ye philanthropists who struggle to*
> *Correct the evils of society!*
> *You've neither rule or plummet.*
> *Here are men*
> *Cloth'd with the everlasting Priesthood: men*

> *Full of the Holy Ghost, and authoriz'd*
> *To 'stablish righteousness—to plant the seed*
> *Of pure religion, and restore again*
> *A perfect form of government to earth.*

That form of government was not only to be established in the stakes of Zion, as later generations of Latter-day Saints would come to understand it, but also on earth in the territory of Utah. She makes this point in the *Deseret News* by repeatedly declaiming at line-break points of poetic emphasis the word "here":

> If elsewhere men are so degenerate
> That women dare compete with them, and stand
> In bold comparison: let them come *here*;
> And *here* be taught the principles of life
> And exaltation.
> Let those fair champions of "female rights"
> Female conventionists, come *here*. Yes, in
> These mountain vales; chas'd from the world, of whom
> It "was not worthy" *here* are noble men
> Whom they'll be proud t' acknowledge to be far
> Their own superiors, and feel no need
> Of being Congressmen; for *here* the laws
> And Constitution our forefathers fram'd
> Are honor'd and respected. Virtue finds
> Protection 'neath the heav'n-wrought banner *here*.
> 'Tis *here* that vile, foul-hearted wretches learn
> That truth cannot be purchas'd—justice brib'd;
> And taught to fear the bullet's warm embrace,
> Thro' their fond love of life, from crime desist,
> And seek a refuge in the States, where weight
> Of purse is weight of character, that stamps
> The impress of respectability.
> "Knowledge is pow'r." Ye saints of Latter-day!
> You hold the keys of knowledge. 'Tis for you

To act the most conspic'ous and the most
Important parts connected with the scenes
Of this New Year: To 'stablish on the earth
The principles of Justice, Equity,—
Of Righteousness and everlasting Peace.[17]

As Maureen Ursenbach Beecher wrote, "Eliza adopted ideas from
whatever source she trusted—Joseph Smith's utterances would be received without question—and worked them meticulously into a neatly-
packaged theology with the ends tucked in and the strings tied tight."[18]
Eliza R. Snow endorsed Brigham Young's vision of a theocratic Utah
governed by white priesthood holders.

We see this explicit conjoining of Church and territory on February
5, 1852, the day after the passage of the "Act in Relation to Service"
and the day the legislature established voting rights (white men only)
in Cedar City and Fillmore. Young used the occasion to hold forth
extemporaneously and at length on the status of whites, Blacks, and
others in matters spiritual and temporal. Records from this day are
the first contemporary document of a theologically rationalized ban
on full participation by Black Africans and African Americans. Young
declared that African Americans were descendants of Cain and thus
bearers of a curse that prohibited them from holding the priesthood.
Further, he stated that any who intermarried with African Americans
would bear the same curse and that it would be a blessing to them to
be killed. Finally, he outlined principles for establishing the "Church"
as the "kingdom of God on the earth," returning again and again to
the ideal of white "rule" as he had in his January 5 journal entry:

I know that they cannot bear *rule* in the preisthood, for the curse on
them was to remain upon them, until the resedue of the posterity of
Michal and his wife receive the blessings. . . . Now then in the kingdom
of God on the earth, a man who has has the Affrican blood in him
cannot hold one jot nor tittle of preisthood; . . . In the kingdom of
God on the earth the Affricans cannot hold one partical of power in
Government. . . . The men bearing *rule*; not one of the children of old

Cain, have one partical of right to bear *Rule* in Government affairs from first to last, they have no business there. this privilege was taken from them by there own transgressions, and I cannot help it; and should you or I bear *rule* we ought to do it with dignity and honour before God. . . . Therefore I will not consent for one moment to have an african dictate me or any Bren. with regard to Church or State Government. I may vary in my veiwes from others, and they may think I am foolish in the things I have spoken, and think that they know more than I do, but I know I know more than they do. If the Affricans cannot bear *rule* in the Church of God, what business have they to bear *rule* in the State and Government affairs of this Territory or any others? . . . If we suffer the Devil to *rule* over us we shall not accomplish any good. I want the Lord to *rule*, and be our Governor and dictater, and we are the boys to execute. . . . Consequently I will not consent for a moment to have the Children of Cain *rule* me nor my Bren. No, it is not right. . . . No man can vote for me or my Bren. in this Territory who has not the privilege of acting in Church affairs.

Shorthand Pitman transcriptions of the speech provide an even stronger sense of Brigham Young's perspective:

I tell you this people that commonly called Negros are children of Cain I know they are I know they cannot bear rule in priesthood first sense of word for the curse upon them was to continue on them was to remain until the residue of posterity of [Adam] and his wife receive the blessings they should bear rule and hold the keys of priesthood until times of restitution come . . . in kingdom of God on earth a man who has the African blood in him cannot hold one one jot nor tittle of priesthood now I ask for what for upon earth they was the true eternal principles Lord Almighty has ordained who can help it angels cannot all powers cannot take away the eternal I Am what I Am I take it off at my pleasure and not one particle of power can that posterity of Cain have until the time comes the Lord says have it that time will come. . . . In the kingdom of God on the earth the Africans cannot hold one particle of power in government they are the subjects the eternal servants of

residue of children and the residue of children through the benign influence of the Spirit of the Lord have the privilege of saying to posterity
of Cain inasmuch as the Lord [is?] will you may receive the Spirit of
Lord by baptism that is the end of their privilege and no power on earth
give them any more power . . . let my seed mingle with seed of Cain
brings the curse upon me and my generations reap the same rewards
as Cain in the priesthood tell you what it do if he were to mingle their
seed with the seed of Cain bring not only curse upon them selves but
entail it on their children get rid of it . . . again to the principle of men
bearing rule not one of children of old Cain as any right to bear rule in
government affairs from first to last no business there it was taken from
them by their own transgression and I and I cannot help it and you and
I bear rule or do with dignity before God I am [as] much opposed to
the principle of slavery as any man because it is an abuse I am opposed
to abusing that which God has decreed and take a blessing and make
a curse of it greatest blessings to all the seed of Adam to have seed of
Cain for servants those that serve who use them with all the heart the
feeling use their children and their compassion should reach over them
around them and treat them as kindly as mortal beings can be and their
blessings in life great in proportion than those provide bread and dinner
for them. . . . I will not consent for one moment to have an African to
dictate me nor my brethren with regard church and state government
I may vary from others and they may think I [am] foolish and short
sighted who think they know more than I do I know I know more than
they do consequently if they cannot bear rule in church of God what
business have they in bearing rule in state and government affairs of
territory of those whose by right God should reign the nations of earth
should control kings. . . . I will not consent for a moment to have the
children of Cain rule me nor my brethren when it is not right. Why not
say some thing of this in constitution allow me the privilege to tell it
right out it is not any of their damned business what we do so we do not
say anything about and it is for them to sanction and it is for us to say
what we will about it it is written right out that every male citizen. . . .
I have given you the true principles and doctrine no man can vote for

38

me my brethren in territory has not the privilege of voting acting in church affairs.[19]

Brigham Young's white supremacy was posited primarily but not exclusively in relation to African Americans. In the same speech, Brigham Young envisioned a day when people might emigrate to Utah from the "Islands," or "Japan," or "China." They too, Young averred, would have no understanding of government and would have to be governed by white men.[20] This speech suggests that the legalization of slavery and Young's exclusion of Blacks from the priesthood were elements of a larger vision in which the Kingdom of God on earth was to be established with whites avoiding intermixture with Blacks except so as to rule over them.

The legal establishment of Black servitude in Utah territory managed to preserve the slaveholding interests of a few influential white Mormons while discouraging voluntary emigration to Utah territory by free Blacks, even as free Blacks were setting out to seek their fortunes in other western states. In December 1852, Young told the legislature that the act "had nearly freed the territory of the colored population."[21] The 1860 census found 59 African Americans in Utah, constituting .14% of the territorial population. In neighboring Nevada, the census found 45 African Americans constituting .6% of the territorial population, and in California, 4,086 African Americans constituting 1.1% of the population.[22]

One of the consequences of "freeing the territory" was eliminating the possibility that white Mormon people would interact with African Americans as neighbors, coworkers, friends, or coreligionists. The limited extent of Black servitude also "freed" white Mormons from engaging to any significant extent with the national controversy over slavery's abolition. Outsiders who visited Salt Lake City were struck by white Mormons' lack of engagement with the issue. B. H. Roberts's *History of the Church* commemorates the lack of abolitionist sentiment in Utah, as noted by Horace Greeley at the Salt Lake City banquet in his honor in 1859:

I have not heard tonight, and I think I never heard from the lips or journals of any of your people, one word in reprehension of that national crime and scandal, American chattel slavery, this obstinate silence, this seeming indifference on your part, reflects no credit on your faith and morals, and I trust they will not be persisted in.[23]

Greeley wondered at the "obstinate silence" and "seeming indifference" of white Mormons. But he misunderstood. Silence did not mean white Mormons were indifferent on race. The legal and theological architects of "the Kingdom of God on earth" had established Utah territory as a white supremacist space. Brigham Young used his conjoint role as LDS Church president, territorial governor, and empire builder to implement anti-Black racism as a means of consolidating relationships among the young territory's key operatives and as a foundational step toward realizing a theocratic Mormon kingdom where white men "ruled."

* * *

Two years after the death of Brigham Young, in May 1879, LDS Church President John Taylor traveled to a conference of the Utah Valley Stake in Provo. Presiding over the stake was Abraham O. Smoot. Smoot had a long history of close connection with Brigham Young. After his conversion in Kentucky in 1833, Smoot proved himself a loyal, strong-tempered, battle-ready defender of the Mormon movement, fighting in 1838 alongside Porter Rockwell among the Danites, and serving as a Nauvoo policeman. He migrated with his wife Margaret to Utah in 1847 as the leader of two companies of fifty; subsequently, Smoot captained three additional companies in 1850, 1852, and 1856, and served as well a number of foreign missions. Brigham Young acknowledged his leadership by appointing him superintendent of one of the valley's first sugar factories and bishop of the Sugar House ward, which set Smoot on a path to become alderman from the Sugar House district of Salt Lake, and then mayor of Salt Lake City from 1857 to 1866. It was Smoot who, in July 1857, discovered with Porter Rockwell the advance of US Army troops toward Utah and turned around from

Missouri to ride back to Utah and personally warn Brigham Young. In 1868, at the instruction of Brigham Young, Smoot moved to Provo, where he became the region's effective governor—simultaneously serving as Provo city mayor (1868–1881), Utah Valley stake president (1868–1881), and the first head of the Board of Trustees of Brigham Young University. Smoot played an elemental role in the creation and consolidation of key LDS institutions and in Utah's early theocracy.[24]

Smoot was also a solid proponent of slavery. As a missionary in Alabama in 1844, he refused to distribute political literature for Joseph Smith's 1844 presidential campaign that proposed a gradual emancipation plan. After his move to Utah, historian Amy Tanner Thiriot has confirmed, Smoot owned or hired three slaves. The 1851 census slave schedule held in draft form at the Church History Library shows Abraham and Margaret Smoot in possession of a slave named Lucy; the Great Salt Lake County 1860 census schedule of "Slave Inhabitants" shows "A. O. Smoot" as being in possession of two male slaves, both aged forty.[25] One of these was a man named Jerry who had been the property of David and Duritha Trail Lewis, fellow Kentucky-born converts to the Church. Jerry came to Utah in the company of migrants led by David Lewis in 1851.[26] He remained with the family after David's death in 1855, on November 2, when (as figure 2.2 shows) the Third District Court in Salt Lake County recorded three individuals among the "property" of the deceased:

> 1 coloured man (35 years old) . . . $700
> 1 " woman (16 years old) $500
> 1 " girl (11 years old) $300[27]

On August 4, 1858, Duritha filed a record with the clerk of the Third Judicial District Court for the Utah territory registering these same individuals as her property:

> Duritha Lewis who being duly sworn, states on oath that she is the true and lawful owner of three persons of African blood, whose names and ages are as follows to wit; Jerry, Caroline, and Tampian, aged 38,

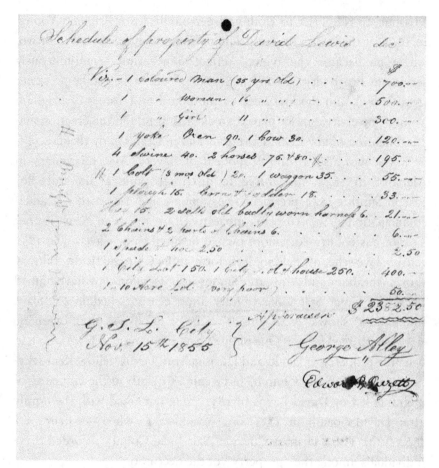

Figure 2.2. Probate records of David Lewis.

Image courtesy of Utah Department of Administrative Services, Division of Archives & Records Service.

18, 14. That she said Duritha Lewis inherited them from her father Solomon Trail according to the laws of the state of Kentucky. That by virtue of such inheritance, she is entitled to the services of the said, Jerry, Caroline, and Tampian, during their lives, according to the Lewis of the said Territory. That she makes this affidavit that they may be registered as slaves according to the requirements, of the said Lewis of the said Territory, for life.[28]

As a widower who had initially been remarried but left that household, Duritha Trail Lewis was in a vulnerable economic position. On
January 3, 1860, Brigham Young wrote to Duritha Lewis to encourage
her to sell Jerry:

Dear Sister Lewis:

I understand that you are frequently importuned to sell your negro
man Jerry, but that he is industrious and faithful, and desires to remain
in this territory: Under these circumstances I should certainly deem it
most advisable for you to keep him, but should you at any time conclude
otherwise and determine to sell him, ordinary kindness would require
that you should sell him to some kind faithful member of the church,
that he may have a fair opportunity for doing all the good he desires to
do or is capable of doing. I have been told that he is about forty years
old, if so, it is not presumable that you will, in case of sale, ask so high
a price as you might expect for a younger person. If the price is sufficiently moderate, I may conclude to purchase him and set him at liberty.

Your brother in the gospel, Brigham Young.[29]

Young's letter is revealing in many respects. First, in noting that
Duritha was "frequently importuned" to sell Jerry in Salt Lake City,
it suggests that demand for slaves was greater than supply in Utah
territory. Second, it documents that Brigham Young was personally
involved in exchanges or trades of slaves: he prevailed upon Duritha
Lewis to advise her on the desirability of sale, to set pricing expecta-
tions, and to encourage her to sell him to another Church member.
Although Young offered to "purchase him and set him at liberty," presumably at a cost discounted from his $700 valuation in 1855, this
sale never materialized. Instead, by June 1, 1860, Jerry (along with
one other forty-year-old Black man) was in the possession of Abraham
Smoot. Both were presumably freed in 1862, though Jerry moved with
the Smoot household to Provo in 1868.

Smoot was a talented entrepreneur whose enterprises included
farming and ranching collectives, the first woolen mills in Utah,

43

lumber mills and lumber yards, and banks. He amassed a substantial fortune that he used at the end of his life to build the Provo Tabernacle and to pay the substantial debts of Brigham Young University, making him its first underwriter. It is unlikely that his few slaves held from the 1850s through 1862 played a substantial role in the growth of these industries or Smoot's wealth. However, it is clear that they played a significant symbolic and ornamental role for Smoot, who as a native Kentuckian and pro-slavery advocate likely viewed slaveholding as an appropriate and necessary status marker for a man of means. Black lives were, to Abraham Smoot, a display of wealth.

After the Saturday morning session of the Utah Valley stake conference, Smoot brought back to one of his four Provo homes President John Taylor, Taylor's secretary John Nuttall, Brigham Young Jr., and Zebedee Coltrin. Coltrin, who had joined the Church in 1831, attended the first School of the Prophets in 1833, emigrated to Utah in 1847, lived in Spanish Fork, and was a member of Smoot's stake. Taylor sought from both men their understanding of Joseph Smith's views on race in connection with a request from Elijah Abel to be sealed in the temple to his spouse. As notes taken by John Nuttall document, Taylor first interviewed Coltrin, who stated that in 1834 Joseph Smith told him "the negro has no right nor cannot hold the Priesthood" and that Abel had been ordained to the Seventy as symbolic compensation for labor on the temple but dropped when his "lineage" was subsequently discovered. Coltrin also testified that he had experienced a deep sense of revulsion while ordaining Abel at Kirtland. Smoot spoke next, indicating that he agreed with Coltrin's statement and providing as additional evidence that Black men should not receive the priesthood his memory when serving a mission in the southern states in 1835–1836 that Joseph Smith had instructed him to neither baptize nor ordain slaves.[30] Having traded for and hired Black men, Smoot understood the legal and social distinctions between free and enslaved Black men, but he did not maintain these differences in the testimony he provided to President Taylor, advancing Joseph Smith's instructions in regard to conversion of slaves—a sensitive issue given the long and complicated history in the United States of proselyting and religious instruction of slaves, compounded by rumors in border and southern states that Mormons might seek to foment slave revolt—as though they were to pertain to Black men at large.

Smoot and Coltrin did not provide correct testimony. Elijah Abel himself held and provided Church leaders with documentary evidence of his ordination as an elder on March 3, 1836, a fact reaffirmed in his patriarchal blessing, given by Joseph Smith Sr. He also owned and provided evidence of his ordination to the Third Quorum of the Seventy in the Kirtland Temple on December 20, 1836, which was commemorated in two certificates affirming his membership in the quorum in the 1840s and 1850s. In fact, just a few months before the interview at Abraham Smoot's house, on March 5, 1879, as historian Paul Reeve has discovered, Abel spoke and shared his recollections of Joseph Smith at a meeting of the Quorums of the Seventies at the Council House in Salt Lake City.[31] In the face of Abel's open, ongoing, and uncontested participation in LDS leadership, Smoot and Coltrin's testimony was bold, controversial, and socially violent. Even more striking is the fact that both Coltrin and Smoot were contemporaneous, living witnesses to Elijah Abel's ordination to the Third Quorum of the Seventy on December 20, 1836, in Kirtland. It was, in fact, Zebedee Coltrin himself who had ordained Abel, as records show, along with six other new members of the Third Quorum of the Seventy—including Abraham Smoot, that very same day in that same place.[32]

It appears that Smoot and Coltrin jointly agreed to arrange their recollections to support a position opposing Black ordination and temple participation. They did so even though they themselves had been primary witnesses to Abel's ordination: Coltrin performed it, and Smoot was certainly present at the occasion and may have witnessed the actual ceremony. Both men withheld this vital testimony from President Taylor. Both men instead purposefully provided testimony that obscured the ordination, obscured vital differences between slave and free, and attributed an anti-ordination stance to Joseph Smith himself. Abraham Smoot and Zebedee Coltrin together bore false witness to bar full participation by Black men in the priesthood and temple ceremonies.

How do we understand what happened at the home of Abraham Smoot that day? How do we understand the dynamics that led both Coltrin and Smoot to arrange their testimonies to align and to obscure important facts in order to advance Black exclusion? It would be perfectly human for Abraham Smoot to allow his own views on the status of African Americans, views that had been fully supported by President Brigham Young who helped broker Smoot's purchase of one of his slaves, to influence him. He would have felt justified in doing so not only by the personal support of Brigham Young but also by the culture of theocratic expediency in which he had risen to power, and by the near-complete absence of a culture of white abolitionism or emancipation in Utah in the 1850s, 1860s, and 1870s. He would have felt completely assured, in the majority, and in the right, advancing his interest in Black exclusion. Zebedee Coltrin never owned slaves. In fact, after settling in Spanish Fork in 1852 and surviving three subsequent years of failed crops, his family had survived on pigweed and the food carried to them by a Black slave belonging to the Redd family—likely Marina Redd. Poverty had been a persistent feature of Coltrin's postemigration life. When Brigham Young instructed Abraham Smoot to organize the United Order in Spanish Fork in 1873, Zebedee Coltrin was among those who joined, and even though he was not among those Smoot put forward as its slate of officers on May 2, 1874, Coltrin vocally encouraged his fellow high priests in Spanish Fork to deed their property to the order—as he had in all likelihood done himself. Smoot presided over the United Order and held the deeds to land, including the land on which Zebedee Coltrin's land and home stood.[33] Had he wanted to enlist Coltrin's loyalties, to arrange their joint recollections to support Black exclusion, had he wanted to steer the meeting—held at his own home, with his own testimony to close—Smoot was certainly in a position to do so. He effectively owned Coltrin's land, home, and life chances. And it would have been in his best economic and social interests for Coltrin to comply. In fact, to resist the implicit and explicit pressure of the situation, Coltrin would have to have been a man of exceptional clarity, resolve, and independence. The very nature of the testimony he provided that day does not suggest this was the case.

Additional insights are provided from the surviving text of Coltrin's recollections, as documented in Nuttall's journal. Coltrin recalled that he had always opposed the ordination of Black men, and that upon return from the Zion's Camp expedition, in 1834, he had put the question directly to Joseph Smith: "When we got home to Kirtland, we both went into Bro Joseph's office together . . . and [Brother Green] reported to Bro Joseph that I had said that the Negro could not hold the priesthood—Bro Joseph kind of dropt his head and rested it on his hand for a minute. And said Bro Zebedee is right, for the Spirit of the Lord saith the Negro had no right nor cannot hold the Priesthood." As recollected by Coltrin, the story is arranged to feature Coltrin's primary connection with Joseph Smith, to highlight his own advance discernment of prophetic revelation, and to ascribe to Joseph Smith an affirmation of "Bro Zebedee's" "rightness." Relationship, discernment, and rightness have been among the most powerful forms of social capital in Mormonism, and Coltrin arranged his recollections to claim all three for himself. His memory of Smith having "dropt his head" also suggests a micropolitics of fealty. Coltrin also claimed to have heard Smith announce in public that "no person having the least particle of Negro blood can hold the priesthood."[34] The word "particle" can actually be traced to various speeches of Brigham Young on the question of Black ordination. Coltrin demonstrated his own fealty to Young by putting his words in the mouth of Joseph Smith in the presence of Young's son Brigham Young Jr. and his successor John Taylor. Coltrin, who, despite his ordination to Church patriarch in 1873, had become a minor player in the affairs of the Church due in part to his financial and geographical marginalization in Spanish Fork, enjoyed something of a personal renaissance after this interview, as he was invited by John Taylor to accompany him to temple dedications in his official capacity as patriarch in years following. Relationship, discernment, rightness, and loyalty or fealty shaped this pivotal moment in LDS history. The joint witness provided by Smoot and Coltrin, the consensus of two white men, was believed over documentation provided by a single Black man, Elijah Abel. Especially after the death of Elijah Abel in

1884, the Smoot-Coltrin consensus came to serve as a basis for LDS Church policy.

* * *

These three key points in early Mormon history present micropolitical instances when white Mormons opted to build the Mormon movement, Utah territory, and LDS Church priesthood by preferring relationships among whites over a sense of obligation to the human rights of Blacks, Black enfranchisement, and the lived reality of Black testimony. Nineteenth-century Mormons, as historian Paul Reeve has convincingly shown, were on the "wrong side of white": repeatedly racialized and marginalized in popular opinion, in the press, and by political and legal institutions.[35] Building the movement and securing a space for the free exercise of our religion required tactical concessions and agreements, and in the absence of a strongly developed, even singular religious commitment to Black emancipation, it was in every respect expedient to operationalize a variety of white privilege and pass as white. This desire for the protections and privileges of whiteness created a climate generally unwelcoming to African Americans, which thus reinscribed white supremacy by "freeing" white Mormons of lived relationships with and accountability to Black fellow Saints and neighbors.

White Mormons in key decision-making roles actively and intentionally privileged white relationships, loyalty, solidarity, and "rule" over Black lives and Black testimonies at the expense of theology, integrity, and ethics but to the benefit of institutional growth and dominion. This is the definition of white supremacy. White supremacy guided the formation of key LDS institutions—the theocratic territory of Utah, the modern correlated orders of the priesthood, even Brigham Young University, whose founding trustee and major funder bore false witness and influenced others to do the same to block Black Mormons from full access to priesthood and temple rites. At each instance, we witness intentional human decisions to advance white over black.

Thus we find at work at formative nodes in Mormon history an anti-Black racism differentiated from the anti-Black racism of the American South by important distinctions in economic, cultural, and religious contexts, but one just as intense and pervasive.[36] Did Black lives matter in early Mormon Utah? Even before the full consolidation and institutionalization of the anti-Black priesthood and temple ban, stories flashing up at the joints of history suggest that they did not. They reveal, in fact, an active toleration and even celebration of anti-Black violence. Robert Dockery Covington, the leader of the "Cotton Mission" organized by Brigham Young in 1857 to establish a cotton industry in southern Utah and an LDS bishop, recounted to fellow settlers (according to a contemporaneous record) stories of his physical and sexual abuse (including rape) of African American men, women, and children. His statue stands today in downtown Washington, Utah, and the name of Dixie College in St. George commemorates the area's ties to the American South.[37] In 1863, Brigham Young preached at the Tabernacle on Temple Square in Salt Lake City that intermarriage between blacks and whites was forbidden by God on penalty of blood atonement—death. Declaring himself opposed to both slavery as practiced in the South and its abolition, Young declared: "The Southerners make the negroes and the Northerners worship them."[38] In December 1866, Thomas Coleman, an African American man, was found murdered in Salt Lake City—stabbed and his throat cut, a method of killing resembling "penalties" affixed in early Mormon temple rituals. An anti-miscegenation warning was inscribed on a sheet of paper and "attached" to his corpse, as reported by the *Salt Lake Daily Telegraph* on December 12.

There are, of course, other instances in LDS history when even Church members who were deeply embedded in Mormonism's theocratic contexts raised a voice of conscience to oppose anti-Black racism and white supremacy. On January 27, 1852, Orson Pratt raised a voice of opposition to Brigham Young and the "Act in Relation to Service." In this speech, which survives only in shorthand, Pratt refused to allow that slavery or any other oppression of Black people was authorized by God's curse on Cain. "Shall we assume the right without the voice of Lord speaking to us and commanding us to [allow] slavery into our territory?" he asked. Refusing slavery "would give us a greater influence among the other nations of earth and by that means save them. . . .

I look for the welfare of nations abroad who will never hear the gospel of Jesus Christ if we make a law upon this subject . . . for us to bind the African because he is different from us in color enough to cause the angels in heaven to blush."[39] Pratt had felt the pressure to accede to Church leadership time and time again—even in so tender a circumstance as being pressured by Joseph Smith to reject the testimony of Pratt's wife that Smith had sought to marry her. But he had told Brigham Young in December 1847 during an argument over the relationship of the president of the Church to the Quorum of the Twelve:

> I av remarked we av hitherto acted too much as machines[,] heretofore—
> instead of as councillors—[A]s to following the Sp[irit], we have been
> machines. T]hat is what I believe in. . . . I will confess to my own shame
> I av decided contrary to my own feelings many times. I av been too
> much a machine—[B]ut I mean hereafter not to demean myself as to let
> my feelings run contra[ry] to my own judg[men]t.

On the issue of anti-Black racism, Orson Pratt refused to be a "machine." He sided with conscience, and he continued to do so, even when his exhortations failed, when he on February 5, 1852, voted against the bills for the incorporation of Fillmore and Cedar City, which prohibited Black franchise.[40] Pratt's is just one example that shows that at every decisive micropolitical moment in Mormon history it would have been possible to do differently on matters of race. But as we established the foundational institutions of our religion, white Mormons did not choose that path. Neither, really, did any predominantly white American Christian institution.

NOTES

1. Noel Ignatiev, *How the Irish Became White* (New York: Verso, 1995); Karen Brodkin, *How Jews Became White Folks and What That Says About Race in America* (New Brunswick, NJ: Rutgers University Press, 1998).

2. George Lipsitz, *The Possessive Investment in Whiteness: How White People Profit From Identity Politics* (Philadelphia: Temple University Press, 2006), vii.
3. Max Mueller, *Race and the Making of the Mormon People* (Chapel Hill: University of North Carolina Press, 2017).
4. Matthew L. Harris and Newell G. Bringhurst, eds., *The Mormon Church and Blacks: A Documentary History* (Urbana: University of Illinois Press, 2015), 29. See also Martin B. Hickman, "The Political Legacy of Joseph Smith," *Dialogue: A Journal of Mormon Thought* 3.3 (1968): 23; Richard D. Poll and Martin Hickman, "Joseph Smith's Presidential Platform," *Dialogue: A Journal of Mormon Thought* 3.3 (1968): 19–23.
5. On Lewis, see James Oliver Horton, "Generations of Protest: Black Families and Social Reform in Ante-Bellum Boston," *New England Quarterly* 49.2 (1976): 242–256; Connell O'Donovan, "The Mormon Priesthood Ban and Elder Q. Walker Lewis: 'An example for his more whiter brethren to follow,'" *John Whitmer Historical Association Journal* 26 (2006): 48–100.
6. On early Mormonism's treatment of African Americans, see Lester E. Bush Jr. "Mormonism's Negro Doctrine: An Historical Overview," *Dialogue: A Journal of Mormon Thought* 8:1 (Spring 1973): 225–294; Ronald K. Esplin, "Brigham Young and Priesthood Denial to the Blacks: An Alternate View," *BYU Studies* 19.3 (1979): 394–402; Newell G. Bringhurst, *Saints, Slaves, and Blacks: The Changing Place of Black People within Mormonism* (Westport, CT: Greenwood Publishing Group, 1981); Newell G. Bringhurst, "The Mormons and Slavery: A Closer Look," *Pacific Historical Review* 50.3 (1981): 329–338, www.jstor.org/stable/3639603; Armand Mauss, *All Abraham's Children: Changing Mormon Conceptions of Race and Lineage* (Urbana: University of Illinois Press, 2003), 212–230; Newell G. Bringhurst, "The 'Missouri Thesis' Revisited: Early Mormonism, Slavery, and the Status of Black People," in *Black and Mormon*, ed. Newell Bringhurst and Darron Smith (Urbana: University of Illinois, 2004), 13–33; Newell G. Bringhurst, "Joseph Smith's Ambiguous Legacy: Gender, Race, and Ethnicity as Dynamics for Schism Within Mormonism After 1844: 2006 Presidential Address to the John Whitmer Historical Association," *John Whitmer Historical*

Association Journal 27 (2007): 1–47; Matthew L. Harris and Newell G. Bringhurst, eds., *The Mormon Church and Blacks: A Documentary History* (Urbana: University of Illinois Press, 2015); W. Paul Reeve, *Religion of a Different Color: Race and the Mormon Struggle for Whiteness* (New York: Oxford University Press, 2015); Max Mueller, *Race and the Making of the Mormon People* (Chapel Hill: University of North Carolina Press, 2017); Ronald Coleman, "The African-American Pioneer Experience in Utah," lecture delivered August 30, 2017, Wellsville Historical Society, https://www.youtube.com/watch?v=frD1lLeo75A. On estimated counts of early African American LDS Church members, see Reeve, 178.

7. William W. Phelps, "Free People of Color," *Evening and Morning Star* 2.14 (1833): 217–218.

8. See, for example, the experience of an African American man named Chism, as described in Bringhurst (1981) and Max Mueller, *Race and the Making of the Mormon People* (Chapel Hill: University of North Carolina, 2017), 132.

9. Bringhurst (1981), 335; Reeve, 149.

10. Harris and Bringhurst, 32–35; Reeve, 148–159; John Turner, *Brigham Young: Pioneer Prophet* (Cambridge, MA: Harvard Belknap, 2012), 225–226.

11. Orson Hyde, "Slavery Among the Saints," *The Latter-day Saints' Millennial Star* 13 (April 15, 1851): 63, http://contentdm.lib.byu.edu/cdm/ref/collection/MStar/id/2335.

12. See Bringhurst (1981), Nathaniel R. Ricks, "A Peculiar Place for the Peculiar Institution: Slavery and Sovereignty in Early Territorial Utah" (MA thesis, Brigham Young University, 2007); Christopher B. Rich Jr. "The True Policy for Utah: Servitude, Slavery, and 'An Act in Relation to Service,'" *Utah Historical Quarterly* 80 (2012): 54–74; Harris and Bringhurst, 32–35.

13. Rich, 55.

14. Reeve, 155.

15. "History of Brigham Young," entry dated January 5, 1852, in Church Historian's Office Records Collection, LDS Church Archives; quoted in Ricks, 114.

16. Jonathan Stapley, *The Power of Godliness: Mormon Liturgy and Cosmology* (New York: Oxford University Press, 2018), 21.

17. E. R. Snow, "The New Year 1852," *Deseret News*, January 10, 1852, 1; see also Jill Mulvay Derr and Karen Lynn Davidson, *Eliza R. Snow: The Complete Poetry* (Salt Lake City: BYU Press, 2009), 419–420.

18. Maureen Ursenbach Beecher, "The Eliza Enigma," *Dialogue* 11 (1978): 40–43, http://www.dialoguejournal.com/wp-content/uploads/sbi/articles/Dialogue_V11No1_33.pdf.

19. Church History Department Pitman Shorthand transcriptions, 2013–2017; "The Lost Sermons" publishing project files, 1852–1867; Brigham Young, February 5, 1852; Church History Library, https://catalog.lds.org/record/5df3b7da-d0a5-437b-8268-7dde8a87c76e/comp/fc314280-4158-4286-a6c7-6571eccf11ad?view=browse (accessed March 26, 2019).

20. Brigham Young Addresses, Ms d 1234, Box 48, Folder 3, dated February 5, 1852, located in the LDS Church Historical Department, Salt Lake City, Utah. See also https://archive.org/details/CR100317B0001F0017.

21. Bringhurst (1981), 335; Ricks, 131.

22. The United States Census, US Census, 1860, https://www.census.gov/library/publications/1864/dec/1860a.html.

23. B. H. Roberts, *A Comprehensive History of the Church*, vol. 4 (Salt Lake City: Church of Jesus Christ of Latter-day Saints, 1930), 533.

24. C. Elliot Berlin, "Abraham Owen Smoot: Pioneer Mormon Leader" (MA thesis, Brigham Young University, 1955), http://scholarsarchive.byu.edu/cgi/viewcontent.cgi?article=5522&context=etd.

25. Amy Tanner Thiriot, personal correspondence, November 10, 2017; "Schedule" (June 1860), http://www.rootsweb.ancestry.com/~utgenweb/Census/1860US/SaltLake/PageP24.jpg.

26. "David Lewis Company, 1851," *Mormon Pioneer Overland Travel*, https://history.lds.org/overlandtravel/companies/185/david-lewis-company.

27. Third District Court, Salt Lake County Probate Case Files, no. 39, "in the Matter of David Lewis" (1855), http://images.archives.utah.gov/cdm/ref/collection/p17010coll30/id/590.

28. Text of statement reprinted in "Duritha Trail Lewis," Our Family Heritage, July 3, 2011, http://ourfamilyheritage.blogspot.com/2011/07/duritha-trail-lewis.html.

29. Letter reprinted in Margaret Blair Young and Darius Gray, *Bound for Canaan* (revised and expanded) (Salt Lake City, UT: Zarahemla Books, 2013).
30. Bush (1973), 31–32; Calvin Robert Stephens, "The Life and Contributions of Zebedee Coltrin" (MA thesis, Brigham Young University, 1974), 53n55; Reeve, 196–197.
31. Reeve, 196–197.
32. Stephens, 53–55. See also Paul Reeve, "Guest Post: Newly Discovered Document Provides Dramatic Details About Elijah Able and the Priesthood," Keepapitchinin, January 18, 2019, http://www.keepapitchinin.org/2019/01/18/guest-post-newly-discovered-document-provides-dramatic-details-about-elijah-able-and-the-priesthood/.
33. Stephens, 77–78, 86–88.
34. Stephens, 55.
35. Reeve, 138.
36. Dennis Lythgoe observed in his 1966 University of Utah MA thesis, "Negro Slavery in Utah," that the Mormon "position on the Negro closely resembled that of the South" (84).
37. Brian Maffly, "Utah's Dixie Was Steeped in Slave Culture, Historians Say," *Salt Lake Tribune*, December 10, 2012, http://archive.sltrib.com/article.php?id=55424505&itype=CMSID.
38. Bringhurst and Harris, 43.
39. Margaret Blair Young, "A Few Words From Orson Pratt," Patheos, June 11, 2014, http://www.patheos.com/blogs/welcometable/2014/06/a-few-words-from-orson-pratt/.
40. Gary James Bergera, "The Orson Pratt—Brigham Young Controversies: Conflict Within the Quorums, 1853–1868," *Dialogue: A Journal of Mormon Thought* 13.2 (1980): 7–49; see also Gary James Bergera, *Conflict in the Quorum: Orson Pratt, Brigham Young, Joseph Smith* (Salt Lake City: Signature Books, 2002).

CHAPTER 3

ORIGINALISM, INFALLIBILITY, AND THE INSTITUTIONALIZATION OF WHITE SUPREMACY

1880s-1940s

When a predominantly white religious community casts its lots, chooses whiteness, and designates its Black scapegoats, history shows that it attributes these outcomes to the will of God—just as Aaron did in Leviticus. White Christians begin to tell ourselves that although Black suffering is regrettable, it is inevitable: "The poor will always be with us," or so God himself ordained. This is how God wants it, and this is how it has always been. Actual histories of white supremacy, the human failings of founders, the intentionality of their betrayals, and the possibility that it could have been otherwise—these critical parts of the story fade into memory. Predominantly white institutions assume the facade of inevitability and timelessness and the exclusion of Black people hardens into a self-perpetuating fact. Legal scholar Thomas Ross has described this dynamic as "black abstraction":

> Black abstraction is the rhetorical depiction of the black person in an abstract context, outside of any real and rich social context. . . . The power of black abstraction is that it obscures the humanness of black persons. We can more easily think of black persons as not fully human so long as we do not see them in a familiar social context. We can accept the absence of stigmatization in de jure segregation, or its self-imposed

Mormonism and white supremacy. Joanna brooks, Oxford University Press (2020). © Oxford University Press.
DOI: 10.1093/oso/9780190081768.001.0001

quality, so long as we resist empathy. . . . The great power of black abstraction is its power to blunt the possible empathetic response.

Black abstraction, Ross observes, was critical to legal opinions such as Dred Scott and Plessy in which US Supreme Court justices could legitimate the dehumanization and segregation of Black people by focusing exclusively on the nation's chartering legal documents—flawed as they may have been—while taking pains to exclude as evidence the impacts of the law on Black lives.

Empathy requires contact, observation, information, understanding, or, failing these, a powerful imagination and a consciousness willing to push beyond the comfort of stereotype. Systematic "modern" knowledge as constituted by whites has been developed not through empathetic engagement with Black and indigenous lives but through abstraction. Virtually every modern knowledge project of scale has served as an expression of the European imperial agenda to appropriate, collect, and organize other lives in other places to exert and enforce material and political domination. Systems of "racial" classification—first legal, then scientific—themselves emerged from a context of imperial violence and in the service of racial domination. Scientists like Linnaeus who produced the first systematic classificatory "racial" schemes rendered their abstract systems from an archive of data shaped down to the point of its origination by colonization. Their systematicity is an alibi for massive crimes. As legal scholar Thomas Ross observed in 1990, "originalism," or the claim that judges were helpless in the face of racial inequality because they could not change the content of the nation's founding documents or the intent of its founders, was key to establishing white racial innocence, the idea that whites as a class were not responsible for the harms of anti-Black racism. Behind every disciplined presentation of system in neatly arrayed and carefully enumerated treatises stands a thousand, if not a million, human encounters and choices, a long discontinuous sequence of micropolitical interactions that in their collected mass provide the weight of "authority" and the appearance of originality. Authors create systems to vest their own perspectives with an aura of originalism: authority, universality, timelessness, coherence, and inevitability. But every system bears telltale marks and traces of the politics from which it emerged.

We can see this in the emergence of a systematic and institutionalized Christian fundamentalism in the United States in the late nineteenth and early twentieth centuries, during what historian Rayford Logan famously termed "the nadir of American race relations." Especially in places with significant Black populations, these decades saw deadly anti-Black vigilantism, lynchings, and white-on-Black riots in places like Tulsa, Oklahoma. They also saw the broad popularization of white supremacy in American culture emblematized in movies like *Birth of a Nation* (1915), the nationwide rise of the Ku Klux Klan, and the institutionalization of Jim Crow laws and economic systems like debt peonage and convict leasing designed to maintain Black labor as a caste. These years also saw racist retrenchment among orthodox white American Christians. J. Albert Harrill explains:

> Antislavery Christianity was forced away from close readings of the text into a less literal reading of the Bible by the moral imperative of the struggle against slavery. The first step in this move was to find a kernel in the gospel and to make that kernel control biblical interpretation. That kernel was found to be Jesus' so-called Golden Rule: "Do unto others as you would have them do unto you" (Matthew 7:12 and Luke 6:31). This egalitarian reciprocity ethic became the interpretive key to unlock the meaning of Jesus' silence on slavery.[1]

Higher criticism, a scholarly approach to the Bible developed in German universities to reconcile the Bible with new scientific theories of evolution, accelerated the shift from literalism to ethical interpretation. Fundamentalist Christianity took shape in the 1880s through the 1920s as a rejection of both the social progressivism and nonliteralism of progressive Christianity, which it countered with a "hermeneutics of plain sense" centering around close readings of scriptural proof texts as the final authority on moral questions. *The Fundamentals* (1910–1915), a set of twelve volumes collecting ninety essays by conservative

Christian theologians, set forth the core dogma of this new conservative Christian consensus around literalism and scripture inerrancy. The project was conceived and sponsored by Lymon Stewart, the founder of Union Oil and a famously pious conservative Presbyterian—who was engaged in an imperial rivalry with John D. Rockefeller, head of Standard Oil, and founding funder (with other progressive American Baptists) of the avowedly liberal University of Chicago and its broadly influential Divinity School—and his partner, Pastor A. C. Dixon, an evangelical Christian whose brother Thomas Dixon had authored the white supremacist novel *The Klansmen*, basis for *Birth of a Nation* (1915). Stewart and Dixon promised to send the set "to every pastor, evangelist, missionary, theological professor, theological student, Sunday school superintendent, YMCA and YWCA secretary in the English-speaking world."[2] A massive exercise in abstraction and originalism, *The Fundamentals* are largely mute on questions of human dignity and racial equality. The only treatment of race in the entire set comes from Dyson Hague, a Canadian Anglican pastor, who contributed an essay on the literal value of Genesis, in which he perpetuated the centuries-old tradition of mapping racial categories onto the sons of Noah:

> The Hamitic nations, including the Chaldean, Babylonia, and Egyptian, have been degraded, profane, and sensual. The Shemitic have been the religious with the line of the coming Messiah. The Japhetic have been the enlarging, and the dominant races, including all the great world monarchies, both of the ancient and modern times, the Grecian, Roman, Gothic, Celtic, Teutonic, British and American, and by recent investigation and discovery, the races of India, China, and Japan. Thus Ham lost all empire centuries ago.[3]

African and African American peoples, according to Hague, were among the descendants of Ham. Christian fundamentalism, the most impactful white American Protestant movement of the century, offered itself from its beginnings in the service of white supremacy.

The movement to create a systematic, Bible-based fundamentalist white American Christianity had white supremacist impulses at its core. It was motivated by a retreat from an engaged, ethical, emancipatory Christianity and by an insistence on using biblical proof texts to apologize for slavery and empire. As James Cone writes, "From the very beginning to the present day, American white theological thought has been 'patriotic,' either by defining the theological task independently of black suffering (the northern liberal approach) or by defining Christianity as compatible with white racism. In both cases, theology becomes a servant of the state, and that can only mean death to blacks."[4] Like other American Christianities, Mormonism too hurried in the late nineteenth and early twentieth centuries to develop its own systematic renditions of its much-maligned theology. It did so at the same moment that it sought to achieve for Utah recognition as a state while yet maintaining a theocratic territorial Mormonism that persisted under the cover of the nation-state (and persists to this day). It did so in a context of Black abstraction as a consequence of decisions by influential Mormon leaders to exclude Black people from Utah territory and the Mormon movement. With only a few dozen African American people living in LDS communities, white Mormons could maintain an untroubled ignorance of Black experience and Black perspectives, then reframe their ignorance as religious knowledge. Just as American Protestant fundamentalists used systematic theology and correlation in these same decades to retreat from urgent ethical questions about race, Mormon theologians produced systematic theologies and curriculum that erased and retreated from responsibility for Black Mormon lives. The systematization of Mormon theology went hand in hand with a centralization and bureaucratization of Mormon religious life at the turn of the century. Consequently, modern Mormonism instituted one of the most rigidly enforced systems of racial segregation in the history of American Christianity. This chapter examines how this happened, and how white Mormon people let this happen—or, more plainly, *did this*—to ourselves.

* * *

Even though it was home to a comparatively small Black population—which grew from 232 in 1880 to 1,446 in 1940, mostly in connection with coal mining and railroads[5]—Utah was by no means absolved from the ruthless anti-Black violence of the late nineteenth and early twentieth centuries. Southern States Mission President John Morgan implicitly endorsed lynching during a sermon at the Church's main Assembly Hall on Temple Square on December 18, 1881, when he recounted witnessing an African American woman taking her purchased seat in a first-class train car in Nashville, Tennessee, displacing him and other white passengers to the second-class smoking car. Morgan described the woman's conduct as "impudence" and proudly recalled that he had remarked to the railroad car "manager" that had an African American man attempted the same twenty-five years earlier "you would have hung him to a lamppost," remarks subsequently published (without criticism) in the *Deseret News* and *Journal of Discourses*.[6] On August 25, 1883, Sam Joe Harvey, an African American man, was arrested for allegedly shooting a police officer, then turned over to a Salt Lake City mob that hanged him and dragged his corpse down State Street. And the last recorded anti-Black lynching in the American West took place in the coal mining town of Price, Utah, on June 18, 1925, when a crowd estimated at 1,000 including families with children carrying picnic baskets gathered to see Robert Marshall, an African American miner and a fellow Mormon, hung from a tree.[7]

It was in this context, during the nadir of American race relations, that what historian D. Michael Quinn has described as the "headquarters culture" of institutional Mormonism took shape. Utah Mormon leaders engaged in a coordinated effort to transition Mormonism from a frontier "sect" to something the rest of the nation would recognize as a Protestant-type "church," a transition manifest in the relinquishment of the public practice of polygamy in 1890 (it has never been dislodged from Mormon doctrine), Utah statehood, and the election and national trial of Utah Senator Reed Smoot. Poststatehood in-migration of non-Mormons to Utah and out-migration of Utah-Idaho-Arizona Mormons seeking economic and educational opportunity on the coasts opened new cultural crosscurrents that also spurred a

greater emphasis among Mormons on conformity with orthodox belief and practice to sharpen the differentiating edges of Mormon identity.[8] Terryl Givens writes, "As the church grew more bureaucratically
sophisticated, populous, and geographically diffuse, the maintenance
of orthodoxy through centralized correlation and control became a
more urgent concern."[9] The Church too, having survived efforts by
the US government to bankrupt and destroy it, was newly challenged
by the demands of consolidating and extending its institutional infrastructure. The Mormon movement could no longer count on charismatic hierarchical leadership, extended family relations, geographical
isolation and concentration, and the familiarity and immediacy of access that came with these to hold it all together.

This "headquarters culture" was forged in and through white solidarity and white supremacy. LDS Church President Joseph F. Smith
(1838–1918) belonged to a select cohort of LDS Church leaders who had
been since 1852 affirming their relationships to one another through
actions and decisions that upheld white interests over Black lives and
white testimonies over Black testimonies. Smith also understood the
necessity of winning acceptance to the mainstream. As historian Paul
Reeve writes: "Their decisions regarding race, priesthood, and temples
at the turn of the century are best viewed as efforts by Mormon leaders
to facilitate Mormonism's transition from charges of racial contam-
ination to exemplars of white purity."[10] During these years, high-
ranking Church leaders hashed out time and again in personal letters
and closed meetings competing rationales for excluding Black LDS
people from the temple and priesthood ordination. For his part, Joseph
F. Smith had maintained if quietly and individually his memory and
testimony that there was a time when Black men had been ordained
to the priesthood. In 1879, Smith had testified to other Church leaders
that Elijah Abel had been ordained to the priesthood by the Prophet
Joseph Smith and contested the recollection of Abraham Smoot and
Zebedee Coltrin that Joseph Smith had renounced the ordination.[11]
He would continue to maintain this memory for the next sixteen
years, going on record again in 1895 at a meeting of Church leaders
convened by President Wilford Woodruff to consider Jane Manning

James's request for temple endowment.[12] But he changed his story on August 26, 1908, at a meeting of the Council of the First Presidency and Quorum of the Twelve. In response to a letter from the recently returned president of the Church's South Africa mission about whether missionaries should teach and baptize individuals of Black African descent, President Smith instructed the council that Elijah Abel had been ordained to the priesthood, but Smith also stated—for the first time on record—that this ordination "was declared null and void by the Prophet himself." He also cited as a precedent the denial of endowment and sealing privileges to Abel and James by Presidents Brigham Young, John Taylor, and (mistakenly) Wilford Woodruff and argued for a "position without any reserve" that Black LDS people were not to be ordained, endowed, or sealed because they bore the "curse" of "Cainan" imposed by "the decree of the Almighty."[13]

What changed for Joseph F. Smith? What made it possible to recant his testimony and accede, finally, to the galvanizing white majority? Perhaps it is no coincidence that Smith changed his story only after the death of Jane Manning James—Mormon pioneer, African American woman, and force of conscience—on April 16, 1908. James was such an iconic figure in Mormon life that within hours her death made front-page headlines in the *Deseret Evening News*, which recalled, "Few persons were more noted for faith and faithfulness as was Jane Manning James, and so of the humble of the earth, she numbered friends and acquaintances by the hundreds. Many persons will regret to learn that the kind and generous soul has passed from the earth." Her funeral just a few days later drew hundreds, including President Smith, who spoke at the occasion. Smith likely shared personal recollections drawn from his own memory, as he had known James from the time he was a five-year-old boy. Assembled mourners also likely heard Jane's life told in her own words, as she had in 1900 dictated her autobiography to a family historian with the specific instructions that it be read at her funeral. In it, Jane Manning James records the welcome she received from Joseph Smith when the nine-member family group she led finished its trek from Wilton, Connecticut, by canal boat and then on foot, to Nauvoo, Illinois:

When we found it, Sister Emma was standing in the door and she kindly said, "Come in. Come in!" Brother Joseph said to some white sisters that was present, "Sisters, I want you to occupy this room this evening with some brothers and sisters that have just arrived." Brother Joseph placed the chairs around the room, then he went and brought Sister Emma and Dr. Bernhisel and introduced them to us. Brother Joseph took a chair and sat down by me and said, "You have been the head of this little band, haven't you?" I answered, "Yes, sir!" He then said, "God bless you! Now I would like you to relate your experience in your travels." I related to them all that I have above stated and a great deal more minutely, as many incidents has passed from my memory since then. Brother Joseph slapped Dr. Bernhisel on the knee and said, "What do you think of that, doctor: isn't that faith?" The doctor said, "Well, I rather think it is. If it had have been me, I fear I should have backed out and returned to my home!" He then said, "God bless you. You are among friends now and you will be protected." They sat and talked to us a while, gave us words of encouragement and good counsel.[14]

James stayed with the Smith family during her first days in Nauvoo and found herself the recipient of empathetic attention from Joseph Smith:

Brother Joseph came into the room as usual and said, "Good morning. Why—not crying, [are you]?" "Yes sir," [I said,] "the folks have all gone and got themselves homes, and I have got none." He said, "Yes you have, you have a home right here if you want it. You musn't cry, we dry up all tears here." I said, "I have lost my trunk and all my clothes." He asked how I had lost them; I told them I put them in care of Charles Wesley Wandle and paid him for them and he has lost them. Brother Joseph said, "Don't cry, you shall have your trunk and clothes again." Brother Joseph went out and brought Sister Emma in and said, "Sister Emma, here is a girl that says she has no home. Haven't you a home for her?" "Why yes, if she wants one." He said, "She does," and then he left us.[15]

James lived with and worked for the Smith family until Joseph Smith's assassination in 1844, when she transitioned into the employ of Brigham Young, whom she called "Brother Brigham." She married a fellow Black Mormon and in 1847 made the trek across the plains to Utah, giving birth to a son named Silas at Winter Quarters on the trail. She established a home in Salt Lake City, eighth ward; had six more children; served in the Relief Society; and petitioned repeatedly for access to sacred temple rites, which she was denied by every LDS Church president from John Taylor forward. Still, she maintained her generosity toward and activity in the Church and was recognized, if only symbolically, for her historic role in the Mormon movement: at major events in the Mormon Tabernacle, authorities routinely reserved front-and-center seats for Jane and her brother Isaac Manning.[16] She took and held this complicated and constricted place of high visibility with dignity, even as mobs in Salt Lake City lynched Black men in the streets, and Church leaders voiced base prejudices that had far more to do with the white supremacist culture of the United States than with the principles of the Mormon faith. She knew the empathy of Joseph and Emma Smith and the reality of later leaders' anti-Black racism, and by insisting on having her story told in her own words at her funeral, she made sure to leave Latter-day Saints with a firsthand account of their own devolution from the spirit of their founder. Perhaps Jane Manning James wanted to hold Mormonism and its leaders accountable.

Jane Manning James had lived with and worked for Joseph Smith, and she called him "Brother Joseph." She called Brigham Young "Brother Brigham." All subsequent LDS Church presidents she called by their last names. Mormonism had consolidated and disciplined it-self from a religious movement into a modern, hierarchical religious institution. With this institutional consolidation, Mormonism's treat-ment of Black members also moved from informal and relational to formal and institutional. With her death, Mormonism lost its last living Black witness to the generosity of Joseph Smith and the original possibilities of an expansive, anti-racist way of practicing the faith. Not having Jane Manning James in the front row to look them in the eyes meant that the LDS Church leaders who took the stand at major events in the Mormon Tabernacle could tell the Mormon story as they wished, freed from the constraints of historical accountability.

Indeed, it seems likely that President Smith found in the death of Jane Manning James freedom from accountability—from the pain of bearing false witness in the presence of someone who knew it was false—to the last living witness to the reality of Abel's ordination. The death of Jane Manning James made it possible to deny and ignore the complicated facts of Black Mormon history and the reality of Black Mormon testimony. It contributed to the abstraction of Black lives from decision making by LDS Church leaders and to the erasure of stories of Black Mormon lives from LDS Church official publications. It made it possible for Church leaders like Joseph F. Smith to remake Mormon history, to deny that Joseph Smith had ever truly meant to ordain Black men, and to instead produce a new theological rationale for anti-Black discrimination and segregation that attributed exclusion to the original will of God from the beginning of time.

* * *

The first step to dislodging a lived history is to generalize beyond its details. This is the necessary step that transforms the chaotic creative energy of an emergent faith into a proper and respectable theology. The first theologian to undertake this work in the domain of Mormonism was James Talmage (1862–1933), a member of the Church's Quorum of the Twelve Apostles and the first Mormon to receive a PhD. Talmage compiled *The Articles of Faith* (1899), a landmark work of LDS systematic theology organized around the thirteen Articles of Faith composed by Joseph Smith in 1841. The impetus to systematize and organize is evident throughout the text, down to its composition in carefully numbered paragraphs. Notably, the work makes no mention of race nor of restricting priesthood by race, though that was by 1899 the Church's effective practice. Similarly, John Widtsoe (1872–1952), who was educated at Harvard and received his PhD from the University of Goettingen, Germany, made no mention of the priesthood and temple ban in his *Rational Theology* (1915), a similarly motivated effort to systematize Mormon belief and practice but through a humanistic framework. Widtsoe in fact goes so far as to say: "In the Church, all men who have attained sufficient experience hold or should hold the Priesthood."[17] Talmage and Widtsoe avoided what James Cone characterizes as the theological issue of "black suffering," but they also avoided any mention of the Church's exclusionary practices. They wrote about the priesthood as though there were no exclusions at all. Making the exclusion of Black Mormons invisible abstracted Black lives and Black experience.

Mormon theologian B. H. Roberts took it one step further. He developed a systematic theology that rationalized white racism as an essential part of Mormonism and incorporated secular anti-Black racism into the LDS print canon and Church curriculum. Roberts (1857–1933) was born and raised in a working-class home in Lancashire, England; his parents converted to Mormonism the year he was born. His father, reportedly an alcoholic, later abandoned the family; his mother followed, emigrating to the United States and finally to Utah. At the age of nine, B. H. left England with his sister and also emigrated, reunited with his less-than-welcoming mother, and settled in Bountiful, Utah. After working first as a miner and then apprenticing as a blacksmith, B. H. learned to read and entered the University of Deseret. An insatiable autodidact, he was also a tough-minded if contrary stalwart who served on recovery missions to bring the bodies of murdered missionaries home from Cane Creek, Tennessee, in 1884, and a committed polygamist who largely evaded federal arrest and prosecution. He was, to be sure, as hard-headed, contrary, pugilistic, and controversy-loving as they come. He was also early Mormonism's most prolific systematic theologian and historian, compiling a seven-volume *History of the Church of Jesus Christ of Latter-day Saints* (now known as the *Documentary History of the Church*, or DHC) (published 1902–1912) and another three-thousand-page seven-volume *Comprehensive History of the Church*, which he badgered the Church into publishing in 1930. He also engaged in studies of the controversies surrounding the Book of Mormon, on the theory that Mormonism must face the questions directly, reaching conclusions that have left some question as to whether he himself maintained an orthodoxly faithful view of LDS scripture.[18]

As early as 1885, in his role as editor of LDS Church magazine *The Contributor*, in an article entitled "Instructions to Youth," Roberts brought into the LDS Church print canon an arcane theological speculation conjured up by the early Mormon thinker Orson Hyde in 1844. Hyde imagined that racial differentiation among humans reflected the relative valor of their conduct in a premortal spiritual existence; Roberts introduced verses from the recently canonized LDS book of scripture the Pearl of Great Price (first published in the United States in 1878 and canonized in 1880) invoking it as scriptural support for this view. Roberts theorized that Ham, already under punishment from his father, Noah, for having betrayed him in his nakedness, disqualified his posterity from receiving the priesthood by marrying "Egyptus," a woman whose name and brief mention in the Pearl of Great Price Roberts takes as evidence of descent from Cain and inheritor of his accursedness: "I believe that race is the one through which it is ordained those spirits that were not valiant in the great rebellion in heaven should come; who, through their indifference or lack of integrity to righteousness, rendered themselves unworthy of the Priesthood and its powers, and hence it is withheld from them to this day."[19]

In 1907, Roberts fortified, extended, and further institutionalized this line of thought in his seven-volume *Seventies' Course in Theology* (1907), which was published as instructional manuals for adult priesthood-holding men across the LDS Church. Roberts's systematic "method" in developing this course of study was to frame a lesson plan in a sequence of enumerated points, then provide selected scriptural proof texts for group study. By reading through and discussing together these selected proof texts in a given order, Mormon priesthood holders could develop study habits that joined individual reflection with an orthodoxly conservative perspective on important elements of Mormon doctrine. It was a pedagogy well suited to a modestly educated but intellectually curious Mormon grassroots, an all-comers way of doing theology that persists in Mormon Sunday schools to this day.

LDS Church historian Leonard Arrington remembered that books like those written by Widtsoe and Roberts filled a void (especially for out-migrating LDS people) where there had been only "a few books intended for educated LDS people" that sought to "reconcile secular learning and Latter-day Saint scholarship."[20] That Mormonism could produce a coherent, "systematic" account of itself in polite, recognizable language, and in print, was essential to its transition from marginal sect to respectable and recognizably Protestant "church" in the early twentieth century. And like all purportedly neutral systems, the design of Roberts's *Course on Theology* reveals the preoccupations, prejudices, blind spots, and antipathies of its author. And what stood behind B. H. Roberts's *Course on Theology*, volume 1, part 5, lesson VIII, "The Law of the Lord in Ancient and Modern Revelation Applied to the Negro Race Problem," was not ancient scripture or modern revelation but Reconstruction-era white supremacist thought, developed in the American South and incorporated silently into a defining work of Mormon theology (figure 3.1).

Roberts felt "the Negro Race Problem" was so significant that it warranted attention in volume one of the seven-volume *Course*, immediately following lessons on the history of the Quorums of the Seventy and each of the books of LDS scripture and before lessons on essential elements of LDS theology. Roberts structured the lesson around a sequence of topics that guided Church members to deduce from the history of white supremacist domination of Blacks in the United States "the law of God." The sequence ran as follows:

I. The American Negro Race Problem
  1. The Advent of the Negro Race in America
  2. Slavery and the Abolition of It
  3. Political Enfranchisement of the Black Race—Its Wisdom or Unwisdom
  4. Present Status of the Negro Race Problem
II. The Law of the Lord as Affecting the Negro Race Problem
  1. The Progenitor of the Race
  2. The Manner of Its Preservation Through the Flood
  3. The Curse Put Upon It by Noah

LESSON VIII.

SCRIPTURE READING EXERCISE.

(SPECIAL LESSON.)

THE LAW OF THE LORD IN ANCIENT AND MODERN REVELATION APPLIED TO THE AMERICAN NEGRO RACE PROBLEM.

SUBJECT.

I. The American Negro Race Problem.
  1. Advent of the Negro Race in America.
  2. Slavery and the Abolition of It.

  3. Political Enfranchisement of the Black Race—Its Wisdom or Unwisdom.

  4. Present Status of the Negro Race Problem.

II. The Law of the Lord as Affecting the Negro Race Problem.
  1. The Progenitor of the Race.

  2. The Manner of Its Preservation through the Flood.
  3. The Curse Put Upon it by Noah.
  4. In what Respects a Forbidden Race.
  5. From all the Foregoing Deduce the Law of God in the Question.

REFERENCES.

History of the United States by Alexander Stephens, pp. 36, 88, 366. Same Author's, "War Between the States. Old Virginia and Her Neighbors (John Fiske), Vol. I, p. 18, 19, Vol. II. pp. 7, 29, 41, 172-222, 228-231, 235-6.

Emancipation Proclamation (Abraham Lincoln), War Between the States. Vol. II. Appendix to Papers and Messages of the Presidents' Vol.

For Present Status of the Question see "The Color Line," Wm. Benjamin Smith, McClure Phillips & Co., N .Y.

Book of Moses—Pearl of Great Price, Chap. v, verses 5-8, 22; Chap. viii: vehses -8, 2; Chap. viii: 12-15. Gen. ix: 18-27.

Book of Abraham, Chap, i: 9-11, 21-28. Compare Gen. ix: 18-27; also "The Book of Abraham—A Divine and Ancient Record," (Reynolds), p. 6, 7. Smith's Old Testament History, Chap. iii.

SPECIAL TEXT: "Let not man join together what God hath put asunder."—"THE COLOR LINE," chap. i.

Figure 3.1. Contents for B. H Roberts, "Lesson VIII," Part 5, Volume 1, *Course on Theology*, 1907.

Image courtesy of Marriott Special Collections Library, University of Utah.

4. In What Respects a Forbidden Race
5. From All the Foregoing Deduce the Law of God in the Question

A column at the right provided references: proof texts for individual and collective study to guide reflection and discussion. Proof texts in previous lessons had come from scripture, Church history, and reference works on scripture history developed by clergy of other Protestant faiths.

For this lesson on race, Roberts sourced references from the Old Testament, the Pearl of Great Price, Alexander Stephens's *The History of the United States* (1881), Stephens's *A Constitutional View of the War Between the States* (1868), and William Benjamin Smith's *The Color Line: A Brief on Behalf of the Unborn* (1905), as shown in figure 3.2.

Alexander Stephens (1812–1883) served as the vice president of the Confederacy during the US Civil War. In his famous Confederate "Cornerstone Speech" of 1861, Stephens had declared: "Our new government is founded upon exactly [this] idea; its foundations are laid, its cornerstone rests upon the great truth, that the negro is not equal to the white man; that slavery—subordination to the superior race—is his natural and normal condition. This, our new government, is the first, in the history of the world, based upon this great physical, philosophical, and moral truth." Slavery, he argued, "is the proper status of the negro in our form of civilization."[21] Roberts sourced to Stephens's *History,* written to serve as a history textbook for the former states of the Confederacy, a view of African slaves as "supposed descendants of Ham" whose importation as slaves to the Virginia colony was the "source of so much subsequent trouble" and was opposed by early Virginia settlers not out of "feelings of humanity" toward the enslaved but out of a concern for "the best interests and future welfare of the colony." Roberts also followed Stephens in characterizing moves to abolish slavery by the US Congress beginning in 1790 as a betrayal of the "federal system" and a compromise of states' rights and the ultimate abolition of slavery in 1863 as "merely a war measure" designed to provide an advantage to the Union in the Civil War. How B. H. Roberts came to espouse a view of American history according to the Confederacy and its white supremacist intellectuals is not entirely clear but may stem from his service as the leadership of the Southern States Mission in the 1880s or from his activity as a populist Democrat in national political circles. (Despite being duly elected by his home

REFERENCES.

History of the United States by Alexander Stephens, pp. 36, 88, 366. Same Author's, "War Between the States. Old Virginia and Her Neighbors (John Fiske), Vol. I, p. 18, 19, Vol. II. pp. 7, 29, 41, 172-222, 228-231, 235-6.

Emancipation Proclamation (Abraham Lincoln), War Between the States. Vol. II. Appendix to Papers and Messages of the Presidents' Vol.

For Present Status of the Question see "The Color Line," Wm. Benjamin Smith, McClure Phillips & Co., N .Y.

Book of Moses—Pearl of Great Price, Chap. v, verses 5-8, 22; Chap. viii: vehses -8, 2; Chap. viii: 12-15. Gen. ix: 18-27.

Book of Abraham, Chap, i: 9-11, 21-28. Compare Gen. ix: 18-27; also "The Book of Abraham— A Divine and Ancient Record," (Reynolds), p. 6, 7. Smith's Old Testament History, Chap. iii.

Figure 3.2. References for B. H Roberts, "Lesson VIII," Part 5, Volume 1, *Course on Theology*, 1907.

Image courtesy of Marriott Special Collections Library, University of Utah.

district in 1898, Roberts was banned from taking a seat in Congress after national debate by a 260-to-58 vote of his would-be congressional colleagues on the grounds that he was a polygamist. When William Jennings Bryan campaigned for president in Utah in 1900, Roberts campaigned for him, introducing him at one Salt Lake City event as a man like Thomas Jefferson "who had been provided by God to steer the ship of state from the shoals that designing men had set for it."[22])

These were the historical source texts Roberts introduced into LDS Church Quorums of the Seventy for mass study. LDS lay priesthood curriculum relied on Confederate history.

Source texts for contemplating the "wisdom or unwisdom" of the "political enfranchisement of the Black race" Roberts drew from William Benjamin Smith's *The Color Line*. Smith (1850–1934) was a professor of mathematics at Tulane University who had published in the 1890s the first in what would be a series of studies of a "pre-Christian Jesus," the idea that Jewish religious groups had worshipped a purely divine Jesus figure, which he intended as a counterargument to higher criticism's presentation of the "historical Jesus" as an actual, historically discernable human being. Smith took time from his mathematical and theological pursuits in 1905 to write and publish *The Color Line*. His reason for doing so Smith declares in the work's opening paragraph:

> The following pages attempt a discussion of the most important question that is likely to engage the attention of the American People for many years and even generations to come. Compared with the vital matter of pure Blood, all other matters, as of tariff, of currency, of subsidies, of civil service, of labour and capital, of education, of forestry, of science and art, and even of religion, sink into insignificance. For, to judge by the past, there is scarcely any conceivable educational or scientific or governmental or social or religious polity under which the pure strain of Caucasian blood might not live and thrive and achieve great things for History and Humanity; on the other hand, there is no reason to believe that any kind or degree of institutional excellence could permanently stay the race decadence that would follow surely in the wake of any considerable contamination of that blood by the blood of Africa.[23]

In six chapters following, Smith lays out arguments for the innate inferiority of African Americans, designed not only to make a case for the permanent segregation of the races but also to counter the work of American anthropologist Franz Boas, a public opponent of scientific racism. Smith's book draws its "evidences" from an imperial mish-mash of source texts in comparative physiology, anthropometry, and population science to argue that inferiority was rooted in the Black body and to argue vociferously against interaction with Blacks as a danger to the physical superiority of the white race, maintained in the purity of white "blood." Smith's emphasis on blood aligned neatly with Mormonism's theological emphasis on literal "blood" inheritance from the House of Israel as a factor in the survival and restoration of sacred religious rites and the modern-day gathering of God's elect.[24] This may have been one reason Roberts used Smith. But the fact that more than half of the lesson on the "Negro Problem" is quoted directly from Smith suggests that its appeal went even deeper. Militancy against social interaction and marriage between the races had been a driving preoccupation for Brigham Young and had deeply influenced his successors in the LDS Church leadership. Roberts hones in on this very issue in his *Course*, citing not from within the Mormon tradition or the statements of Brigham Young but from external "scientific" sources in "biological science" as per William Benjamin Smith. Roberts concludes his references with this quote from *The Color Line*: "That the negro is markedly inferior to the Caucasian is proved both craniologically and by six thousand years of planet-wide experimentation; and that the commingling of inferior with superior must lower the higher is just as certain as that the half-sum of two and six is only four" (see figure 3.3).

The second half of the lesson builds on this rhetorical foundation of white supremacist history and "biological science" a sequence of scripture proof texts designed to guide the LDS priesthood holder through the argument Roberts had hammered out in his 1885 *Contributor* article: that from Cain the Black race had descended, that Cain's descendent Egyptus had married the Noah-accursed Ham, that in their posterity the curse persisted through the flood, and that the curse pertained to the priesthood. "From all the Foregoing," the final prompt in the discussion outline instructed, "Deduce the Law of God in the Question." Roberts guided Church members to deduce from the alleged physical inferiority of Blacks their accursedness as

4. **The Race Question as Affecting the Southern States**: Perhaps the most convincing book in justification of the South in denying to the negro race social equality with the white race is the one written by William Benjamin Smith, entitled "The Color Line, A Brief in Behalf of the Unborn," from which the following is a quotation:

"Here, then, is laid bare the nerve of the whole matter: Is the south justified in this absolute denial of social equality to the negro, no matter what his virtues or abilities or accomplishments?

"We affirm, then, that the south is entirely right in thus keeping open at all times, at all hazards, and at all sacrifices an impassible social chasm between black and white. This she must do in behalf of her blood, her essence, of the stock of her Caucasian race. To the writer the correctness of this thesis seems as clear as the sun—so evident as almost to forestall argument; nor can he quite comprehend the frame of mind that can seriously dispute it. But let us look at it closely. Is there any doubt whatever as to the alternative? If we sit with negroes at our tables, if we entertain them as our guests and social equals, if we disregard the color line in all other relations, is it possible to maintain it fixedly in the sexual relation, in the marriage of our sons and daughters, in the propagation of our species? Unquestionably, No! It is certain as the rising of tomorrow's sun, that, once the middle wall of social partition is broken down, the mingling of the tides of life would begin instantly and proceed steadily. Of course, it would be gradual, but none the less sure, none the less irresistible. It would make itself felt at first most strongly in the lower strata of the white population; but it would soon invade the middle and menace insidiously the very uppermost. Many bright mulattoes would ambitiously woo, and not a few would win, well-bred women disappointed in love or goaded by impulse or weary of the stern struggle for existence. As a race, the Southern Caucasian would be irrevocably doomed. For no possible check could be given to this process once established. Remove the barrier between two streams flowing side by side—immediately they begin to mingle their molecules; in vain you attempt to replace it. * * * * The moment the bar of absolute separation is thrown down in the South, that moment the bloom of her spirit is blighted forever, the promise of her destiny is annulled, the proud fabric of her future slips into dust and ashes. No other conceivable disaster that might befall the South could, for an instant, compare with such miscegenation within her borders. Flood and fire, fever and famine and the sword—even ignorance, indolence, and

Figure 3.3. Conclusion, B. H Roberts, "Lesson VIII," Part 5, Volume 1, *Course on Theology*, 1907.

Image courtesy of Marriott Special Collections Library, University of Utah.

the "forbidden race" and hence God-ordained exclusion. *Quod erat demonstratum.*

Roberts's systematic theology presented alleged biological inferiority, read through the prism of scriptural proof texts, as a rational basis for an anti-Black theology. Presenting racism in this apparently disciplined way, with a "logical" catechistic infrastructure rooted in a carefully arranged set of scripture verses and validated externally by "science" in an official course of study, vested it with an aura of authority, inevitability, and inarguability. This is precisely the kind of work systematic methodologies are meant to do: they are designed to manage and obscure, to vest what is actually a field of information and experience shot through with historical conflict and relations of power with a timeless inevitability that sacralizes as concept its preferred conceits and erases all that does not fit within them. Talmage and Widtsoe nervously failed to mention Blacks at all rather than attempt to manage the contradiction of their exclusion; B. H. Roberts raised their exclusion to the sacred status of concept. Talmage and Widtsoe erased the whole history of conflict on the subject of Black exclusion; B. H. Roberts attributed the erasure to the "Law of God."

The theological system of instruction developed by Roberts played a critical role in LDS institutional history. The publication of Roberts's *Course in Theology* inspired LDS Church President Joseph F. Smith to create a "Correlation Committee" that very year to develop a systematic curriculum for the Church's priesthood quorums. In April 1908, Smith also announced at the Church's General Conference a new initiative to redevelop the organizational infrastructure of priesthood, citing a specific concern that the "lesser" quorums of the priesthood should do more to engage young men and "make them interested in the work of the Lord."[25] It would have required an exceptional commitment to racial equality to advance Black ordination at this pivotal moment when the focus was on making priesthood association attractive to participation and commitment from young white Mormon men. That commitment is nowhere in evidence among LDS Church leaders at this historical moment. Instead, the imperative to organize and systematize gave new energy and force to the imperative to exclude African Americans: formally institutionalizing Black exclusion was one of the elements of priesthood reformation. On April 18, 1908, the LDS Church publication *Liahona: The Elders Journal*, which was distributed to all LDS missions, published an article on "The Negro and the Priesthood" drawing out extensive rationale for the ban from the Pearl of Great Price and the Old Testament, and offering as well without scriptural basis the "more comprehensive explanation" that "negroes," who came from the lineage of Cain and Ham and were thus forbidden from holding the priesthood, were "predestined" to this lineage as a just "deserts" for their conduct in the pre-existence.[26] It also quoted remarks attributed to Brigham Young on the spiritual unsuitability of Black people for priesthood ordination. From this point in time forward, responses from Church headquarters to inquiries by letter from mission field officials were consistent in their advice that missionaries should not seek to proselyte among Black African populations.

Apostle Joseph Fielding Smith, a son of the recently deceased Joseph F. Smith, published another article on "The Negro and the Priesthood" in the Church's monthly *Improvement Era* in April 1924. While indicating that there was no scriptural basis for the pre-existence hypothesis that "prevail[ed] to a considerable extent" among LDS people and that it was not advisable to "dwell" on "speculation" about how premortal life may have shaped "nation[al]" differences, Smith gave anti-Black segregation of the priesthood and temple its own eternal life:

> It is true that the negro race is barred from holding the Priesthood, and this has always been the case. The Prophet Joseph Smith taught this doctrine, and it was made known to him, although we know of no such statement in any revelation in the Doctrine and Covenants, Book of Mormon, or the Bible. . . . Let it suffice that the negro is barred from the Priesthood and the reason we may someday understand.[27]

It was the first time an official Church publication declared in print (see figure 3.4) that the ban was entirely ahistorical, that it had "always been the case" and had been "made known" as the will of God through the Prophet Joseph Smith. Originalism took hold here.

Joseph Fielding Smith expanded his *Improvement Era* essay and extended it into a multipage narrative of the cursed line of Cain-Egyptus-Ham in his 1931 book *The Way to Perfection*, repeatedly attributing the origins of this "doctrine" to Joseph Smith. This finalized the abstraction of Black Mormon lives and the complicated human history writer says: "The belief prevails to a considerable extent that when the plan of redemption was laid before the spiritual hosts in heaven, that one-third remained neutral, also that from this source the negro race sprung. Are there any scriptural proofs, that will substantiate such a belief?"

We know of no scripture, ancient or modern, that declares that at the time of the rebellion in heaven that one-third of the hosts of heaven remained neutral. This thought has developed from the fact that the Lord states that one-third of the hosts of heaven rebelled and were cast out with Lucifer and became the devil and his angels. Doc. and Cov. 29:36-38.

It is true that the negro race is barred from holding the Priesthood, and this has always been the case.. The Prophet Joseph Smith taught this doctrine, and it was made known to him, although we know of no such statement in any revelation in the Doctrine and Covenants, Book of Mormon, or the Bible. However, in the Pearl of Great Price, we find the following statement written by Abraham: "Now this first government of Egypt was established by Pharaoh, the eldest son of Egyptus, the daughter of Ham, and it was after the manner of the government of Ham, which was patriarchal. Pharaoh, being a righteous man, established his kingdom and judged his people wisely and justly all his days, seeking earnestly to imitate that order established by the fathers in the first generations, in the days of the first patriarchal reign, even in the reign of Adam, and also of Noah, his father, who blessed him with the blessings of the earth, and with the blessings of wisdom, but cursed him as pertaining to the Priesthood." Pearl of Great Price, Abraham 1:25-26.

President Brigham Young, in a discourse given in 1855, speaking of the negro said: "It is their privilege to live so as to enjoy many of the blesings which attend obedience to the first principles of the gospel, though they are not entitled to the Priesthood." Journal of Discourses, 2:184.

That one-third of the hosts of heaven remained neutral and therefore were cursed by having a black skin, could hardly be true, for the negro race has not constituted one-third of the inhabitants of the earth.

It is a reasonable thing to believe that the spirits of the pre-mortal state were of varying degrees of intelligence and faithfulness. This thought is conveyed in many passages of scripture, such as Acts 17:24-27; Deuteronomy 32:8; Abraham 3:19-26. However, to dwell upon this topic and point out certain nations as having been cursed because of their acts in the pre-existence, enters too much on the realm of speculation. Therefore, let it suffice that the negro is barred from the Priesthood and the reason some day we may understand.—*Joseph Fielding Smith*.

Figure 3.4. Joseph Fielding Smith, "The Negro and the Priesthood," *Improvement Era*, April 1924, 565.

Image courtesy Marriott Special Collections Library, University of Utah.

of priesthood exclusion from LDS doctrine and vested it through the mechanisms of systematic theology and institutionally coordinated curriculum with self-evident authority. Just as B. H. Roberts claimed that the ban was in fact an expression of the "Law of God," Joseph Fielding Smith rewrote history to suggest that the doctrine originated through revelation of the "Law of God" to Mormonism's founders. Thus, when the Church's First Presidency was moved to settle lingering questions about race and the priesthood with an official statement on the issue in August 17, 1949, it could declare: "The attitude of the Church with reference to the Negroes remains as it has always stood. It is not a matter of the declaration of a policy but of direct commandment from the Lord, on which is founded the doctrine of the Church from the days of its organization." The ban's move from human to divine, from historical to timeless, from micropolitical to institutional, from uneven to correlated, from speculation to doctrine, was thus complete.

If Christian fundamentalists had beat back the encroachments of science and history and retreated from ethical engagement with racial issues by establishing through "systematic" argument, publishing, and distributing a new orthodox consensus around biblical inerrancy, Mormonism's conservatives in the early twentieth century made a parallel move by establishing through "systematic" argument, publishing, and institutionalizing a new orthodox consensus around the inerrancy or infallibility of Mormon prophets. Prophetic infallibility was essential to the survival and institutional development of the modern LDS Church, to its transition from marginal sect to marginally respectable Protestant faith, and to its development of an internal infrastructure capable of maintaining membership and sustaining growth beyond the period of its territorial isolation, against the incursions of increased interaction with the outside world, and through its own rapid geographical expansion through out-migration-coordinated administration. "The Lord will never permit me or any other man who stands as President of this Church to lead you astray," LDS Church President Wilford Woodruff had told the faithful assembled at the General Conference in October 1890, shortly after asking them to accept as "authoritative" the end to the public practice of polygamy. "It is not in the programme. It is not in the mind of God. If I were to attempt that, the Lord would remove me out of my place, and so He will any other man who attempts to lead the children of men astray from the oracles of God and from their duty." His statement was canonized in 1908 after having been reiterated for more than eighteen years by his apostles and successors to overcome deep divisions among Latter-day Saints over whether the end of polygamy was a survival tactic or truly the will of God. The charismatic authority of a prophet, collective reverence for the prophet, and shared accession to a newly institution-alized doctrine of prophetic infallibility produced coherence out of the confusion, contradiction, and dramatic reversals that characterized polygamy's official end. Accession to declared prophetic infallibility also produced coherence out of the confusion, contradiction, and dra-matic reversals that characterized the official institutionalization of Black exclusion from the priesthood and temple rites. Prophets said that prophets had always said so, because God himself said so, and God would not allow prophets to get it wrong. No matter how cruel or unethical anti-Black racism seemed to humans, God had his reasons, to be known in due time. And that's how the story would stand.

* * *

The LDS Church claim that the priesthood and temple ban originated with God and was communicated through revelation to the religion's founders despite living testimony and historical documentation to the contrary constituted its own powerful form of "originalism." The claim that the ban was the "Law of God" or the will of God as re-vealed to infallible prophets allowed every successive generation of leaders and rank-and-file members to claim that they were helpless to change the ban and thus innocent of anti-Black racism. Nothing could be done, we told ourselves, until God himself ordered a change.

But we ourselves did a great deal to carry out the anti-Black es-sence of the ban and extend it far beyond priesthood ordination and temple worship. Once institutionalized in the marrow of LDS doctrine and practice, anti-Black segregation practices radiated out into civil society in geographical areas where Mormons were concentrated. In the 1940s and 1950s, LDS Church leaders including J. Reuben Clark advocated for the racial segregation of Utah hospital blood banks so that white LDS people would not have their blood "mixed" through transfusions from black donors and lose eligibility for priesthood, a practice that held in some areas in Utah through the 1970s.[28] George Albert Smith, J. Reuben Clark, and Mark E. Peterson encouraged local LDS leaders to join and support ordinances and organizations that would prevent Black citizens from moving into white neighborhoods in Utah and California.[29] At the LDS Church's April 1965 General Conference, Apostle Ezra Taft Benson (who became LDS Church president in 1987) encouraged members worldwide to oppose the civil rights movement: "President David O. McKay has called communism the greatest threat to the Church—and it is certainly the greatest threat this country has ever faced. What are you doing to fight it? . . . I [have] warned how the communists were using the Civil Rights movement to promote revolution and eventual takeover of this country. When are we going to wake up? What do you know about the dangers [of] Civil Rights Agitation in Mississippi?"[30]

The institutionalized ban also continued to shape the global growth of the Church and practices of discrimination in LDS Church–owned institutions. In the 1940s and 1950s, after abandoning the instruction to teach only Brazilians of European descent, Church leaders in Brazil developed "circulars" directing missionaries to screen potential converts for Black African lineage by scrutinizing phenotypic features—hair, skin, features—at the door when tracting and to avoid teaching potential converts of African descent. The missionary lessons as delivered in Brazil also included a special "dialogue" scripted to detect African lineage and to teach converts that "Negroes" were not eligible for priesthood. Converts of African descent who persisted had their baptismal certificates marked with a "B" for Black, "C" for Cain, "N" for Negro, or similar, a practice that persisted into the 1970s.[31] In the 1950s, high-ranking LDS Church leaders Mark E. Petersen and Bruce R. McConkie delivered remarks and published as authoritative "doctrine" anti-Black speculative theology supporting segregation, opposing interracial marriage, and claiming that African Americans were cursed by God and that white supremacy was God's will. Their words were, in Petersen's case, circulated in typescript among Brigham Young University religion faculty through the 1960s, and in McConkie's case remained in print with only minor revisions in the book *Mormon Doctrine* until 2010. Following these official remarks, Brigham Young University sought to discourage applications and enrollments from Black students in the 1960s. Harold B. Lee wrote to Brigham Young University Ernest Wilkinson that he would hold him "responsible" if a "granddaughter of mine should ever go to BYU and become engaged to a colored boy there."[32]

But perhaps the most pernicious and far-reaching impact of the institutionalization of the priesthood ban through a systematic, "correlated" theology that erased historical memory was that it intensified the Church's commitment to prophetic infallibility. To manage the theological incoherence of an anti-Black stance on ordination and temple ordinances with Christian ethics, the Mormon movement developed not only a *possessive investment in whiteness* but also *a possessive investment in rightness* that it used to insulate itself against dissent from within the Church and pressure from without. No matter the cost to its own integrity or dignity, the Church and its members would do as God wanted, and had always wanted, and as prophets had always taught—or so we were led to believe. The possessive investment in rightness that emerged from Mormonism's possessive investment in whiteness uses prophetic infallibility to excuse, cover for, and render innocent the white supremacist choices of Mormon individuals and institutions.

NOTES

1. J. Albert Harrill, "The Use of the New Testament in the American Slave Controversy: A Case History in the Hermeneutical Tension Between Biblical Criticism and Christian Moral Debate," *Religion and American Culture: A Journal of Interpretation* 10.2

(Summer 2000): 149–186; see also Mark Noll, *Between Faith and Criticism: Evangelicals, Scholarship, and the Bible in America* (Vancouver: Regent College Publishing, 2002).

2. *The Fundamentals*, ed. R. A. Torrey et al., vol. 1, chap. 1, 4, https://archive.org/details/fundamentalstest17chic.

3. Dyson Hague, "The Doctrinal Value of the First Chapter of Genesis," in *The Fundamentals*, ed. R. A. Torrey et al., vol. 1, chap. 14, https://archive.org/details/fundamentalstest17chic. On the tradition of mapping Blackness onto Noah's son Ham, see also Stephen R. Haynes, *Noah's Curse: The Biblical Justification of American Slavery* (New York: Oxford University Press, 2002) and Sylvester Johnson, *The Myth of Ham in Nineteenth-Century American Christianity* (New York: Palgrave Macmillan, 2004).

4. James Cone, *Black Theology of Liberation* (Maryknoll, NY: Orbis Books, 2010), 4–5.

5. Pamela Perlich, "Utah Minorities: The Story Told by 150 Years of Census Data," Bureau of Economic and Business Research, Eccles School of Business, University of Utah, October 2002, http://gardner.utah.edu/bebr/Documents/studies/Utah_Minorities.pdf.

6. "The Southern States Mission . . . Discourse by Elder John Morgan, Delivered in the Assembly Hall, Salt Lake City, Sunday Afternoon, December 18, 1881," *Journal of Discourses* 23.6 (1883), http://scriptures.byu.edu/jod/jodhtml.php?vol=23&disc=06.

7. Tammy Walquist, "Utah Lynching May Have Been Last," *Deseret Morning News*, June 19, 2005, https://www.deseretnews.com/article/600142549/Utah-lynching-may-have-been-last.html; James Brooke, "Memories of Lynching Divide a Town," *New York Times*, April 4, 1998, http://www.nytimes.com/1998/04/04/us/memories-of-lynching-divide-a-town.html.

8. On this transitional period, see Ethan R. Yorgason, *Transformation of the Mormon Culture Region* (Urbana: University of Illinois Press, 2003); Kathleen Flake, *The Politics of American Religious Identity: The Seating of Senator Reed Smoot, Mormon Apostle* (Durham: University of North Carolina Press, 2005); Armand Mauss, *The Angel and the Beehive: The Mormon Struggle with Assimilation* (Urbana: University of Illinois Press, 1994).

9. Terryl Givens, *Wrestling the Angel: The Foundations of Mormon Thought: Cosmos, God, Humanity*, vol. 1 (Oxford: Oxford University Press, 2014), 15.
10. Reeve, 204.
11. Lester Bush, "Mormonism's Negro Doctrine: An Historical Overview," *Dialogue: A Journal of Mormon Thought* 8 (Spring 1973): 11–68, https://www.dialoguejournal.com/2012/mormonisms-negro-doctrine-an-historical-overview/.
12. Reeve, 202.
13. Bush, 61n135; Reeve, 209–210.
14. Jane Manning James, "The Autobiography of Jane Manning James: Seven Decades of Faith and Devotion," ed. James Goldberg, *LDS Church History*, December 2013, https://history.lds.org/article/jane-manning-james-life-sketch?lang=eng; Quincy D. Newell, *Your Sister in the Gospel: The Life of Jane Manning James, a Nineteenth-Century Black Mormon* (New York: Oxford University Press, 2019).
15. Jane Manning James, "The Autobiography of Jane Manning James: Seven Decades of Faith and Devotion," ed. James Goldberg, *LDS Church History*, December 2013, https://history.lds.org/article/jane-manning-james-life-sketch?lang=eng; Quincy D. Newell, *Your Sister in the Gospel: The Life of Jane Manning James, a Nineteenth-Century Black Mormon* (New York: Oxford University Press, 2019).
16. Linda King Newell and Valeen Tippetts Avery, "Jane Manning James," *The Ensign* (August 1979), https://www.lds.org/ensign/1979/08/jane-manning-james-black-saint-1847-pioneer?lang=eng#note19-.
17. James Widtsoe, *Rational Theology* (Salt Lake City: Deseret Book Company, 1937), 102, https://archive.org/details/rationaltheology-widtsoe.
18. See Terryl L. Givens, *By the Hand of Mormon: The American Scripture that Launched a New World Religion* (New York: Oxford University Press, 2002), 110–111; Brigham D. Madsen, "B. H. Roberts's Studies of the Book of Mormon," *Dialogue: A Journal of Mormon Thought* 26 (Fall 1993): 77–86, and "Reflections on LDS Disbelief in the Book of Mormon as History," *Dialogue: A Journal of Mormon Thought* 30 (Fall 1997): 87–97.

19. Bush, 34.
20. Leonard Arrington, "Dialogue's Valuable Service for LDS Intellectuals," *Dialogue: A Journal of Mormon Thought* 21.2 (1987): 135, https://www.dialoguejournal.com/wp-content/uploads/sbi/articles/Dialogue_V21No2_136.pdf.
21. Originally published in Henry Cleveland, *Alexander H. Stephens, in Public and Private: With Letters and Speeches, Before, During, and Since the War* (Philadelphia, 1886), 717–729, http://teachingamericanhistory.org/library/document/cornerstone-speech/.
22. Herbert Cihak, "Bryan, Populism, and Utah" (MA thesis, Brigham Young University, August 1975), 65, https://scholarsarchive.byu.edu/cgi/viewcontent.cgi?referer=https://www.google.com/&httpsredir=1&article=5601&context=etd.
23. William Benjamin Smith, *The Color Line: A Plea for the Unborn* (New York: McClure and Phillips, 1905), ix, https://ia800504.us.archive.org/7/items/colorlinebriefinoosmit/colorlinebriefinoosmit.pdf.
24. See Armand L. Mauss, *All Abraham's Children: Changing Mormon Conceptions of Race and Lineage* (Urbana: University of Illinois Press, 2003), "In search of Ephraim: Traditional Mormon Conceptions of Lineage and Race," *Journal of Mormon History* 25.1 (1999): 131–173, and "Mormonism's Worldwide Aspirations and Its Changing Conceptions of Race and Lineage," *Dialogue: A Journal of Mormon Thought* 34.3–4 (2001): 103–133.
25. William Hartley, "The Priesthood Reform Movement, 1908–1922," *BYU Studies* 13.2 (1973): 3.
26. Harris and Bringhurst, 58.
27. Joseph F. Smith, "The Negro and the Priesthood," *Improvement Era* 27.6 (April 1924): 565, https://archive.org/stream/improvementera2706unse#page/564/mode/2up.
28. Harris and Bringhurst, 68.
29. Harris and Bringhurst, 171.
30. Harris and Bringhurst, 78–79.
31. Harris and Bringhurst, 103.
32. Darron Smith, 90–91.

CHAPTER 4

THE PRODUCTION
OF NATIONAL
RACIAL INNOCENCE
1950s–1960s

Since when and on what grounds have white American Christians declared ourselves innocent of the sins of our generations? When did white American Christianity—at least Protestantism—excuse itself from grappling with the most serious and far-reaching human abuses, the Cain-slew-Abel on a global scale, to make as its object instead the perpetuation of an undisturbed and unchallenged hold on continuity and capital? Recall again the words of James Baldwin in his 1962 letter to his nephew, "My Dungeon Shook":

> They have destroyed and are destroying hundreds of thousands of lives and do not know it and do not want to know it. One can be—indeed, one must strive to become—tough and philosophical concerning destruction and death, for this is what most of mankind has been best at since we have heard of war; remember, I said most of mankind, but it is not permissible that the authors of devastation should also be innocent. It is the innocence which constitutes the crime. . . . These innocent people . . . are in effect still trapped in a history which they do not understand and until they understand it, they cannot be released from it.[1]

White became right early in American Christianity, and even more so with religious movements' institutionalization and mass production of theologies and religious curricula designed not to unsettle but to stabilize and consolidate power. Such theologies have vested

Mormonism and white supremacy. Joanna brooks, Oxford University Press (2020). © Oxford University Press.
DOI: 10.1093/oso/9780190081768.001.0001

the mechanisms of white supremacy with an originalism that erases the facts of Black experience and conveys blamelessness on whites. Thus, it has sold "morality" as the unknowing blamelessness of children rather than the hard-won wisdom of adults who make difficult choices. White American churches have offered rites, performances, and salvific formulas that in exchange for a specific individual performance of piety (typically defined by heteronormatively married sexual monogamy, polite manners, deference to authority) promise moral exculpation from the wrongs of history.[2] Moreover, white American Christian cultures have serviced white supremacy at large by offering to American publics spectacles and entertainments that convey a sense of absolution or transcendence without moral responsibility. White American religiosity has served as a technology for the production of white racial innocence.

As Robin Bernstein has argued in her book *Racial Innocence* (2011), during the nineteenth century, in novels like *Uncle Tom's Cabin*, white American audiences connected imaginatively with innocent child characters like Little Eva as a way to evade taking responsibility for racism:

> To be innocent was to be innocent *of* something, to achieve obliviousness. This obliviousness was not merely an absence of knowledge, but an active state of repelling knowledge—the child's "holy ignorance." . . . Innocence was not a literal state of being unraced but was, rather, the performance of not-noticing, a performed claim of slipping beyond social categories.[3]

By taking delight in the performance of "obliviousness" or "forgetting" through the figuration of children, white American adults found a way to convince themselves that they were innocent of racist wrongs and bore no responsibility for addressing racist power structures. This willed innocence sustained white supremacy.[4]

The advent of mass media extended exponentially the power of white Christian religiosity to convey moral innocence through spectacle, and it did so at the very same moment Black emancipation struggles nationalized due to twentieth-century Black migration and the advent of a nationwide civil rights movement. In truth, Black freedom was never a regional struggle, but it was easy for white majorities in the north and west to imagine so, and thus to exculpate themselves from moral responsibility. These silent white Christian majorities contributed mightily to the perpetuation of white supremacy. If we are to understand the role religion played in white supremacy in the United States, we have to look beyond the familiar and highly visible stories of the roles Black churches and white evangelicals in the South played in advancing and contesting segregation and white supremacy to this broader national dynamic: how white American churches across the country communicated to the people in the pews that they could be good, moral, and redeemed without seriously confronting America's brutality toward African Americans, past and present. Many mainstream white churches maintained silent agreements to "overlook" such issues or to embrace religious figures who harbored unethical views on race. Good Christians, after all, were expected not to bring contention or division into the house of God.

Theologian James Cone once called on scholars to "sound out" the silent agreements that stand behind white racism. For my part, I will use this chapter to "sound out" the way my coreligionists during the advent of mass media and the decades of the civil rights movement provided to the white American public spectacles that satisfied white supremacy's need to assert its moral superiority while at the same time disclaiming moral responsibility for its wrongs. As it sought to transition organizationally from a marginal sect to a mainstream church in the twentieth century, the LDS Church institutionalized a formerly loose and contradictory set of views on the role of African Americans in the faith into coherent policies and practices of anti-Black racism and segregation. The LDS Church also sought in these years to win broader social acceptance from the white American public, and it did so through public relations programming that promoted an image of Mormons as deeply patriotic, morally trustworthy, conservative white Americans.[5] Key to this public relations effort were the Mormon Tabernacle Choir and the Osmond family. Founded in 1847, the

360-member choir, an official body of the LDS Church, served as the primary media instrument through which mainstream America transitioned its imaginings of Mormons away from the sensationalized, sinister depictions of Mormon polygamy, deceit, sexual divergence, and separatism provided by nineteenth- and early twentieth-century political cartoons. Through its nationally syndicated radio broadcast *Music and the Spoken Word* and an ambitious touring schedule, the Mormon Tabernacle Choir offered a new image of Mormons as clean, disciplined, industrious, wholesome, and patriotic. It achieved remarkable mainstream success including a Billboard Top 20 hit with "The Battle Hymn of the Republic" (1959), which also won a Grammy, and invitations to perform at the White House and the presidential inaugurations of Lyndon B. Johnson (1965), Richard Nixon (1969), and every Republican president who followed, including Ronald Reagan, who called the Mormon Tabernacle Choir "America's Choir." By the late 1960s, the choir's programs were broadcast regularly on more than four hundred radio stations and thirteen television stations in the United States. When their broadest public popularity dipped in the late 1960s, they were succeeded in the public eye by the Osmonds of Ogden, Utah, a family musical group featured regularly through the 1960s on the Andy Williams Show, peaking in popularity in the 1970s, before youngest siblings Donny and Marie scored number one hits and their own Friday night television show, which ran from 1976 to 1979 on ABC. The Osmonds, though not officially sponsored by the Church, made Mormonism a major element of its public presence.

At almost no point during the 1950s, 1960s, or 1970s did white American audiences who patronized the Mormon Tabernacle Choir or the Osmonds express concerns about the explicit anti-Black racism of the LDS Church. As Jan Shipps, an eminent scholar of Mormonism, wrote in her assessment of media coverage of Mormonism during these decades, "the LDS Church had what Americans who embraced the civil rights movement regarded as a retrograde position on race, one noted and commented on in the print media, especially *Time, Newsweek,* the *Christian Century,* and elite newspapers on the East Coast and West Coast. But that encumbrance was usually overlooked in radio and television broadcasts."[6] "Overlooked" may not be strong enough a term. White American audiences openly *embraced* the most visible public emissaries of an officially racially segregated faith. This embrace entailed a silent agreement between white Mormon performers and their white audiences. This chapter focuses on this silent agreement between Mormon performing acts and white American audiences: how it worked, why it mattered, and how it enabled white Mormons to continue uncritically in their anti-Black religious beliefs and practices. The Mormon Tabernacle Choir and the Osmonds enacted a spectacle of innocence that normalized anti-Black racism as an unremarkable element of a "wholesome" morality. Their performances engaged audiences in a silent agreement to "forget" racism and to claim a moral high ground without taking responsibility for the oppression of people of color. Twentieth-century Mormon performers like the Mormon Tabernacle Choir and the Osmonds thus played into an older pattern of American culture in which white American publics sought in cultural spectacle ways to absolve themselves of the sins of their generations. And in exchange for doing this form of white supremacist cultural labor, Mormons were rewarded with a modicum of social acceptance. White American audiences admitted Mormon performers into the mainstream not only because Mormons aspired to join it but also because Mormons served as surrogates for the white American aspiration to willed innocence and obliviousness.

* * *

Founded in Salt Lake City in 1847 by a band of recently migrated volunteers, the Mormon Tabernacle Choir evolved over the century that followed into Mormonism's most important ambassadors to the world. Especially after the creation of the *Music and the Spoken Word* radio program in 1929, the choir logged a series of appearances at World's Fairs, a national and international tour, and even invited visits to the White House. It was a 1955 Mormon Tabernacle Choir tour of Europe that convinced the Church to create its own publicity bureau—the Church Information Service—which played a critical role in placing articles in the *Saturday Evening Post* (1958) and *Look* magazine (1958) celebrating the Church's welfare programs, emphasis on patriarchal families, and members' abstinence from alcohol and tobacco as emblematic of "wholesomeness." The choir's 1958 "Grand America" tour included stops at Carnegie Hall and on the *Ed Sullivan Show*. Choir President Lester Hewlett explained in a 1958 letter to George Romney, then president of the American Motors Corporation: "Our only reason for going out like this and spending several hundred thousand dollars is to break down prejudice so that our missionaries can get entrance into more homes," an effort more likely to achieve conversions than, as Hewlett characterized the LDS missionary experience, "just hammering doors like you and I did years ago."[7]

In the late 1950s, the choir had toured on a repertoire of sacred music like "the Lord's Prayer" and classical choruses by Bach, Schubert, and Haydn. But it included as the last track on its 1959 LP *The Lord's Prayer* an arrangement of "The Battle Hymn of the Republic." Columbia records released it as a 45-rpm single. By the end of October 1959, it peaked on the *Billboard* pop charts at number thirteen, charting under Bobby Darin's number one "Mack the Knife" and hits by Paul Anka and the Everly Brothers. Choir historian Michael Hicks writes that "Battle Hymn" catered to "nationalist fervor," "a self-promotional enthusiasm now fueled by *Sputnik* and the competitiveness between the Soviet Union and the United States."[8] That same fall, the choir won the Grammy for "Best Performance by a Vocal Group or Chorus," beating out the Ames Brothers, the Kingston Trio, the Browns, and the Robert Shaw Chorale. A one-hour patriotic television special "Let Freedom Ring" produced by Salt Lake City's KSL television station centering around the choir and its rendition of "Battle Hymn" won a Peabody Award for public service in television in 1961. The success of "Battle Hymn" sealed the association between Mormonism, religious "wholesomeness," and Cold War patriotism.

The moment that epitomized the choir's iconic value not only to Mormonism but also to American nationalism came on July 23, 1962, when it appeared as the featured musical number in a US government–backed propaganda television special filmed at Mount Rushmore and broadcast in Europe via satellite, the first satellite-televised program in history. NASA had launched the AT&T-developed Telstar satellite on July 10, and the nation's three major television networks—ABC, NBC, and CBS—collaborated to produce a broadcast special interspersing musical numbers by the choir, including "Battle Hymn" and Martin Luther's "A Mighty Fortress Is our God," with images of President John F. Kennedy, baseball games, and stampeding buffalo.[9] The broadcast, writes one media critic, captured the "conjunction of technology, geopolitics, and religious striving"; marked a "high point of assimilation for the choir and the church"; and reached an estimated hundreds of millions of viewers in seven voiced-over languages in eighteen countries. This and similar televised visual depictions of Mormonism in the 1960s, Jan Shipps has observed, positioned LDS people against the Left or the emerging counterculture, with the claim that Mormons were "more American than the Americans" a common refrain.[10]

The choir continued to hold its iconic place in the national spotlight, singing when President John F. Kennedy spoke at the Mormon Tabernacle in 1963 and again at a special national broadcast organized to mourn his assassination, appearing at the World's Fair in New York City, and honoring an invitation from President Lyndon B. Johnson to sing at the White House in July 1964. But the contexts around the choir were shifting in ways that would impact in the longer run Mormonism's prospects for continuing assimilation and influence in American life. The growth of the civil rights movement put institutionalized racism and anti-Black segregation at the center of national conversation. Mormons, a contemporary survey found, did not stand outside national norms in their views on secular racial integration.[11] In fact, in response to pressure from the NAACP, the Church had issued in 1963 a statement expressing its support for "full civil equality for all of God's children." But the Church steadfastly held to its explicitly anti-Black segregationist policies and Church leaders sought to repress critical discussion within the LDS community of the ban and its origins.[12]

The appearance of the choir at the inauguration of President Johnson in January 1965 came at a particularly momentous time in the national debate over African American civil rights. Johnson had signed the Civil Rights Act forbidding segregation in government services and public accommodations in July 1964. In his January 4, 1965, "State of the Union" address, he had promised as part of his Great Society effort to pursue equality for African Americans through "enforcement of the civil rights law and elimination of barriers to the right to vote."[13] Just days before the inauguration, on January 15, Johnson spoke by phone with Martin Luther King Jr., who had just launched the Selma Voting Rights campaign, and agreed to push for the legislation that would become the Voting Rights Act (1965). When the choir took the stage on January 20 to sing "Battle Hymn of the Republic" as the inauguration's closing number, King and others were organizing in Selma. Just a few weeks later, on March 9, as King led marchers across the Edmund Pettis bridge, African American activists in Utah protested at LDS Church headquarters, and the most prominent Mormon of his time, Michigan Governor George Romney, led a march of ten thousand in Detroit to support voting rights and demonstrate solidarity with the Selma marchers. It seems remarkable that an all-white choir from an officially segregated religion took and held center stage to perform "Battle Hymn of the Republic" at this contested moment in American life—even more so when one notes that Greek Orthodox Archbishop Iakovos, who gave the closing prayer at the inauguration, joined King and the Selma marchers on March 15.

The nature of a silent agreement is that its terms are never spoken aloud. For this reason, there is no extant evidence to document why President Johnson gave the choir a "pass" on its racial politics in a historic moment suspended between the Civil Rights Act and the Voting Rights Act, a moment when the president was engaged in one-to-one conversations about mounting tensions in Selma with Martin Luther King Jr. It seems plausible that the inaugural committee either did not recognize what it meant to invite a racially segregated choir to the nation's ceremonial mainstage or did not find Mormonism's anti-Black racism sufficiently objectionable. It may be that Johnson felt he had bigger battles to fight—with George Wallace, with Southern Democrats—and bigger stakes to consider in the rights and lives of African Americans. It may be that as westerners, from Utah, from a historically outsider culture, Mormons seemed to transcend the historic sectional divides onto which the nation had projected its racial politics. Or it may be that Johnson and his committee actually embraced the Mormon Tabernacle Choir performance as a chance for white citizens to indulge what Robin Bernstein would call a "holy obliviousness." The choir held a space at the center of national politics where both they and the public could by silent agreement co-construct and indulge in a spectacle of racial innocence.

It is even more significant that the song that made the choir a national icon was "The Battle Hymn of the Republic." From its origins as a tribute to the radical abolitionism of John Brown through its transition by the hand of Julia Ward Howe in 1861 into an anthem for Union troops, "Battle Hymn" had by the 1950s detached from its earliest anti-racist origins and been reappropriated as a hymn of Cold War conservative nationalism. Evangelist Billy Graham had adopted it as the theme song for his "Hour of Decision" radio program in the 1950s and his crusades. In his use of "Battle Hymn," Graham aligned the song's sense of militant preparation for moral crisis with anti-Communist fervor. As John Stauffer and Benjamin Soskis write, he sought to "[inspire] Americans in their apocalyptic battle against international communism, [saying . . .] 'When you turn from your sins to Christ, you redeem America'" and to herald the "triumph of traditional American values."[14] The choir cannily sought to step out of its regional and religious specificity into the conservative Protestant national mainstream when it made "Battle Hymn" the signature element of its repertoire.

"Battle Hymn" had by 1961 receded from use as a hymn of the civil rights movement, overtaken in popularity by "We Shall Overcome." Martin Luther King Jr. had referenced it passingly in numerous speeches during the early 1960s. But he returned to it with special emphasis in an extended riff on "Battle Hymn" at the conclusion of the Selma March to Montgomery, on March 24, 1965, just eight weeks after the all-white choir from an officially segregated religion had deployed "Battle Hymn" on the national mainstage. Selma marchers sang "Battle Hymn" as they entered the capitol, and King himself had concluded his speech with a recitation of the hymn's first and second stanzas, wrenching the song back into its originating contexts of anti-racist militancy. Perhaps there was a limit to the contradictions some American audiences were willing to accept.[15]

Columbia Records and commercial audiences of the era showed no such qualms. From 1961 to 1968, the choir released six records—three with the Philadelphia Orchestra—in the Columbia Masterworks series, creating a middle-of-the-road repertoire of Americana that willed in-nocence to the implications of American historical music and anthems for the present political moment: *Songs of the North and South* (1961), which included "Battle Hymn," "Dixie," and "Sometimes I Feel Like a Motherless Child"; *The World's Great Songs of Patriotism and Brotherhood* (1963); *God Bless America* (1965); *This Land Is Your Land* (1965); and *Beautiful Dreamer* (1967), a collection of songs by Stephen Foster, a key creator of the minstrel song genre. Perhaps the most egregiously contradictory release was the album *Mormon Pioneers* (1965), a collection of Mormon folk songs and hymns, which included a forty-eight-page booklet of essays, including an introduc-tory essay by Columbia executive Goddard Lieberson, who extolled the "family" values represented by the choir and compared Mormons to other American minorities that had fled "bigotry," "intolerance," and "prejudice," going so far as to draw a parallel between nineteenth-century mob persecutions of Mormons and the "brutality" visited on Native Americans.[16] Columbia Records executive John McClure captured the place of the choir in its catalog in a letter of March 1968: "Thanks to the unique collaboration of our two organizations, you become increasingly each year a cultural necessity in millions of American homes." Not just entertainment, but a "cultural neces-sity"—the choir offered a patriotism defined by willed obliviousness to contemporary political struggles, especially to the thorny moral re-sponsibility entailed in institutional racism. The choir's religious char-acter served elementally in this bestowal of innocence by gesturing toward a transcendence of racial issues that cost whites nothing and left segregation and white supremacy completely intact.

A provocative artifact from this time period is coverage of presidential candidate George Wallace's campaign trail visit to the Mormon Tabernacle on October 12, 1968. Candidates for the presidency from major political parties customarily spoke at the Tabernacle. Wallace's American Independent Party bid drew substantial support in Utah, including the endorsement of high-ranking LDS Church official and former secretary of agriculture Ezra Taft Benson. He appeared before what the *New York Times* described as "an overflow crowd of more than 10,000," which contrasted sharply with the decidedly smaller and less enthusiastic reception Wallace received elsewhere in the American West. Wallace was pleased with his reception. Speaking at the historic Tabernacle, the geographical center of religious Mormonism, Wallace told the crowd, "This is a high point of our travels. . . . We are alike— we see the dangers that confront the American people today."[17] Karl Rove, who grew up in Utah and attended the event, remembered:

> Wallace was angry, belligerent, and nasty, and even to my untrained ears, a pure demagogue. A protester heckled, and the Alabama governor taunted him back, saying that if the protester lay down in front of Wallace's limousine, it would be the last one he'd lie down for. The crowd screamed in agreement.[18]

Photos accompanying *New York Times* coverage convey an indelible image of the Mormon Tabernacle Choir performing behind Wallace, like back-up singers. Wallace sought spectacle, and both LDS Church leaders and the choir cooperated in the name of patriotic neutrality. Like the willed racial innocence of whiteness, this neutrality was not earned transcendence or the holy embrace of agonistic moral reasoning with one another, but a silent agreement not to see and not to challenge white supremacy but to give it a pass, as the Church had been given a pass on so many things mainstream white Americans found noncredible or distasteful.

But this silent agreement could not hold forever. As protests from university sports teams refusing to play Church-owned Brigham Young University teams mounted through late 1968, "the Mormon priesthood position came to be portrayed more frequently" in the press as "an affront" to a national consensus that had shifted in favor of "civil equality," writes media scholar J. B. Haws.[19] Historian Michael Hicks notes that internal correspondence reflects hesitation about using the Mormon Tabernacle Choir among members of the inauguration organizing committee, who cited the Church's controversial stance on African American equality. But the choir did perform at Nixon's January 1969 inauguration, and Nixon afterward wrote to thank them "for what you have come to mean to our country and for the sake of our country. Continue on."[20] Nixon recognized the role the choir played in providing the nation with a religious spectacle of transcendence that gestured beyond racial politics without demanding moral responsibility for white supremacy. That function was valuable enough for Nixon and others to forgo demanding accountability of the choir and the LDS Church for its own commitment to anti-Black racial segregation. The co-construction of innocence benefited both Mormons and white America: it benefited Mormons by allowing them to access the status, visibility, and respectability of the inaugural stage and presidential sanction, and it benefited white America by affirming the moral respectability of white supremacy and of silent agreements among whites not to trouble that supremacy.

African American audiences were not willing to put up with these spectacles indefinitely. In Denver, the Reverend Roy Flournoy, founder of the Church of the Black Cross and author of works on Black theology, announced a boycott of the Mormon Tabernacle Choir and its products (as well as travel to Utah and an end to missionary passports, tax exemptions, and other benefits to Mormons) effective November 15, 1969. Rev. Flournoy and his efforts were featured in *Jet* magazine in January and February 1970, as shown in figure 4.1. Significantly, Flournoy refused to allow a disconnect between the Church's religiously argued racial segregation and the standing of African Americans in civil society, telling *Jet*, "If a church can make blacks second-class Christians, then it's easy to justify making them second-class citizens."

Black Church Wages War On Mormon Church

An effort to reform the Church of Jesus Christ of Latter-Day Saints (Mormon), which discriminates against blacks, was initiated by the Church of the Black Cross in Denver, Colo. Rev. Roy Flournoy, consultant-in-chief, and his members are calling for an interracial boycott of Mormon Tabernacle Choir records,

Rev. Flournoy displays bumper sticker used in drive against church bias.

tourist travel to Utah and a denial of missionary passports, jobs, tax exemptions, grants and contracts to Mormons. Rev. Flournoy said, "If a church can make blacks second-class Christians, then it's easy to justify making them second-class citizens." The Mormon Church denies the priesthood and marriage within the church to blacks and teaches the doctrine that blacks are denied a place in Heaven. Rev. Flournoy said he believes many Mormons would remove such doctrines. George Romney, Secretary of Housing and Urban Development who is a Mormon, said, "If my church prevented me from working to eliminate social injustices and racial discrimination . . . I would not belong to it," during his campaign for Republican nominee for President in 1968. Other notable figures who are of the Mormon faith are David Kennedy, Secretary of Treasury; Stewart Udall, former Secretary of the Interior; Ezra Taft Benson, former Secretary of Agriculture, and actress Laraine Day. Recently Stanford University President Kenneth Pitzer said the Palo Alto, Calif., school would not schedule any competition with Mormon-operated Brigham Young University due to the church's racial policy.

51

Figure 4.1. Rev. Roy Flournoy of Denver, Colorado, publicizes his Mormon Tabernacle Choir boycott in *Jet* Magazine, January 8, 1970, and February 19, 1970.

Just weeks after Flournoy announced his boycott, on December 2, the choir auditioned and admitted an African American soprano named Marilyn Yuille, who performed immediately, on December 4. By January 1970, according to the *New York Times*, the choir had admitted two Black sopranos—Yuille and Wynetta Martin—and was considering a male tenor.[21] But it would be eight years more before the Church rescinded its ban on Black ordination to the priesthood and Black access to sacred temple rites, a position that grew more strained and divergent from national consensus each year. The choir did not perform at Nixon's swearing-in ceremony at the US Capitol at his second inauguration in 1973, but instead a group of thirty choir members performed in the White House for a postinauguration devotional. In fact, the choir did not return in any capacity until Ronald Reagan invited them to perform in his inaugural parade and ceremony in 1981, after the ban had officially ended.

* * *

The commercial staying power of the Mormon Tabernacle Choir owed not only to the spectacle of willed innocence it provided white Americans—"for the sake of *our country*," as Nixon put it—but also to the stubbornness of the corporate leadership of Columbia Records, whose head, Goddard Lieberson, had steadfastly kept the label out of rock and roll, preferring Mitch Miller, Broadway, and classical through the end of his career in the early 1970s. But just as the choir's popularity took a downturn, Mormon culture came through with a successor: the Osmond family.

The Osmonds got their start when four Osmond brothers—Alan, Wayne, Merrill, and Jay—started singing close barbershop harmonies for paying audiences in and around their hometown Ogden, Utah, to raise money to send two older Osmond brothers, Virl and Tom, on proselytizing missions for the LDS Church. After a failed attempt to audition for Lawrence Welk in Southern California, the family was "discovered" while visiting Disneyland and subsequently performed on "Disneyland After Dark" in 1962. From 1962 to 1969, five Osmond brothers (now including Donny) were regulars on the *Andy Williams*

Show and headlined print advertisements for the program. After joining *The Jerry Lewis Show* in 1969, the group transitioned to bubblegum pop, scoring several top ten hits in the United States and the United Kingdom in 1971–1973. The Osmond family openly sought to use "Osmondmania" to the benefit of LDS Church growth, with some Osmond brothers opting to forgo proselytizing missions because they judged their singing careers more effective means of introducing potential converts to the faith. (A March 11, 1972, feature in the LDS Church–owned *Church News* captured the Osmond family leaving the LDS Church Office Building after a meeting with high-ranking Church officials.) The family, the *Church News* reported, received thousands of letters of fan mail each week including letters from fans inquiring about the Church, which they devotedly answered.[22] As a solo act, Donny scored four top ten hits in 1971–1972 and attained *Tiger Beat* teen idol status. Marie's first single, a cover of Anita Bryant's "Paper Roses," became a chart-topping country hit in 1973. Hit duets with Donny followed, and by 1976, the brother-and-sister duo had landed their own Friday night variety show on ABC, which ran through 1979.

The ascendance of the Osmond family facilitated a critical pivot in media representation of the LDS Church. In November 1969, following protests by African American athletes at the University of Texas El Paso and University of Wyoming, Stanford University suspended its athletic contests with Brigham Young University to protest racial segregation. On December 15, the Church issued an internal statement to clarify what it portrayed as "confusion" over its views on "the Negro both in society and in the Church." The statement opened with a recitation of early LDS histories of persecution by mobs in nineteenth-century American frontier states, then asserted the view that the US Constitution was in the Church's view a "sacred" document. "We believe the Negro, as well as those of other races, should have his full Constitutional privileges as a member of society," the statement continued, "and we hope that members of the Church everywhere will do their part as citizens to see that these rights are held inviolate." But it carved out a separate domain under constitutional law for "matters of faith, conscience, and theology." The statement incorrectly asserted that Joseph Smith opposed Black ordination and portrayed the ban as the will of God as revealed to Mormon prophets, quoting current LDS Church President David O. McKay: "The seeming discrimination by the Church toward the Negro is not something which originated with man; but goes back into the beginning with God."[23] The Stanford decision and the subsequent Church statement received wide attention in the press, including critical scrutiny by both *Time* and *Newsweek* on January 19, 1970. The fullest criticism came from the weekly magazine *Christian Century*, which called the Church's separation of civil and religious equality an unacceptable "moral dualism" and criticized its official rationales as an "incredibly primitive reassertion of obscurantist doctrine concerning race" and a reflection of contemporary Mormons' enthrallment to "the literalist white supremacy" of past Mormon leaders.[24] *Christian Century* and Wallace Turner of the *New York Times* continued to cover Mormon anti-Black racism in the early 1970s.

While the Church took modest internal steps to address its own racial issues, including organizing an official fellowship group for African American Mormons, it also undertook a new public relations effort focused on promoting the LDS Church as a champion of "families." The Church's emphasis on families derived in large part from a unique theology that held that family bonds were to persist in the afterlife. This theology as translated through the vernacular of American culture and politics also fostered a dedicated focus in Church programming and Mormon life on heterosexual, monogamous married couples with young and school-aged children. In 1972, the Church launched through its subsidiary television stations and production companies the "Homefront" series of public service announcements advocating time spent with family. Within four years, Church officials reported, the series was playing on 95% of American television stations.[25] During the same time period, media profiles of prominent Mormon "success stories"—such as journalist Jack Anderson, golfer Johnny Miller, and hotel magnate Bill Marriott, scion of a large multigenerational Mormon family—ran in dozens of periodicals from *Forbes* to *Newsweek*, depicting their subjects as clean-living, dedicated "family men."[26] Even the *New York Times*, which along with the *Christian Century* had been the media organization to most consistently cover the Church's racist policies, devoted a full-page human interest feature on June 4, 1973, to the Church's "Family Home Evening Program." As staff writer Judy Klemsrud put it:

> To many casual observers, the American family of the mid-20th century appears headed down the drain in a swirl of divorce, drugs, venereal disease, alcohol, adultery and group sex. "Marriage is passe!" is a rallying cry of many young people. Children are passe, they say. The family is passe. But for at least one sizable group in American society, the family is still the thing. The group is The Church of Jesus Christ of Latter-day Saints (Mormon), and their way of attacking delinquency and deteriorating morality is to strengthen family solidarity through a Monday night get-together in the home called the "family home evening."

Klemsrud's article implicitly mobilizes a racialized notion of wholesomeness that positions white patriarchal, heterosexual families against "delinquency" and "deteriorat[ion]" evidenced in behaviors associated in the white national imagination with counterculture, urban, and minority communities. The article featured an interview with and photographs of the Osmond family but did not mention the Black priesthood and temple ban.[27]

Media coverage of the Osmonds promoted the idea of Mormon innocence in three major ways. First, the Osmonds were celebrated as a "blue-eyed soul" alternative to groups like the Jacksons, who were viewed by white audiences through racializing prisms that associated soul with anti-Black stereotypes of sexual promiscuity. Teenaged Osmonds were also queried time and again on their dating interests and habits, focusing in on the sexual purity of Donny and Marie, Marie especially not being allowed to date by her religion and her older brothers. Finally, the media provided celebrity-magnitude amplification to this Church-grown public relations emphasis on Mormonism as the champion of "the family." Features in *Newsweek* (September 3, 1973), *Atlantic Monthly* (October 1973), *Rolling Stone* (cover article, March

1976), and *TV Guide* (August 1976) connected the Osmond family's success to its religiosity, including the religiously valued focus on the patriarchal, heterosexual, monogamously married family.[28] "Each and every Osmond is a devout member of the Church of Jesus Christ of Latter-Day Saints (*sic*), a fact that indelibly colors the image, lifestyle, and music of this most successful household," wrote Tom Nolan in his six-page feature in *Rolling Stone* (with photographs by Annie Leibovitz) entitled "The Family Plan of the Latter-day Osmonds." Nolan predictably positioned the Osmonds as a foil to the so-called counterculture: "While many rock stars are known to sniff coke, the Osmonds don't even drink it." Noting the "hermetic," isolated, idyllic atmosphere of the "Land of Os," Nolan did nothing to trouble it: he asked Donny about what kind of girls he liked but did not take issue in print with their support for anti-Black racial segregation.[29]

That silent agreement ended in February 1978, when Barbara Walters brought her production team to Osmond Studios in Orem, Utah, for an in-depth interview with twenty-year-old Donny and eighteen-year-old Marie. The interview opened with a sequence featuring the extended Osmond family—including patriarch George and wife Olive and their fifteen grandchildren—holding Family Home Evening on the set and with a voiceover by Walters reciting the commonplace media characterizations: "To understand the Osmonds is to know that they are Mormons," she said. Their religious identity and emphasis on family stood behind their success as a "conglomerate of millionaires." "They are also genuinely nice," Walters intoned, "and that's pretty refreshing all by itself."[30] Sitting down to probe Donny and Marie more closely, Walters asked deeper questions about Osmond—and, thus, Mormon—views on marriage, family, dating, and premarital sex. "Our religion is everything to us," said Marie. Walters then asked the question that had never been asked of so high profile a Mormon in such a widely distributed, live media format:

BW: Look, I have to ask you something that I know that you have heard about, and if I don't ask it people will wonder why I didn't. And that is, in the strength of your religion, the whole business about Blacks not being allowed to be priests in the Mormon religion.

DO: Mmm hmm.

BW: Tell me how you feel about it and what the explanation for that is, would you Donny?

DO: You bet. [Looks at ground.] Well, I'm not an authority on the subject [looks sidelong at Walters, returns gaze to ground] but uh I will mention that uh we are not prejudiced people [looks sidelong at Walters, returns gaze to ground] we offer more I think than any other religion to the Black person [looks sidelong] [cut] and uh if you really want a good explanation from someone who has an authority about it you should really talk to the general authorities of our church. [Marie turns gaze from Donny to look at Walters, and nods affirmatively.] Um. They are not allowed to hold the priesthood in this [pause] right right now and I don't know why but that's the way the Lord wants it.

Walter's lead-in—"if I don't ask it people will wonder why I didn't"—suggests something had shifted in the long-standing silent agreement of mutually affirmed innocence between overtly religious Mormon performers and the white American public, enough at least that it felt to Walters that her professional credibility could be impacted if she didn't ask the question.

Donny Osmond's answer to Walters suggests that the brother-and-sister pair had rehearsed for the question (as they did for every other aspect of their public appearances) and that they had done so in an exclusively Mormon environment. Donny is completely un-self-conscious as he expresses no objection to the ban: highly observant and politically conservative Mormons like the Osmonds would have considered public expression of dissent evidence of impiety. His attempt to draw a distinction between the Church's anti-Black policy and general racial "prejudice" was also a commonplace of LDS rhetoric, including the Church's formal 1969 statement on the ban. The claim that Mormonism "offer[ed] more to the Black person" than any other religion was also commonplace rhetoric among Mormons, premised on the belief that the LDS Church through the mechanism of "continuing revelation" to prophets offered the most authentic and complete religious truth and the most efficacious rites; "the Church is true" is how observant LDS people put it, and even a partial access to that "truth"—Black people could after all be baptized and learn Church doctrine—was "more" than "any other religion" could offer. This phrase, which exemplifies the "abstraction" of Black lives necessary to legal claims of white innocence, seemingly originated with a remark made by LDS Church President Joseph Fielding Smith to a *Look* magazine reporter in 1963, and persisted.[31] In fact, Ruffin Bridgeforth, an African American Mormon and member of the Church's "Genesis" fellowship group, made a similar remark to *Jet* magazine on May 25, 1978: "In this church a Black man can do more than he can in any other church." Those who coached Donny and Marie had also provided them with a way to evade moral responsibility for the ban, as Donny's carefully scripted repetition of the term "authority" indicates: "I'm not an *authority* on the subject," he begins; "you should talk to the general authorities of our church." Church leaders since the time of Brigham Young had often remarked that someday God could in fact permit Black ordination. Donny's remark "in this [pause] right right now" is a stumbling allusion to this idea. But his concluding sentence, "I don't know why but that's the way the Lord wants it," reiterates his commitment to the orthodox Mormon view of prophetic leadership as inerrant, as God's own foregone conclusion. Osmond's answer to Walters's question exemplifies legal-rhetorical tactics of white innocence such as "originalism" and "helplessness" identified by legal scholar Thomas Ross that allowed whites to disclaim responsibility for racism by characterizing it as the will of an original power—whether the authors of the US Constitution or God themself.

Just as the Mormon Tabernacle Choir had traded on "innocence" to play an iconic role for white American audiences in the 1950s and 1960s, the Osmonds sought to maintain innocence to hold a place in 1970s pop culture. But the social and media contexts in which they attempted to do so had changed over the decades. The silent agreement to overlook Mormonism's explicit anti-Black segregation expired by 1978. So did the priesthood and temple ban. As Donny and Marie sat down with Barbara Walters, high-ranking LDS Church leaders were preparing to end anti-Black restrictions on full Church participation, a change announced on June 8, 1978.[32]

Performances of white innocence by overtly religious performers allowed national audiences to enjoy, bond around, and experience affirmation of their moral superiority while ignoring segregation. Donny and Marie's cringeworthy answers to Barbara Walters in 1978 are embarrassing to thoughtful Mormons for what they reveal about our own insularity and incredibility, but they say just as much about bad faith and duplicity on the part of mainstream white audiences. "I believe in 1978 / God changed his mind about Black people," sings Elder Price, the protagonist in the Broadway hit musical *Book of Mormon* (2011). The line is a major laugh-getter; the play has now grossed over $500 million. In the musical, as in the 1960s and 1970s, the Mormon willingness to voice out loud and without reservation white supremacist sentiments held broadly but in silence by mainstream American Christians made our religion good entertainment. To this day, mainstream audiences have been happy to keep Mormons as the butt of the national joke.

There were, of course, Mormons who were in 1965 and 1978 using public venues to ask much harder questions of their faith, their leaders, and American racism. I will profile them in chapter 5. Their experience reflects the ongoing struggle within the Mormon movement between those who sustain the inerrancy of Church leaders by keeping silence around elements of Mormonism that have been morally objectionable and those who believe that Mormonism's better angels require us to keep seeking and naming and repairing our own shortcomings as a people. Our struggle in this way is no different than that of any other American Christian denomination—or American society writ large. But along the way Mormons learned that so long as we mirrored back white American fantasies of innocence and moral superiority, we would be excused from answering the hard questions that should define honorable participation in a civil society. "They have destroyed and are destroying hundreds of thousands of lives and do not know it and do not want to know it," wrote James Baldwin of white innocence. "They are in effect still trapped in a history which they do not understand and until they understand it, they cannot be released from it."[33] Because it served white supremacy, Mormons were kept in a state of innocence like children, our lack of credibility an open secret, the butt of the joke, but a small cost (or so it seemed) to pay for the benefits of assimilation, especially if it meant Mormon missionaries—our sons, our brothers, our nephews—found more success in the proselyting field because of the Osmonds or the Mormon Tabernacle Choir, or at least were not treated so discouragingly on the doorstep.

Mormons have scarcely begun to count the costs to our own humanity of more than a century of persistent internal anti-Black segregation, nor of the forty years of denial—characterized at times by the same proud ignorance evidenced by Donny and Marie—let alone the costs exacted by this willed innocence on our coreligionists of color. At the time of my writing, Donny Osmond still defends the Church's internal segregation as the will of God.[34] Mormonism has observed the fortieth anniversary of the ban with no official apology from the Church for its errors and a suffocating stasis around anti-Black racism among orthodox believers, most of whom still refuse to acknowledge that we were wrong. As one who grew up idolizing Donny and Marie—they were the only people like me I saw on television—and feeling just about the same way they did about the priesthood and temple ban, I can say that the mainstream white audiences who bought into and subsidized our white "innocence" did us no favors.

NOTES

1. James Baldwin, "My Dungeon Shook: Letter to My Nephew on the One Hundredth Anniversary of the Emancipation," in *The Fire Next Time* (New York: Dial Press, 1963), 21.
2. K. D. Guitterrez, "White Innocence," *International Journal of Learning* 12.10 (2005): 223–229; Dalia Rodriguez, "Investing

in White Innocence: Colorblind Racism, White Privilege, and the New White Racist Fantasy," in *Teaching Race in the 21st Century: College Teachers Talk About Their Fears, Risks, and Rewards,* ed. L Guerreo (New York: Palgrave, 2008), 123–124; Jennifer Seibel Trainor, "'My Ancestors Didn't Own Slaves': Understanding White Talk About Race," *Research in the Teaching of English* 40.2 (2005): 140–167.

3. Robin Bernstein, *Racial Innocence: Performing American Childhood and Race From Slavery to Civil Rights* (New York: New York University Press, 2011), 6.

4. White innocence does not always present in this way, as Gloria Wekker has recently observed in her study of white supremacy among the Dutch; there is also "smug ignorance," which can present with rage and violence. See Gloria Wekker, *White Innocence: Paradoxes of Colonialism and Race* (Durham: Duke University Press, 2016), 18.

5. J. B. Haws, *The Mormon Image in the American Mind: Fifty Years of Public Perception* (New York: Oxford University Press, 2015), 47–73.

6. Jan Shipps, *Sojourner in the Promised Land: Forty Years Among the Mormons* (Urbana: University of Illinois Press, 2000), 100.

7. Haws, 22–29; Michael Hicks, *The Mormon Tabernacle Choir: A Biography* (Urbana: University of Illinois Press, 2015), 118.

8. Hicks, 115.

9. Kirk Johnson, "Mormons on a Mission," *New York Times,* August 20, 2010, http://www.nytimes.com/2010/08/22/arts/music/22choir.html?pagewanted=all; last accessed January 30, 2018.

10. Haws, 36.

11. Haws, 60.

12. Haws, 50–51.

13. Lyndon B. Johnson, "Annual Message to Congress on the State of the Union, January 4, 1965," *The American Presidency Project*, http://www.presidency.ucsb.edu/ws/index.php?pid=26907, last accessed January 30, 2018.

14. John Stauffer and Benjamin Soskis, *The Battle Hymn of the Republic: A Biography of the Song That Marches On* (New York: Oxford University Press, 2013), 230, 242.

15. John Stauffer and Benjamin Soskis, *The Battle Hymn of the Republic: A Biography of the Song That Marches On* (New York: Oxford University Press, 2013), 230, 242.

16. Hicks, 125.

17. Roy Reed, "Wallace Seeks Mormon Votes; Draws Big Tabernacle Crowd," *New York Times,* October 13, 1968, https://timesmachine. nytimes.com/timesmachine/1968/10/13/317688762.html, last accessed January 30, 2018.

18. Karl Rove, *Courage and Consequence: My Life as a Conservative in the Fight* (New York: Threshold Books, 2010), 11.

19. Haws, 59.

20. Hicks, 132.

21. Wallace Turner, "Mormon Liberals Expect No Change," *New York Times,* January 25, 1970, http://www.nytimes.com/1970/01/ 25/archives/mormon-liberals-expect-no-change-smith-mckays- successor-backs.html, last accessed January 30, 2018; *Salt Lake Tribune,* February 21, 1970.

22. "35 Memorable Photos From the Church News Archives," *Deseret News,* September 29, 2014, https://www.deseretnews.com/top/ 2740/2/Donny-Osmonds-wedding-35-memorable-photos-from-the- LDS-Church-News-archives.html, last accessed January 30, 2018.

23. Harris and Bringhurst, 82–83.

24. Stephen W. Stathis and Dennis L. Lythgoe. "Mormonism in the 1970s: Popular Perception," *Dialogue: A Journal of Mormon Thought* 10.3 (1977), 107.

25. Haws, 79–81.

26. Haws, 83–85.

27. Judy Klemsrud, "Strengthening Family Solidarity with a Home Evening Program," *New York Times,* June 4, 1973, 46, http:// www.nytimes.com/1973/06/04/archives/strengthening-family- solidarity-with-a-home-evening-program.html, last accessed January 30, 2018.

28. Sara Davidson, "Feeding on Dreams in a Bubble Gum Culture," *Atlantic Monthly,* October 1973: 72. See also Haws, 84.

29. Tom Nolan, ""The Family Plan of the Latter-day Osmonds," *Rolling Stone,* March 11, 1976, 46–52.

30. "The Barbara Walters Special: Donny and Marie Osmond," February 1978, published February 14, 2012, https://www.youtube.com/watch?v=bPWIEfmPYxo, last accessed January 30, 2018.

31. Matthew L. Harris and Newell G. Bringhurst, eds., *The Mormon Church and Blacks: A Documentary History* (Urbana: University of Illinois Press, 2015), 83n104.

32. See especially Edward Kimball, "Spencer W. Kimball and the Revelation on Priesthood," *BYU Studies* 47.2 (2008): 5–78; Mark L. Grover, "The Mormon Priesthood Revelation and the Sao Paulo, Brazil Temple," *Dialogue: A Journal of Mormon Thought* 23.1 (1990): 39–53, http://www.dialoguejournal.com/wp-content/uploads/sbi/articles/Dialogue_V17No3_25.pdf, last accessed January 30, 2018.

33. James Baldwin, *The Fire Next Time* (New York: Dial Press, 1963), 21.

34. Donny Osmond, "My Beliefs: Questions and Answers," donny.com, https://donny.com/my_beliefs/do-you-honestly-think-black-people-worldwide-dont-deserve-public-apology/, last accessed January 30, 2018.

CHAPTER 5

WHITE PRIVILEGE, RACIAL INNOCENCE, AND THE COSTS OF ANTI-RACIST DISSENT, MORMON EXAMPLES 1940s-1980s

No one is *born* white—it is only possible to *become* white, to be enlisted and acculturated into whiteness, and white American Christian churches are among the many venues for that acculturation. Just as white Christians develop silent agreements among ourselves to define morality in individual terms that take no responsibility for systematic anti-Black racism, white Christian churches develop means for managing and disciplining adherents who do take on anti-Black racism in a serious and discomfiting way. Marginalizing or repressing anti-racist dissent is necessary to maintaining a hold on the story that anti-Black racism is how it has always been and how God intends for it to be or, at least, is content enough with it not to intervene. The attribution of intentionality and inevitability to the systems of white supremacy that hurt Black people takes shape in more conservative white American Christian contexts as belief in infallibility—whether in the text of the Bible, the pope, or the leaders of the LDS Church. Infallibility kills: it kills the bodies of those marked expendable, it kills relationships with those who dissent, and it kills the souls who suffocate on their own ignorance and privilege. It kills courage, it kills hope, it kills faith, and it kills the kind of historical memory that helps a religious community understand itself and find its next steps toward holiness.

Mormonism and white supremacy. Joanna brooks, Oxford University Press (2020). © Oxford University Press.
DOI: 10.1093/oso/9780190081768.001.0001

It is easier take a principled stance as a white American Christian against white supremacy and anti-Black racism in the nation at large than to confront the quiescence mistaken for reverence that preserves the workings of white supremacy in the church. Witness the case of Michigan Governor George Romney, who took bold and principled public stands against anti-Black racism in the secular world. Just days after Selma, in 1961, Governor Romney helped organize and walked at the head of a march of ten thousand demonstrators in Detroit. He provided state support and full endorsement for the Martin Luther King Jr.–led Detroit Walk to Freedom on June 23, 1963; he did not walk in the Sunday event due to his observance of the Sabbath, but he did lead a march with NAACP leaders through the suburb of Grosse Pointe just a few days later. His outspoken stance earned him private pushback from high-ranking Church leaders, in particular, a member of the Church's Quorum of the Twelve Apostles named Delbert Stapely, who in January 1964 had written a personal letter to Romney conveying concern on the part of several others unnamed that his public support for civil rights was not aligned with the teachings of Joseph Smith and warning him that activism on Black human and civil rights causes had, in several recorded instances, led to untimely death for the activist.[1] In no moment, though, was the membership or worthiness of George Romney, the most prominent Mormon in America besides the Mormon Tabernacle Choir, put into question. Nor did Romney openly question the Church's segregationist policies. He did go so far as to call out "social injustice based on race and color" during a Sunday meeting of an LDS congregation in faraway Anchorage, Alaska, when he was on the presidential campaign trail in February 1967, a statement cannily recognized by the *New York Times* as Romney's effort to differentiate his "personal position" from that of the Church itself and demonstrate his principled independence from its teachings on matters of racial equality.[2] He went even further during his term of service as President Nixon's secretary of housing and urban development by refusing to consider government support for housing projects that did not support racial integration, earning strong pushback from Nixon that contributed to Romney's loss of his position.

But with his own Church Romney had struck a silent agreement: he would conduct himself as he felt his principles demanded in the realm of politics, and he would allow them to conduct Church business as they saw fit. Maintaining public silence on discriminatory Church policies while working assiduously to advance desegregation and anti-discrimination in the public sphere was Romney's way of striking a tenuous balance between honoring his conscience and honoring religious vows he had made to "consecrate" his time and resources to the Church and sustain its leaders. A thousand painstaking calculations must have factored into his choices, as they do for every Mormon who finds him/her/theirself at odds for reasons of conscience with the institutional LDS Church. It matters in this calculus whether you are white, Black, or brown; male or female; straight or LGBTQ; rich or poor; married or not; highly observant or less so. It matters whether you have a current volunteer position in the Church and what that position is—whether one of greater or lesser responsibility. It matters who the local leaders are who are charged with assessing your personal worthiness. It matters whether your ancestors came across the plains as pioneers and where Brigham Young sent them after they did—Idaho, Arizona, southern Utah, Mexico; whether they practiced polygamy; and how closely they maintained their ties with the elite networks of families who have constituted the majority of the Church's leadership. It matters where you work, for whom, and how LDS social networks influence your customer base. And it matters how you express your dissent: written or oral; public or private; book, newspaper, or television; time, place, and manner; down to the tone of your voice and your vocabulary, grammar, and punctuation—it matters. All of these and more factor into the complex calculus of conscientious dissent in the contemporary Mormon movement, especially inasmuch as Mormonism has sought to hold on to the modicum of social acceptance it gained in the mid-twentieth century.

This is in many respects remarkable for a faith tradition that began as an open rejection of and revolt against mainstream American Protestantism, just as Protestantism itself began as a revolt against Catholicism. Eventually, though, the broadly distributed "charisma" of the movement, which empowered every believer to enjoy individual access to revealed truth, gave way to a hierarchical order that centralized charismatic and prophetic authority into a limited number of Church leaders—in Protestantism and Mormonism alike. Tensions between the democratic and authoritarian tendencies of Mormonism persisted, mediated sometimes by the so-called Law of Common Consent, articulated by Joseph Smith in 1830 and commemorated in the LDS scripture The Doctrine and Covenants, section 25, and sometimes leading to the formation of dozens of splinter groups and offshoot movements. Those who remained with the Church of Jesus Christ of Latter-day Saints entered in what Mormon historians Linda Thatcher and Roger Launius have characterized as a "contract": "the assumption that personal feelings must bow below that of the church, that no disagreement be allowed to harm the church." Those who tested the limits of this contract tended, according to Thatcher and Launius, to have some footing or standing in the secular world, to believe that they stood for an "honest minority" opinion, or to feel that the affordances of belonging were no longer worth the costs of submission. Given the political, economic, and social dimensions of Mormon community life, these affordances can include access to education, employment, and marriage as well as continuity of family and community relations. The costs of breaking the contract in a way that leads to excommunication and shunning could be stark, especially in pre-assimilation Mormon communities. Consequently, dissent was stigmatized in the twentieth-century LDS Church, preventing, according to Thatcher and Launius, the development of healthy tolerance for "social conflict."[3]

Every white American Christianity exacts its own kind of silent agreements with its memberships to preserve its racial innocence and, in exchange, to convey certain rewards. Mormonism has provided for people of all economic classes and national, racial, and ethnic identities "a theological and ritual salve for profound personal losses but also a resource that promised middle-class stability, security, social mobility, . . . access to education and broadened perspectives," and even continuity of kinship networks, language, and identity through Church-sponsored social groups, schools, universities, colleges, and labor/employment programs. But as I observed with Maori Mormon womanist scholar Gina Colvin in *Decolonizing Mormonism*:

> These modest affordances came at a cost. LDS institutional spaces were deeply structured by mid- and late-twentieth century American Mormon conservatism, which was itself driven in part by the LDS Church's hunger to transform itself from an outlier sect to a mainstream American Protestant church. These spaces, from wardhouses to Church-sponsored university classrooms, did not support nor equip Mormons to participate in the critical conversations about power and resources colonized peoples around the world were engaging in from the 1940s and 1950s onward. Education in LDS Church colleges and universities and the culture of LDS congregations focused on preparing a globalizing membership to assume local responsibility for the administration of LDS Church units according to American bureaucratic norms. Limited cultural accommodation came at the cost of surrendering critique and sustaining a false sense of political innocence. Stability interlocked with the status quo.

Twentieth-century Mormonism brokered a sort of compact with its global membership. "This compact allowed limited accommodations for traditional cultural practices and identities and promised access to worldly opportunities and moments of spiritual transcendence, to stable supportive institutions, and to theological and social comfort in the face of loss and pain," in our view. "But the cost of this accommodation and access was obedience to LDS Church hierarchy and a bracketing of critique of the status quo, including the forms of systematic and structural violence and inequality that contributed to or created loss and pain."[4]

In places where the Church or networks of LDS people also maintained a degree of power over political, social, material, environmental, and economic resources, this contract or compact—that critique would be exchanged for the affordances of belonging—was leveraged to secure consent from local peoples to projects that may have compromised their dignity, autonomy, or political and economic values.

Hokulani Aikau writes powerfully in *A Chosen People, a Promised Land* of how Church leaders utilized an "ideology of faithfulness"—that is, "faithfulness to church business and managerial practices"—to extract consent from local peoples to the use or appropriation of indigenous land and labor in the service of LDS enterprises, religious and secular.[5] The Church's twentieth-century growth put distance between international leadership and local congregations, constraining what had been within Mormon tradition the possibility of voicing dissent to leaders in the context of familial or community relations. Church leaders maintained the "illusion of personal relationships" through affectionate norms in their public addresses and internationally televised conferences but relied ever more heavily on the ideology of faithfulness to elicit cooperation and marginalize dissent.

This chapter will explore the nature of the silent agreement between LDS Church leaders and members and the conditions under which Mormons have publicly dissented from the Church's anti-Black racism and segregation. Its goal in part is to challenge the idea that anti-Black racism was inevitable—in Mormonism, or in any white American Christian faith. There were always believers who found within faith another way of seeing and being. Their stories matter because they rescue our hearts and minds from the suffocating pretenses of inevitability and infallibility and inspire us to think otherwise. This chapter seeks to reconstruct and make available a lost archive of conscientious objection by white Mormons to the Church's anti-Black segregation and discrimination. Because information and publication in the Mormon movement has been from the 1950s to the 2000s largely managed by the institutional LDS Church, and because the Church itself does not have a professional clergy or professional theological schooling that can support reasoned discussion and conflict, these statements have never been a part of any LDS curriculum or canon. As a lifelong member of the LDS Church and a scholar of race and gender, I was not even aware of them until I researched this book. They constitute an archive of unorthodox lay theologies that broaden our ways of being Mormon to include models of persistent, unapologetic objection to anti-Black racism that refuse racial innocence. (Because they are not broadly accessible, I will use this chapter to provide longer excerpts from the original documents.) But they also encourage us to reflect critically on how the ability to protest racism and stay in good standing in the church is conditioned by privilege, and they vest those of us who do experience privileged identities within Mormonism and other predominantly white Christian faiths with a responsibility to leverage that privilege as meaningfully as possible.

* * *

Born in 1893 and raised in rural Ferron, Utah, to a multigenerational white Mormon family, Lowry Nelson earned degrees from Utah State University (then Agricultural College) and the University of Wisconsin. After working for state agriculture agencies, he joined Brigham Young University faculty and served as a dean of applied sciences. He left Brigham Young University in 1934 after having been reported to high-ranking church authorities for stating to a colleague that immortality was a hypothesis not testable by scientific means. After serving various rural relief agencies and projects during the 1930s, he took a faculty position in sociology at the University of Minnesota, during which time he conducted sociological studies of the Caribbean—including Cuba—for the Department of State, eventuating in the publication of his book *Rural Cuba* (1950). (He would return to Cuba during the 1960s for six years to study life after the Cuban Revolution.) In addition to his academic writing and publishing, Nelson wrote occasionally for the *Nation*, maintained an extensive correspondence, and wrote poems.

On June 20, 1947, President Herbert Meeks of the Church's Southern States Mission, a childhood friend of Nelson's, wrote to Nelson at the University of Minnesota:

I would appreciate your opinion as to the advisability of doing missionary work particularly in the rural sections of Cuba, knowing, of course, our concept of the Negro and his position as to the Priesthood, Are there groups of pure white blood in the rural sections, particularly in the small communities? If so, are they maintaining segregation from the Negroes? The best information we received was that in the rural communities there was no segregation of the races and it would probably be difficult to find, with any degree of certainty, groups of pure white people.[6]

The query came in a critical decade for Mormon scholars and writers, a decade in which out-migration, increased access to education, and moderate accommodation of US norms on the part of LDS people ended cultural isolation and contributed to a new capacity for critical reflection on Utah Mormon experience. This so-called Lost Generation, in terms first used by Mormon literary historian Edward Geary, saw the emergence of writers and works such as Vardis Fisher's Harper prize–winning novel *Children of God* (1939), Virginia Sorenson's *A Little Lower Than the Angels* (1942), and Maureen Whipple's *The Giant Joshua* (1941), a critical reflection on Mormon polygamy, their plotlines often depicting a younger protagonist grappling with the weight of Mormon authoritarianism and Mormon history and the isolation of rural Mormon life.[7] Historian Fawn Brodie was excommunicated after her publication of *No Man Knows My History* (1945), a frank, scholarly quality biography of Joseph Smith Jr. Grassroots historian Juanita Brooks, a southern Utah organic intellectual, published with the assistance of the Huntington Library, Wallace Stegner, and Stanford University Press a direct, nonhagiographic history of the *Mountain Meadows Massacre* (1950), an ambush and mass killing of white emigrants through southern Utah ordered (as Brooks's research showed) by top-ranking Church leaders but blamed on local indigenous people and Mormon renegades. While the book received praise from American studies luminaries like Henry Nash Smith for its "probity," even Stanford University Press's director warned Brooks that she might be excommunicated. She said in response: "I do not want to be excommunicated from my church for many reasons, but if that is the price that I must pay for intellectual honesty, I shall pay it— I hope without bitterness." Brooks's father had offered her advice that pertained to her entire "Lost Generation" of newly critical LDS thinkers and writers, comparing the position of the loyal dissident writer to the cowboy who rides "not in the middle of the herd," nor "abandon[s] it altogether," but "ride[s] on the edge where she might be able to alter its course."[8]

From his position on the edge of the herd—as an observant multi-generational Mormon in a secular university far outside the Mormon corridor—Nelson may indeed have hoped to alter its course. His June 26 response to Meeks reflects honest surprise that customs and folklore mitigating against welcoming Black Mormons into full fellowship had taken on the status of doctrine:

> The attitude of the Church in regard to the Negro makes me very sad. Your letter is the first intimate I have had that there was a fixed doctrine on this point. I had always known that certain statements had been made by authorities regarding the status of the Negro, but I had never assumed that they constituted an irrevocable doctrine. I hope no final word has been said on this matter. I must say that I have never been able to accept the idea, and never shall. I do not believe that God is a racist. But if the church has taken an irrevocable stand, I would dislike to see it enter Cuba or any other island where different races live and establish missionary work. The white and colored people get along much better in the Caribbean and most of Latin American than they do in the United States. Prejudice exists, there is no doubt, and the whites in many ways manifest their feelings of superiority, but there is much less of it than one finds in USA, especially in our South. For us to go into a situation like that and preach a doctrine of "white supremacy" would, it seems to me, be a tragic disservice. I am speaking frankly, because I feel very keenly on this question. If world brotherhood and the universal God idea mean anything, it seems to me they mean equality of races. I fail to see how Mormonism or any other religion claiming to be more than a provincial church can take any other point of view, and there cannot be world peace until the pernicious doctrine of the superiority of one race and the inferiority of others is rooted out. This is my belief.

Writing as a sociologist, Nelson also upbraided Meeks for the idea that there was "pure" whiteness. He praised what the Church could provide rural communities through its lay priesthood structure and high level of organization in terms of social infrastructure, leadership development, and even self-sufficiency, but weighed the value of that against its racism:

> Because I think our system of religious organization could serve the rural Cuban people as perhaps no other system could, I am sad to have to write you and say, for what my opinion is worth, that it would be better for the Cubans if we did not enter their island—unless we are willing to revise our racial theory. To teach them the pernicious doctrine of segregation and inequalities among races where it does not exist, or to lend religious sanction to it where it has raised its ugly head would, it seems to me, be tragic. It seems to me we just fought a war over such ideas. I repeat, my frankness or bluntness, as you will, is born of a fervent desire to see the causes of war rooted out of the hearts of men. What limited study I have been able to give the subject leads me to the conclusion that ethnocentrism, and the smugness and intolerance which accompany it, is one of the first evils to be attacked if we are to achieve the goal of peace.

A handwritten note from Nelson to his wife found on the back of the author's copy, now held in Special Collections at the University of Utah, provides insight into Nelson's frame of mind. "I was so angered by the complacency of the Meeks letter, I had a hard time containing myself."

Nelson did not, in fact, contain himself. He copied his response to Herbert Meeks to LDS Church President George Albert Smith, with the following cover:

> Perhaps I am out of order, so to speak, in expressing myself as I have. I have done so out of strong conviction on the subject, and with the added impression that there is no irrevocable church doctrine on this subject. I am not unaware of statements and impressions which have been passed-down, but I had never been brought face to face with the possibility that the doctrine was finally crystallized. I devoutly hope

that such crystallization has not taken place. The many good friends of mixed blood—through no fault of theirs incidentally—which I have in the Caribbean and who know me to be a Mormon would be shocked indeed if I were to tell them my Church relegated them to an inferior status. As I told Heber, there is no doubt in my mind that our Church could perform a great service in Cuba, particularly in the rural areas, but it would be far better that we not go in at all, than to go in and promote racial distinction. I wanted you to know my feelings on this question and trust you will understand the spirit in which I say these things. I want to see us promote love and harmony among peoples of the earth.

Nelson's letter to Smith reflects the deference to hierarchy—"perhaps I am out of order"—expected of an observant Latter-day Saint. But he also boldly claims for himself a place within the Protestant tradition of the priesthood of all believers, that is, the idea that every believer has the right to study and interpret the sacred texts of the tradition and develop their own understanding. Nelson was in fact correct that over the course of almost one century the Church had abandoned its original practice of ordaining Black men to the priesthood, denied its own history, and instead gradually consolidated with the formal correlation of institutional priesthood programs in the early twentieth century first a policy against ordination and then, through accretion and repetition without interrogation or counterpoint, religious folklore that finally assumed the stature of doctrine. Rather than lend his silent assent to the inerrancy of the doctrine, Nelson emphasizes its historicity, its contingency—"I had never been brought face to face with the possibility that the doctrine was finally crystallized." He holds both to historical memory and to an essential commitment to humane and religious principles—"love and harmony"—that transcend doctrine.

President Smith and his counselors, David O. McKay and J. Reuben Clark, responded on July 17:

The basic element of your ideas and concepts seems to be that all God's children stand in equal positions before Him in all things. Your knowledge of the Gospel will indicate to you that this is contrary to the very fundamentals of God's dealings with Israel dating from the time of His promise to Abraham regarding Abraham's seed and their position vis-a-vis God Himself. Indeed, some of God's children were assigned to superior positions before the world was formed. We are aware that some Higher Critics do not accept this, but the Church does.

Here, President Smith and his counselors reassert an originalist, counterhistorical view of scripture, openly rejecting the rational, historicist "higher criticism" popularized in university-based theology in the nineteenth century and reasserting the Church's claim that its practices honor an intentional godly pattern revealed directly and unchanged from ancient times, or even earlier—premortality. They continue to assert Mormonism's distinctive doctrine, established in books of scripture such as the Book of Mormon and the Pearl of Great Price and reaffirmed in 1918 in a later-canonized revelation to LDS Church President Joseph F. Smith, that souls were created in a premortal sphere and developed a body of experience pertinent to their embodied lives on earth:

> Your position seems to lose sight of the revelations of the Lord touching the preexistence of our spirits, the rebellion in heaven, and the doctrines that our birth into this life and the advantages under which we may be born, have a relationship in the life heretofore.

Even as they correct Nelson for "los[ing] sight" of this revealed doctrine, Smith, Clark, and McKay "lose sight" of and misstate LDS Church history pertaining to Black ordination:

> From the days of the Prophet Joseph even until now, it has been the doctrine of the Church, never questioned by any of the Church leaders, that the Negroes are not entitled to the full blessings of the Gospel.

They close by reasserting the Church's opposition to interracial marriage as a matter not only of social "normalcy" but also of "Church doctrine":

Furthermore, your ideas, as we understand them, appear to contemplate the intermarriage of the Negro and White races, a concept which has heretofore been most repugnant to most normal-minded people from the ancient patriarchs till now. God's rule for Israel, His Chosen People, has been endogenous. Modern Israel has been similarly directed. We are not unmindful of the fact that there is a growing tendency, particularly among some educators, as it manifests itself in this area, toward the breaking down of race barriers in the matter of intermarriage between whites and blacks, but it does not have the sanction of the Church and is contrary to Church doctrine.

Faithfully yours,

Geo. Albert Smith

J. Reuben Clark, Jr.

David O. McKay

The First Presidency[9]

As shown in figure 5.1, the tenor of the final sentence is unmistakably personal: Smith, Clark, and McKay call out Nelson's position as a university-based sociologist and reject his effort to apply rational, historicized understandings of human organization to the timeless patterns assigned to "Modern Israel." The closing line that support for intermarriage is "contrary to Church doctrine" is in fact a warning. The catechism of questions asked by local Church leaders to ascertain a member's "worthiness" to participate in LDS temple worship had since 1934 probed whether members "sustained" and exercised loyalty to Church leaders.[10] To publicly express opinions "contrary to Church doctrine" could be viewed by some local Church leaders as a failure to "sustain" Church leaders and thus lead to a member's loss of access to authority and sacred rites. Nelson would have understood this as a threat to his membership.

But he did not run, nor did he yield. Nelson responded again on October 8, having been delayed by late summer travel but also, perhaps, by what he described as his "disappointment" upon receiving the letter. He "never before had to face up to this doctrine of the Church

July 17, 1947

Dr. Lowry Nelson,
Utah State Agricultural College,
Logan, Utah.

Dear Brother Nelson:

As you have been advised, your letter of June 26 was received in due course, and likewise we now have a copy of your letter to President Meeks. We have carefully considered their contents, and are glad to advise you as follows:

We might make this initial remark: the social side of the Restored Gospel is only an incident of it; it is not the end thereof.

The basic element of your ideas and concepts seems to be that all God's children stand in equal positions before Him in all things.

Your knowledge of the Gospel will indicate to you that this is contrary to the very fundamentals of God's dealings with Israel dating from the time of His promise to Abraham regarding Abraham's seed and their position vis-a-vis God Himself. Indeed, some of God's children were assigned to superior positions before the world was formed. We are aware that some Higher Critics do not accept this, but the Church does.

Your position seems to lose sight of the revelations of the Lord touching the preexistence of our spirits, the rebellion in heaven, and the doctrines that our birth into this life and the advantages under which we may be born, have a relationship in the life heretofore.

From the days of the Prophet Joseph even until now, it has been the doctrine of the Church, never questioned by any of the Church leaders, that the Negroes are not entitled to the full blessings of the Gospel.

Furthermore, your ideas, as we understand them, appear to contemplate the intermarriage of the Negro and White races, a concept which has heretofore been most repugnant to most normal-minded people from the ancient patriarchs till now. God's rule for Israel, His Chosen People, has been endogamous. Modern Israel has been similarly directed.

We are not unmindful of the fact that there is a growing tendency, particularly among some educators, as it manifests itself in this area, toward the breaking down of race barriers in the matter of intermarriage between whites and blacks, but it does not have the sanction of the Church and is contrary to Church doctrine.

Faithfully yours,

The First Presidency

Figure 5.1. LDS Church First Presidency letter to Lowry Nelson, July 17, 1947.

Courtesy of Marriott Special Collections Library, University of Utah.

relative to the Negro," bits and pieces of which had surfaced in various religious settings over the years:

> I remember that it was discussed from time to time during my boyhood and youth, in Priesthood meetings or elsewhere in Church classes; and always someone would say something about the Negroes "sitting on the fence" during the Council in Heaven. They did not take a stand, it was said. Somehow there was never any very strong conviction manifest regarding the doctrine, perhaps because the quesiton was rather an academic one to us in Ferron, where there were very few people who had ever seen a Negro, let alone having lived in the same commuity with them. So the doctrine was always passed over rather lightly I should say, with no Scripture ever being quoted or referred to regarding the matter, except perhaps to refer to the curse of Cain, or of Ham and Canaan.

Nelson expressed his personal reservations about the way Old Testament scripture had been marshaled to explain race, especially since, as a professional sociologist, racialization fell within his field of academic study. His professional training, he explained, had shown him how "ethnocentrism" formed and reformed in human societies across time, implying carefully that what the First Presidency had insisted on as the doctrinal rendition of a God-intended pattern was instead the product of predictably human behavior. He continued:

> Once these things get written down—institutionalized—they assume an aura of the sacred. . . . So we are in the position, it seems to me, of accepting a doctrine regarding the Negro which was enunciated by the Hebrews during a very early stage in their development. Moreover, and this is the important matter to me, it does not square with what seems ann acceptable standard of justice today; nor with the letter or spirit of the teachings of Jesus Christ. I cannot find any support or such a doctrine of inequality in His recorded sayings. I am deeply troubled. Having decided through earnest study that one of the chief causes of war is the existence of ethnocentrism among the peoples of the worlds that war is our major social evil which threatens to send all of us to

destructions and that we can ameliorate these feelings of ethnocentrism by promoting understanding of one people by others, I am now
confronted with this doctrine of my own church which says in effect
that white supremacy is part of God's plan for His children; that the
Negro has been assigned by Him to be a hewer of wood and drawer of
water for his white-skinned brethren. This makes us nominal allies of
the Rankins and the Bilbos of Mississippi, a quite unhappy alliance for
me, I assure you.

Nelson challenged the idea of white supremacy—and Mormon supremacy as well—not only from scholarship but also on the basis of
his admiration for people of color with whom he had interacted in the
professional realm, including "Dr. George Washington Carver, the
late eminent and saintly Negro scientists," who under the emerging
doctrine would be "inferior even to the least admirable white person,
not because of the virtues he may or may not possesss, but because—
through no fault of his own—there is a dark pigment in his skin." He
responded sharply as well to the leadership's instruction that the "social
side" of the Gospel was not a primary concern. "Are the virtues of honesty, chastity, humility, forgiveness, tolerance, love, kindness, justice,
scondary? If so, what is primary? Love of God? Very well. But the
second (law) is like unto it." He concluded in a conciliatory and deferen-
tial tone, admitting that in his concerns he was but one of many faithful
members Church leaders were tasked to lead, guide, and counsel. He
humbly stated that in laying out his thinking so fully in writing he was
"trying to be honest with myself and others" and "trying to find my
way in what is a very confused world," citing his recent time in Europe,
where he witnessed the devastations of World War II, as his motive. He
pleaded for "love," "mutual respect," and "understanding" instead of
a "legalistic" approach to morality. The First Presidency's final reply on
November 12, 1947 (see figure 5.2), yielded nothing:

We feel very sure that you understand well the doctrines of the Church.
They are either true or not true. Our testimony is that they are true.

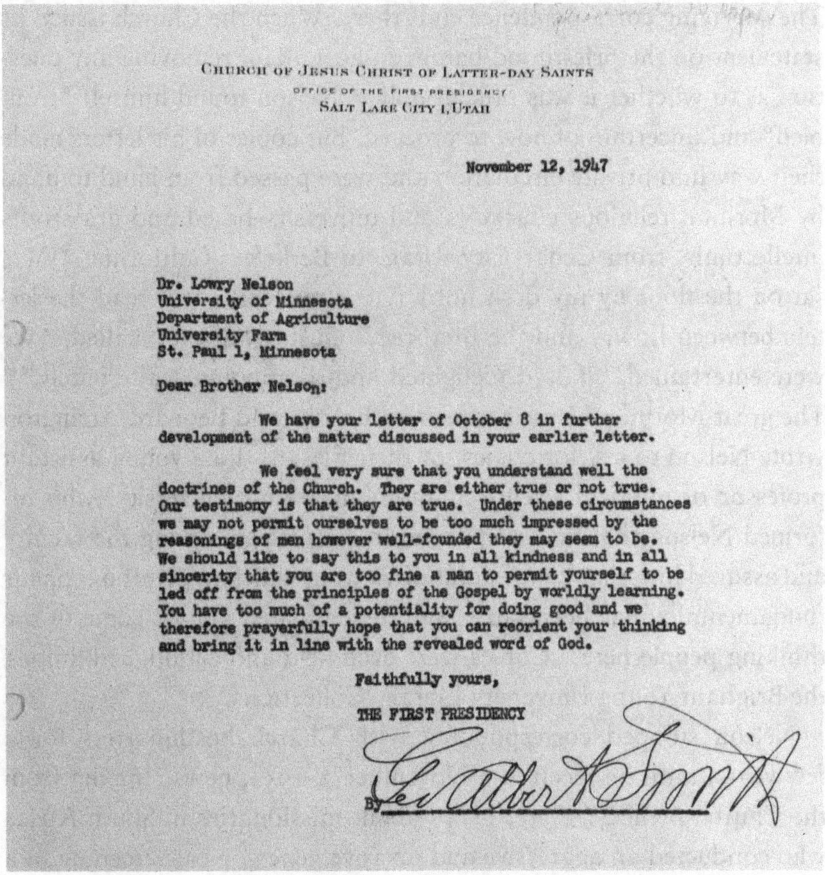

Figure 5.2. LDS Church President George Albert Smith to Lowry Nelson, November 12, 1947.

Image courtesy Marriott Special Collections Library, University of Utah.

Under these circumstances we may not permit ourselves to be too much impressed by the reasonings of men however well-founded they may seem to be. We should like to say this to you in all kindness and in all sincerity that you are too fine a man to permit yourself to be led off from the principles of the Gospel by worldly-learning. You have too much of a potentiality for doing good and we therefore prayerfully hope that you can reorient your thinking and bring it in line with the revealed word of God.

The surviving correspondence ends there. When the Church issued its statement on the priesthood ban in August 1949, removing any question as to whether it was official policy, Nelson found himself "troubled" and uncertain of how to proceed. But copies of his letters made their way into private circulation and were passed from hand to hand by Mormon religious educators and university-based and grassroots intellectuals, from Cedar City, Utah, to Berkeley, California. "[We] sat on the floor by my desk until 1:30 a.m. while [we] read the letters between Lowry and the Brethren," Gustav Larsen recalled. "We were entertained, amused, delighted and disappointed alternately."[11] The great Mormon historians Juanita Brooks and Leonard Arrington wrote Nelson to ask for copies for their files, as did a young assistant professor of political science at Brigham Young University, who informed Nelson that his letters were in circulation among the faculty and assured him that "your point of view, in which many of us concur fundamentally, has been fairly well disseminated among some of the thinking people here." Copies were even held and catalogued among the Brigham Young University Library Collections.[12]

Nelson stopped corresponding with Church headquarters for a few years, until he received a November 7, 1951, news clipping from the Church-owned *Deseret News* about missionaries in South Africa who conducted an aggressive and invasive genealogical screening of a local woman on her deathbed to ascertain whether or not she could be eligible for posthumous temple rites. Nelson later recalled that their efforts "disturbed me all over again," and he resolved to bring greater scrutiny to the priesthood and temple ban.[13] He developed his own report on the Church's anti-Black segregation for publication in *The Nation*, going so far as to send Church leaders the article in advance to make them aware, writing that although he held "the Brethren" in "affectionate regard," anti-Black racism was a "matter of principle which I cannot compromise. . . . I am compelled to publicly issociate myself from adherence to a doctrine which is so incongruous with the Gospel as I had been taught it."[14] He received from the First Presidency's secretary a curt reply that "when a member of the Church sets himself up against doctrines preached by the Prophet Joseph Smith and by those who have succeeded him in the high office which he held, he is moving into a very dangerous position for himself personally." Beyond its aggressive misrepresentation of LDS history, the secretary's letter suggested a direct threat to Nelson's membership. Nelson's article (see figure 5.3) appeared in *The Nation* on May 24, 1952:

ACCORDING to Mormon theology the status of the Negro on earth was determined in the "pre-existent" state, specifically in the War in Heaven (Revelation 12:4, 7). As everyone knows, Lucifer rebelled and was "cast down," taking with him one-third of the hosts of Heaven. These are "the sons of perdition." Michael clearly had a majority with him, some more active supporters than others. Although I can find no Scriptural basis for it, I have heard it said that the active pro-Michael group was no more than one-third. The other third "sat on the fence" refusing to take sides. The latter, in the Mormon lore of my boyhood days, was identified as the Negro. This places him in a sort of never-never land, a twilight zone between the Satanic hosts and those who were ready to be counted on the side of Michael. Thus the blessings of the Mormon Church cannot be extended to anyone with Negro "blood." This unfortunate policy of the church is a source of embarrassment and humiliation to thousands of its members (the writer among them) who find no basis for it in the teachings of Jesus, whom all Mormons accept as the Saviour. The issue has become increasingly important as members of the church outside of Utah and adjacent states have increased rapidly in recent years and are brought into direct contact with Negroes, and who see their fellow Christians engaged in programs to reduce racial prejudice and programs in which they cannot fully participate. Such persons would like to see the policy altered in the interest of peace and simple humanitarianism.

The doctrine of white-race superiority, so much the vogue in the early nineteenth century when Mormonism had its beginning, has been so thoroughly debunked as to catalogue its adherents today as either grossly uninformed or victims of traditional irrational prejudices, or both. Mormons as a group are not ignorant people; they rank high in formal schooling, with an extraordinarily high proportion of college

AROUND THE U. S. A.

Mormons and the Negro

St. Paul, Minn.

ACCORDING to Mormon theology the status of the Negro on earth was determined in the "pre-existent" state, specifically in the War in Heaven (Revelation 12:4, 7). As everyone knows, Lucifer rebelled and was "cast down," taking with him one-third of the hosts of Heaven. These are the sons of perdition. Michael clearly had a majority with him, some more active supporters than others. Although I can find no Scriptural basis for it, I have heard it said that the *active* pro-Michael group was no more than one-third. The other third "sat on the fence," refusing to take sides. The latter, in the Mormon lore of my boyhood days, was identified as the Negro. This places him in a sort of never-never land, a twilight zone between the Satanic hosts and those who were ready to be counted on the side of Michael. Thus the blessings of the Mormon Church cannot be extended to anyone with Negro "blood."

This unfortunate policy of the church is a source of embarrassment and humiliation to thousands of its members (the writer among them) who find no basis for it in the teachings of Jesus, whom all Mormons accept as the Saviour. The issue has become increasingly important as members of the church outside of Utah and adjacent states have increased rapidly in recent years and are brought into direct contact with Negroes, and who see their fellow-Christians engaged in programs to reduce racial prejudice—programs in which they cannot fully participate. Such persons would like to see the policy altered in the interest of peace and simple humanitarianism.

The doctrine of white-race superiority, so much the vogue in the early nineteenth century when Mormonism had its beginning, has been so thoroughly debunked as to catalogue its adherents today as either grossly uninformed or victims of traditional irrational prejudices, or both. Mormons as a group are not ignorant people; they rank high in formal schooling, with an extraordinarily high proportion of college graduates. Many of them naturally find it difficult to reconcile what they learn in college about racial differences and equalities with the stand taken by their church. Curiously the position of the church on the Negro does not carry over to other racial groups. Natives of the South Seas, Mongolians, and American Indians are given a clean bill of health. And Mormons, according to their theology, regard the Jews as their own kin! The doctrine, however, does not mean there is no anti-Semitism among Mormons, but that is another problem.

The basic question remains as to whether the church will modify its present stand on this matter. Perhaps a more important question is, *can* it change? Theoretically the church has a means by which its doctrines may be modified. It was founded upon the idea of "progressive revelation," that as God spoke to the people in Bible days, so He continues to do today through the head of the church. An announcement *ex cathedra* on this question would be accepted by the body of the church; joyfully by some although, no doubt, reluctantly by others. It is recognized, of course, that it is very difficult for a religion based upon revelation to modify its doctrines, but few other denominations have the procedures for change that the Mormon church has. The leaders of this church are men of good will. It is difficult to believe that deep in their own hearts they are not troubled by the ethical problem which this bit of dogma presents.

A very real difficulty is the fact that those who disapprove the church's attitude have no way of expressing their point of view. It is safe to say that most of the one million members give passive assent to the present policy. For most of those living in Utah and adjacent states the Negro question is academic; they hardly ever see Negroes, much less live in the same community with them. In any case, they would find comfortable agreement with the white-supremacy idea because of latent historical prejudices which they share with so many other white people. However, my knowledge of the deep humanitarianism of the Mormon people leads me to think that if the question could be openly discussed they would line up on the side of justice.

Such open discussion, especially in print, however, is a perilous undertaking for any member. It automatically leaves him open to the charge of "disobedience to constituted authority" which may lead to his being excommunicated. The upshot is that discussions by interested persons are largely subrosa. So widespread are such discussion groups that they might be said to constitute a "Mormon underground." The participants are not disloyal church members; rather they are generally active in the church and rationalize their conduct by weighing the many admirable features of their religion against the features with which they disagree.

In writing this article for publication the author does so in a spirit of constructive criticism and in the conviction that his church, with so many admirable qualities and achievements to its credit, is faced by a challenge to place itself alongside those other groups which are laboring against racial bigotry.

LOWRY NELSON

[The writer is a lifelong member of the Mormon Church.]

Bevan Symposium

The Nation will present in an early issue a symposium on Aneurin Bevan's important book, In Place of Fear. Among the contributors will be Stringfellow Barr of the University of Virginia, author of Let's Join the Human Race; Carrol Binder of the Minneapolis *Tribune*; Palmer Hoyt, editor and publisher of the Denver *Post*; Benjamin Javits, author of How the Republicans Can Win in 1952; Murray D. Lincoln, president of the Cooperative League of the U. S. A.; Howard K. Smith, Columbia Broadcasting System's European correspondent and a *Nation* staff contributor, and James P. Warburg, author of How to Co-Exist and many other books. Aneurin Bevan, leader of Britain's left-wing Labor faction, is one of the most colorful political figures in the world today. His book, particularly the sections on foreign policy, is perhaps the most controversial of the year.

Figure 5.3. Lowry Nelson, "Mormonism and the Negro," *The Nation*, May 24, 1952, 2.

graduates. Many of them naturally find it difficult to reconcile what they learn in college about racial differences and equalities with the stand taken by their church. Curiously the position of the church on the Negro does not carry over to other racial groups. Natives of the South Seas, Mongolians, and American Indians are given a clean bill of health. And Mormons, according to their theology, regard the Jews as their own kin! The doctrine, however, does not mean there is no anti-Semitism among Mormons, but that is another problem.

The basic question remains as to whether the church will modify its present stand on this matter. Perhaps a more important question is, *can* it change? Theoretically the church has a means by which its doctrines may be modified. It was founded upon the idea of "progressive revelation," that as God spoke to the people in Bible days, so He continues to do today through the head of the church. An announcement *ex cathedra* on this question would be accepted by the body of the church; joyfully by some although, no doubt, reluctantly by others. It is recognized, of course, that it is very difficult for a religion based upon revelation to modify its doctrines, but few other denominations have the procedures for change that the Mormon church has. The leaders of this church are men of good will. It is difficult to believe that deep in their own hearts they are not troubled by the ethical problem which this bit of dogma presents.

A very real difficulty is the fact that those who disapprove the church's attitude have no way of expressing their point of view. It is safe to say that most of the one million members give passive assent to the present policy. For most of those living in Utah and adjacent states the Negro question is academic; they hardly ever see Negroes, much less live in the same community with them. In any case, they would find comfortable agreement with the white supremacy idea because of latent historical prejudices which they share with so many other white people. However, my knowledge of the deep humanitarianism of the Mormon people leads me to think that if the question could be openly discussed they would line up on the side of justice.

Such open discussion, especially in print, however, is a perilous undertaking for any member. It automatically leaves him open to the charge of "disobedience to constituted authority" which may lead to his being excommunicated. The upshot is that discussions by interested persons are largely subrosa. So widespread are such discussion groups that they might be said to constitute a "Mormon underground." The participants are not disloyal church members; rather they are generally active in the church and rationalize their conduct by weighing the many admirable features of their religion against the features with which they disagree. In writing this article for publication the author does so in a spirit of constructive criticism and in the conviction that his church, with so many admirable qualities and achievements to its credit, is faced by a challenge to place itself alongside those other groups which are laboring against racial bigotry.

The statement is as fine a model of reasoned but faithful LDS dissent and as lucid a depiction of the theological, social, and political conditions of dissent as exists in Mormonism's 180-year history. It also inspired similar attempts to pressure Church leadership from other well-placed LDS scholars including University of Chicago geographer Dr. Chauncy Harris, who maintained a twenty-year correspondence with Nelson, as the two men—and many other like-minded LDS people nationwide—developed private archives of clippings and other documents relating to the issue and attempted to hammer out a strategy for effecting change.[15] In the 1960s and 1970s, Nelson was sought out by scholars like Armand Mauss, Kendall White, and Lester Bush (who would go on to author an essential article on the Black priesthood and temple ban), and John W. Fitzgerald, a Salt Lake–area LDS seminary teacher and high school principal, who had organized with other white LDS people (including Grant Ivins, Sterling McMurrin, and Brigham Madsen) to expose the doctrinal irregularity and insufficiency of the priesthood and temple ban by speaking at civic and non-LDS church events and publishing letters to the editor in the *Salt Lake Tribune*. For making his arguments public, Fitzgerald was excommunicated in late 1972.[16] And yet Lowry Nelson was not excommunicated. It may be that by presenting his case and the threat of excommunication in writing, so clearly, so publicly, in a national venue published outside the Mormon corridor and beyond its domain of territorial knowledge, he gained a kind of immunity from repression, inasmuch as the Church remained invested in not fulfilling its detractors' worst charges of authoritarianism. But his privileged racial and social position also played a role. He again took on the Church's anti-Black segregationism in a 1974 article in the *Christian Century* and, according to one biographer, "needled Church leaders with satirical poems until his death": "The gadfly lived a charmed life as a persistent dissident, possibly because of his age, his eminence, and the fact that he'd known many of the Brethren personally for years."[17] As a Utah-born, white, multigenerational Mormon man with deep connections to the hierarchy, whose writings seemed for the most part limited to academic and liberal audiences, he retained his place at the edge of the herd.

* * *

Over the next decade, the "subrosa" "Mormon underground" of liberal, heterodox, and dissenting LDS people matured enough to develop its own social and print institutions. Most important among them was *Dialogue: A Journal of Mormon Thought*, founded in 1966 by a cohort of Stanford University graduate students. The journal's mission was (and continues to be) to "bring [the Mormon] faith into dialogue with the larger stream of world religious thought and with human experience as a whole and to foster artistic and scholarly achievement based on their cultural heritage." *Dialogue* sought to create a space where Mormons at the edge of the herd could develop shared knowledge, perspective, hopes, and ideas.

From its beginnings, *Dialogue* was one of the most influential forums for exchange of information and opinion on the Church's priesthood and temple ban, as well as on issues of racial and gender equality in Mormonism more generally. Even as the institutional LDS Church from its 1949 statement onward held the counterfactual position that the ban originated with God himself as revealed to the Church's founders, *Dialogue* supported historical scholarship that restored to modern Mormon memory a far more nuanced and complicated historical picture and in so doing challenged the silent compact between the Church and its members not to betray racial innocence or foster critique.

Dialogue's founders represented a sensibility among some white multigenerational Mormon families that it was possible to leverage their relationships and the safety of an unassailable Mormon identity to respectfully challenge authority when warranted. This view was also subscribed to by political families like the Udalls of Arizona, who had made and would continue to make stands on critical issues, even when they placed them on the margins of mainstream Mormonism. Born in 1920 in St. John's, Arizona, Stewart Udall descended from a long line of dissident Mormons. He attended the University of Arizona until service in World War II interrupted his studies; while in the armed forces, Udall joined the NAACP. Upon his return, in 1947, Udall reflected critically on how his wartime experiences impacted his faith: "I find it difficult to be in full fellowship within the Mormon Church," he admitted, citing the fact that "too many members find it easy to be simultaneously devout Mormons and devout anti-Semites, lovers of their fellow men in public and Negrophobes in private."[18] As returning students at the University of Arizona, Stewart and his brother Mo helped desegregate the school cafeteria by escorting Black students who had been restricted to outside dining tables inside and using their stature—social and physical—to resist administration efforts to move them.

After receiving his law degree, Udall entered public service. He cofounded the Tucson League for Civil Unity, an anti-segregationist and anti-discrimination group, and helped implement the desegregation of Arizona schools as a member of the Tucson School Board. Elected to Congress in 1954, Udall was appointed secretary of the interior by President Kennedy in 1960. Among his first acts was to order in March 1961 a survey of Department of Interior properties to screen for racial discrimination in hiring. Legal staff at the department had advised him that the Washington Redskins, the only fully segregated team in the National Football League, had just signed a lease to build a statement on federal property: Anacostia Flats, part of the National

Capital Parks. Udall ordered them to desegregate by October. For this, he was both celebrated and challenged by observers who noted that the secretary of the interior himself belonged to an officially segregated Church.

Although he was considered and, in all likelihood, considered himself a "Jack Mormon"—that is, a nonobservant, nonorthodox Mormon whose ties to the faith are more historical, cultural, and affectional than devotional—Udall took personal responsibility for the priesthood and temple ban. He relayed to LDS Church leadership the embarrassment and conflict the Church's stance created for its progressive members. He also corresponded with his brother, now congressman Mo Udall, to express consternation over egregiously racist public remarks made by LDS Church leaders, including octogenarian LDS Church President Joseph Fielding Smith. Moreover, he developed a personal archive of writings by scholars and rank-and-file Church members that challenged the consensus view of the ban as divinely inspired. After sharing his concerns with Church leaders in writing, he published an open letter to LDS Church President David O. McKay in *Dialogue: A Journal of Mormon Thought* on May 16, 1967. It follows in its entirety:

> For more than a decade we Americans have been caught up in a revolution in thinking about race and human relationships. The Supreme Court has wisely and effectively related the Constitution to the facts of life in the twentieth century; three Presidents and five Congresses have laid new foundations for a society of equal opportunity; most of the churches, with unaccustomed and admirable militance, have enlisted foursquare in the fight for equal rights and higher human dignity.
>
> The whole future of the human race is now keyed to equality—to the ideal of equal opportunity and of equal civil rights and responsibilities, and to the new dignity and freedom which these would bring. The brotherhood of all men is a moral imperative that no religion and no church can evade or ignore. Enlightened men everywhere see now, as their greatest prophets and moral teachers saw long ago, that brotherhood is universal and indivisible.

It was inevitable that national attention would be focused on what critics have called the "anti-Negro doctrine" of the L.D.S. Church. As the Church becomes increasingly an object of national interest, this attention is certain to intensify, for the divine curse concept which is so commonly held among our people runs counter to the great stream of modern religious and social thought.

We Mormons cannot escape persistent, painful inquiries into the sources and grounds of this belief. Nor can we exculpate ourselves and our Church from justified condemnation by the rationalization that we support the Constitution, believe that all men are brothers, and favor equal rights for all citizens.

This issue must be resolved—and resolved not by pious moralistic platitudes but by clear and explicit pronouncements and decisions that come to grips with the imperious truths of the contemporary world. It must be resolved not because we desire to conform, or because we want to atone for an affront to a whole race. It must be resolved because we are wrong and it is past the time when we should have seen the right. A failure to act here is sure to demean our faith, damage the minds and morals of our youth, and undermine the integrity of our Christian ethic.

In her book, *Killers of the Dream*, the late Lillian Smith—whose life was exposed to all the warping forces of a racist culture—wrote these words:

"I began to understand slowly at first, but more clearly as the years passed, that the warped, distorted frame we have put around every Negro child from birth is around every white child also. Each is on a different side of the frame but each is pinioned there. And I knew that what cruelly shapes and cripples the personality of one is as cruelly shaping and crippling the personality of the other."

What a sad irony it is that a once outcast people, tempered for nearly a century in the fires of persecution, are one of the last to remove a burden from the most persecuted people ever to live on this continent. The irony is deepened by the circumstance of history that the present practice of the Church in denying full fellowship to the Negro grew out of troubles rooted in earlier pro-Negro policies and actions. It is well known that Joseph Smith held high ideals of universal brotherhood and

136

had strong pro-Negro leanings that were, in a true sense, prophetic. And it is well known that in the beginning the Church accepted Negroes into full fellowship until this practice offended its anti-Negro neighbors. It then settled for a compromise with its own ideals based on a borrowed superstition that the Negroes are under a divine curse. This anomaly is underscored by the fact that the Church has always enjoyed excellent relations and complete fellowship with all other races. (How different have been our associations with the American Indians, the Spanish-speaking peoples, the Japanese and Polynesians!) What transformations might take place in our spiritual and moral energies if we were to become, once again, moral leaders in improving the lot of the Negroes as we have striven to do with the natives of the South Seas?

At an earlier impasse, the Church, unable to escape history, wisely abandoned the deeply imbedded practice of plural marriage and thereby resolved a crisis of its own conscience and courageously faced the moral judgment of the American people. In 1890 for most Church leaders polygamy was a precious principle—a practice that lay at the very heart of Mormonism. Its proscription took genuine courage, but our leaders were equal to the task. By comparison, the restriction now imposed on Negro fellowship is a social and institutional practice having no real sanction in essential Mormon thought. It is clearly contradictory to our most cherished spiritual and moral ideals.

Every Mormon knows that his Church teaches that the day will come when the Negro will be given full fellowship. Surely that day has come. All around us the Negro is proving his worth when accepted into the society of free men. All around us are the signs that he needs and must have a genuine brotherhood with Mormons, Catholics, Methodists, and Jews. Surely God is speaking to us now, telling us that the time is here.

"The glory of God is intelligence" has long been a profound Mormon teaching. We must give it new meaning now, for the glory of intelligence is that the wise men and women of each generation dream new dreams and rise to forge broader bonds of human brotherhood to what more noble accomplishment could we of this generation aspire?

Stewart L. Udall, Washington, D.C.[19]

Understanding exquisitely well the politics of Mormon culture and its sensitivity to public exposure derived from its nineteenth-century past and its not-too-distant twentieth-century quest for respectability, Udall carefully chose not to directly address Church leadership, which might have been seen as too direct a challenge, nor did he address a broad secular public in an effort to embarrass and expose Church leaders. He wrote, first, to his fellow Latter-day Saints, in an LDS-produced and moderated venue, understanding full well that his national stature would in time bring wider publicity and a broadened audience to witness and support the internal moral deliberations of the Mormon people. And it did. Udall received hundreds of letters and telegrams in response, spanning a range of Mormon opinion, with support coming especially from LDS liberal stalwarts like Esther Peterson, a women's and labor rights activist who also held prominent posts in the Kennedy and Johnson administrations, and Lowry Nelson, who wrote, "I'm proud of you! . . . Would that a little of your courage could get piped into the aenemic [Church] headquarters." Spencer W. Kimball, another rural Arizona Mormon who had ascended into the Church's highest-ranking leadership body, the Quorum of the Twelve Apostles, responded differently. Taking what one historian characterizes as "the tone of an upset and disappointed father," he wrote, "Stewart, I cannot believe it! You wouldn't presume to command your God nor to make a demand of a Prophet of God!" and characterized the letter as a "sincere but ill-advised effort in behalf of the welfare of a minority."[20] Ironically, Kimball's son Spencer L. Kimball, a professor of law at the University of Michigan, had collected his own file of materials on the race issue, including copies of Lowry Nelson's exchange with Church officials, and had stepped away from Church activity over matters of conscience, racism certainly among them.[21]

Another well-placed Arizona-rooted Mormon offered a public rejoinder to Udall in the *New York Times*'s front-page coverage of the letter on May 19, 1967. Udall had sent Romney a handwritten note on May 16 to let him know the piece would shortly appear: "[This] has long been an issue that has troubled my conscience. The brethren must, I am convinced, face it squarely (as the plural marriage issue was faced) sooner or later." Reporter Wallace Turner solicited a quote from Governor George Romney, who despite his own record of vocal and active support for civil rights in the secular sphere did not approve of Udall's efforts: "In light of the fact that church doctrine is not determined by the attitude and expression of the individual members or the leadership, he knows, as do all other informed members of my faith, that his method of accomplishing the religious object he seeks cannot serve any useful religious purpose."[22] Udall's statement and Romney's reply received nationwide newspaper coverage, including front-page coverage in the *New York Times*, with some observers noting that Romney, who was then seeking the Republican Party presidential nomination, had "ducked" the issue to maintain his campaign-trail message that he could not be held responsible for the doctrines of his Church but should instead be measured on racial issues by his conduct as governor.[23]

Both George Romney and Stewart Udall had deep and elite ancestral roots in Mormonism, common ties in the rural Mormon communities of northern Arizona, and national political reputations.[24] Their respective approaches reflect a significant difference in the two men's theories of change in the Mormon movement. Romney subscribed to the silent agreement that he would not openly express opposition to the Church's anti-Black segregation and sustain not only its leadership but also its assertion of innocence. Implicit in this is a theory of change in Mormonism that God will work through the hierarchy of the Church through continuing revelation to Church leaders and that while a well-placed private comment might assist that process, public dissent can only derail it. There is some truth in this viewpoint: as a sharply differentiated religious minority that maintains a strong boundary against "the world," orthodox Mormonism is highly allergic to external scrutiny and pressure, even more so in light of historic persecutions and common mockeries of LDS people. Pressure from the outside may in fact engender retrenchment. But as he weighed the costs and affordances of orthodoxy, Udall found himself in secure enough a position—with footing and public regard in the secular world, and a deeply rooted Mormon identity and sense of belonging not revocable through Church discipline—to step outside the silent agreement and go public. He did so carefully, directing his comments first to other LDS people, not to the public nor directly to Church leadership, which might have been interpreted by the leaders and by more orthodox LDS people as a violent challenge. Implicit in his choices is a recognition that even Church leaders must be held publicly accountable. Until the death of Jane Manning James in 1908, Church leaders had been held accountable by the living presence of Black pioneers who knew the Church's true history on race and stood as living emblems of it, even as that history was erased in institutionally produced, "correlated," orthodox, official histories and curricula. Udall willingly stepped into that role to bear witness and hold Church leaders accountable. Udall's approach also reflects a theory of change that vests hope in the possibility of continuing revelation not only to Church leaders but also to the Mormon people themselves as they apply the tools the faith provides every member—individual prayer, scripture study, contemplation, and personal revelation through the Holy Ghost—to seek truth. Udall's theory of change vested hope in Mormon people as agents of change both within and without the Church. Importantly, it was founded in an understanding that those who lost the most by anti-Black segregation in the LDS Church were not excluded Black people but white Church members themselves who were morally hobbled by their complicity and duplicity. Udall seemed to understand fully the silent agreement to "overlook" Mormon white supremacy sustained by well-placed Mormons like Romney and by the nation's majority itself and how corrosive it was to Mormons ourselves. And he also seemed to understand that without making statements in writing, in public, on the record, articulations of conscience and differences like his would be lost to history—lost to future generations of LDS people who might need role models and exemplars of principled, faithful Mormon dissent. Maintaining racial innocence depended then and depends now on asserting that Mormons had never thought or felt otherwise, that things had been as God intended them, that there had never been struggle, and that struggle was inimical to the Spirit of God. To go along with the silent agreement not to challenge Church leaders on their racism was to surrender even further Mormonism's founding impulses of truth seeking and radical differentiation in the service of twentieth-century white hierarchical institutional security.

* * *

Udall raised a public voice of dissent from a place of privileged security. He knew that as an esteemed public official he would remain secure in his employment. He was not on the Church payroll, and while his Mormon connections were important to his political success, as a federal appointee, he had placed himself beyond whatever ire his stance might draw from LDS voters in his home state of Arizona. Moreover, he knew that as a member of a storied multigenerational Mormon family he would never lose his belonging, community, or identity: he would only by virtue of dissent lose opportunities to serve in a high-ranking position in the Church and the approval of some of its more orthodox leaders and members. As an elite white Mormon man, he had only the discomfort of pushback from other elite white Mormon men to worry about, and in taking his dissent so public, Udall ensured that any pushback would be subject to what elite white Mormon men disliked most—full scrutiny and potential judgment and shame from an American national audience.

But what about the rank-and-file white members who found themselves just as agitated over the Church's anti-Black racism? How did they negotiate the silent agreement? What theories of change did they hold, and how did they put them into action? Lowry Nelson's 1952 piece in *The Nation* spoke of an extensive Mormon "underground" of conscientiously dissenting and heterodox "discussion groups," and by Udall's time that underground had formed its own above-ground print institutions where even geographically far-flung, out-migrated Mormons who may not have had access to critical masses of dissenters in Mormon population centers like Salt Lake could make contact and participate, at least by reading, writing, and thinking. In 1973, the independent historian Lester Bush published in *Dialogue: A Journal of Mormon Thought* "Mormonism's Negro Doctrine: A Historical Overview," a deeply footnoted fifty-seven-page essay composed from archival LDS historical sources tracking the history of the anti-Black priesthood and temple ban. Bush hoped that historicizing the policy—showing it to have been instituted unevenly by human actors with human motivations with shifting rationale—would dislodge the idea that it reflected the will of God from time immemorial as revealed to infallible LDS prophets, the majority view at the time in Mormonism, and have some influence on Church leaders.

Scholarship like that by Lester Bush can play a critical role in helping to shift perspectives. So can taking direct action to disrupt the workings of segregation, and it is the most likely option available to those who were not, as Udall or Bush were, positioned by education and elite access to be able to use writing alone to command attention. But except for working-class Mormons who had taken part in the vibrant and sometimes violent labor struggles of Utah's mining industry in the 1920s and 1930s and those who had participated in demonstrations and strikes after out-migrating (like Esther Peterson), few Mormon people had exposure to or experience in direct action. It was not part of the Mormon political lexicon. The homogeneity and isolation of Intermountain West Mormon communities and the fact that their major struggles were territorial meant that LDS people were more practiced in armed conflict (against the federal government and against indigenous peoples), vigilantism, undergrounding (especially in relation to polygamy), migration (most recently by Mormon polygamous and fundamentalist communities), and the various theatrics of American electoral politics (complicated of course by LDS institutional influence) than in the kinds of mass mobilization associated with popular movements in the nineteenth century and demonstrative civil disobedience theorized by Thoreau and implemented on a mass scale by Mahatma Gandhi that had defined American public protest from the 1950s onward. In the early 1960s, the NAACP had planned or carried out pickets to protest the LDS Church's perceived interference with the passage of civil rights legislation in Utah. By the late 1960s, Black athletes on teams scheduled to play Brigham Young University and their supporters had used nonviolent direct action and civil disobedience to protest the Church's anti-Black segregation, and at times the demonstration crossed over into violence, as when Colorado State fans threw a Molotov cocktail into the basketball arena during a Brigham Young University–Colorado State University contest in Fort Collins in 1970.[25]

But white LDS people who attempted direct action to challenge anti-Black segregation within the Church were very few. An LDS Church member named Douglas Wallace had in April 1976 baptized and ordained a Black man to the priesthood; he was subsequently excommunicated.[26] Wallace continued his pressure by attempting to disrupt General Conference and announcing to the press that he would put LDS Church President Spencer W. Kimball "on trial." Another who took direct action was Byron Marchant. Marchant was one of fifteen children in a multigenerational but nonelite and working-class Salt Lake City Mormon family. His mother, Beatrice Peterson Marchant, came from rural, working-class Utah LDS Democrat stock; worked as a schoolteacher for several years in rural Utah communities; moved to Salt Lake City and raised her children while caring for a disabled husband; and in 1968 was elected to the Utah state legislature, where she fought for the ratification of the Equal Rights Amendment.[27] She was remembered by her grandchildren and greatgrandchildren as a champion of the "underdog," and her personal writings reveal her essentially activist disposition: "I can appreciate and understand the world and the people around me if only I make an effort to do so. I even have the ability to help change the world for better or for worse."[28] Byron had served a proselytizing mission for the Church in France, attended Brigham Young University, married Gladys Smith, and settled in a working-class neighborhood in Salt Lake City, where he taught youth tennis in a local park, took a job as a church meetinghouse janitor, and was appointed by his local congregation to serve as the Scout troop leader. Byron welcomed local non-Mormon African American youth into the troop but was deeply upset when in 1973 local leaders told him that the African American boys were not permitted to assume leadership roles in the troop due to the Church's priesthood-temple ban, and more so when he discovered that the white Mormon Boy Scouts in his troop used the ban to taunt their Black fellow troop members at school. Marchant recalls that the race-based taunting even escalated into a rock fight at one troop campout. It was, to his mind, unacceptable. He worked with the NAACP to bring national attention and pressure to the issue. His actions permanently "split" the family, a nephew later recalled.[29]

Marchant was also a student of Mormon history, and his commitment on the race issue propelled him to research the origins of the Church's ban for himself. With a cluster of Mormon scholars starting to write and publish more openly in venues like *Dialogue* about inconsistencies in the Church's account of its own history on race—the Church had released a statement in 1969 claiming that "Joseph Smith and all succeeding presidents of the Church have taught that Negroes, while spirit children of a common Father, and the progeny of our earthly parents Adam and Eve, were not yet to receive the priesthood, for reasons which we believe are known to God, but which He has not made fully known to man"—Marchant visited the Church Archives on North Temple Street to see for himself the ordination certificate of Elijah Abel, an African American man ordained to the priesthood and the Quorum of the Seventy during the founding decades of the Church. He recalls: "I made a written copy of it (with permission of the archivist there) and proceeded to make a typewritten copy of it at my home from my handwritten copy. The original (public domain) document showed that Joseph Smith, Jr., had signed it." Marchant distributed photocopies of the typewritten facsimile to "the press and public" in August 1977.[30]

As he radicalized around the Church's racism, Marchant and a small cohort adopted direct action tactics, including a weekly picket outside the LDS Church Office Building in downtown Salt Lake City. In October 1977, Marchant took the bold step of introducing direct action and nonviolent resistance tactics into LDS sacred spaces. Twice annually, the Church convened a General Conference in the Mormon Tabernacle on Temple Square. With the entire leadership hierarchy (and the Mormon Tabernacle Choir) seated on the stand, the historic building packed to the rafters with thousands of faithful adherents, and hundreds of thousands more watching on television and listening on radio, General Conference was the most important "rite of assent" (to use Sacvan Bercovitch's term) in Mormon life. Every Conference, a member of the hierarchy asked members attending in person or participating by media to signal with an upraised hand that they "sustained" the leaders of the Church as "prophets, seers, and revelators," an act understood by many orthodox Mormons as a promise not to dissent and as a fulfilling of sacred covenants they had made in LDS temple rites to consecrate themselves entirely to the Church. His nephew Mark Barnes was watching the October 2, 1977, Conference session on local television in Salt Lake City, and recalls:

> As we watched the start of the Saturday afternoon session on October 2, 1977, a familiar voice boomed from the television set. I immediately knew it was Byron. "President Tanner did you note my vote?" First Counselor N. Eldon Tanner looked confused, as he searched for the source of the dissenting vote. Security responded escorting Byron from the building. Byron later explained to the press that his negative vote was meant to highlight the injustice of the priesthood ban.[31]

Byron Marchant had stood in the packed Tabernacle balcony and raised his hand to signal that he did not sustain Church leaders because of their anti-Black discrimination. Moreover, he had called out across the crowded Tabernacle to ensure that his presence registered not only there but also with the hundreds of thousands listening and watching on television, even if the LDS Church camera operators refused to turn their cameras from the pulpit to capture his dissenting image. He was excommunicated twelve days later, on October 14, and subsequently lost his job as a meetinghouse janitor. Marchant was by then a widower. Dissension within the family over his activism and excommunication contributed at least in part to a custody battle that eventuated in the placement of his children with his deceased wife's mother.[32]

Marchant challenged the silent agreement between the Church and its members to maintain its innocence of anti-Black racism, but he had done so from a far more precarious economic and social class position than Udall and through direct action tactics that were arguably more disruptive than Udall's letter. And the costs of revoking his membership would not have been nearly as great to the Church as the potential costs of moving in on someone with Stewart Udall's publicity, esteem, and national stature. As a working-class, nonelite Mormon, Marchant was more expendable, and violating the silent agreement through direct action cost him deeply. He lost access to family, employment, and the social networks that held Mormon life in Salt Lake City together. His story demonstrates the critical role social and class privilege has played and continues to play in Mormon dissent.

* * *

It was even more precarious for members of color who openly opposed the Church's priesthood and temple ban. Elder Boyd K. Packer, a member of the Church's Quorum of the Twelve Apostles, had instructed the Church-sponsored Genesis group—a fellowship auxiliary founded in 1971 serving between twenty and two hundred Black members in the Salt Lake area—to "keep a low profile."[33] Most Genesis members worked through private channels, expressing their desire for priesthood and temple access and sharing their experiences of racism in letters and private face-to-face meetings with Church leaders. Others who became frustrated by the Church's intransigence dropped out of Church activity. In 1976, after Wallace's rogue priesthood ordination of a Black man, some members of the Genesis group did sign a petition calling on the Church to commit to a timeline for ending the ban, a move that exacerbated tensions within the group and led members on both sides of the issue to withdraw.[34]

What would have happened had the leadership of the Genesis group been directly and openly critical of LDS Church racism or taken their disagreements public, breaking the "silent agreement" between the Church and its members to preserve the racial innocence of Mormonism? How did the dynamics of racial and class privilege impact the practice of anti-racist dissent in LDS communities? The experience of George P. Lee suggests that like class privilege, racial privilege determined the extent to which one could conscientiously object and question LDS Church racism without experiencing personal harm. Born in 1943 to the Bitter Water Clan for the Under the Flat-Roofed House People Clan on the Ute Mountain Indian Reservation, George P. Lee (*Ashkii Hoyani*) grew up near Shiprock, New Mexico, and attended Bureau of Indian Affairs boarding schools. Due to the influence of a local Mormon trading post owner, he was among the first indigenous children to participate in the Church's "Indian Placement Program," founded by Elder Spencer W. Kimball. Kimball had fostered and championed a number of initiatives designed to serve indigenous Mormons on the principle that they were the direct descendants of the "Lamanite" peoples in the Book of Mormon, that the Book of Mormon was their heritage and legacy as a "lost tribe" of the "House of Israel," and that their latter-day "blossoming" had been prophesied. In addition to placement, these programs included congregations and conferences for so-called modern Lamanites, and numerous programs to recruit and support American Indian students at Brigham Young University. "In the 1970s," writes John-Charles Duffy, "BYU boasted that it spent more, per student, on American Indian education than on any other undergraduate program and spent more on Indian scholarships than all other colleges and universities in the United States combined; this commitment was explained as an expression of the Church's mission to the descendants of Book of Mormon peoples."[35] Lee participated in a number of these programs, served an LDS mission to indigenous communities in the Southwest, attended Brigham Young University, and married. After attaining a doctoral degree in education, he served as president of the Southwest Indian Mission, the first of several high-profile appointments in Church leadership. He also worked as a teacher, principal, and community college president in reservation schools. In October 1975, he became the first Native American called to serve in the First Quorum of the Seventy; Spencer W. Kimball, who had become the president of the LDS Church, appointed him. Kimball, in addition to sponsoring pro-grammatic supports for indigenous participation in the Church, had also directed that Book of Mormon passages connecting moral decline among the Lamanites with dark skin and redemption with whiteness be revised in 1981. His actions created a climate that fostered confidence in George P. Lee, who wrote and published his autobiography *Silent Courage* in 1987.

During his tenure, Lee developed a Book of Mormon–based theological view that so-called Lamanites and other peoples literally descended from the Biblical House of Israel were the true heirs of the Gospel and bore primary responsibility for the building of the Kingdom of God on earth. White Europeans and their descendants could be "adopted" into the "House of Israel's" "tribe of Ephraigm" through baptism but could never be "blood" lineage descendants. From his new position among the leadership, Lee also observed that attention and opportunities for leadership were directed primarily toward other elite white Mormons, not toward the poor or people of color. The death of President Kimball in 1985 and the subsequent institutional transition to the leadership of Ezra Taft Benson proved difficult for Lee. Under Benson's leadership, the Church scaled back its programming for and focus on so-called Lamanites, bringing Lee into conflict with leaders including Apostle Boyd K. Packer, who was notorious for his irascibility and intransigence. In fall 1987, Lee penned a long letter to Benson and other Church leaders expressing his frustration. The letter opened in the tone of humility and deference toward Church leaders expected of LDS people. "I speak unto you not just for myself but for all of my people the Lamanites as well as the Jews and the Lost Ten tribes," Lee began, before presenting a series of questions:

Who terminated the BYU Indian Education Department?

Who terminated BYU Indian Special Curriculum which helped Indian students succeed in college?

Who is phasing out BYU American Indian Services?

Who is phasing out the Church's Indian Student Placement program?

Who got rid of the church's "Indian Committee"?

Who fired the Indian Seminary teachers and send them out into the cold?

Who pulled the full-time missionaries off Navajo and other Indian reservations?

Who moved the mission headquarters from Holbrook to Phoenix?

Who caused missionary work on Indian reservations to falter and make it almost non-existent?

Who is causing a feeling of rejection among Lamanite members on reservations which resulted in great inactivity among them?

Who terminated Indian Seminary and all related curriculum materials?

In addition to the discontinuation of indigenous-focused programs, Lee interrogated what seemed to be an abandoning of Kimball's theological focus on "Lamanites" as the heritage peoples of the Book of Mormon and heirs to a special destiny as literal members of the House of Israel:

Who is teaching that the "Day of the Lamanites" is over and past?

Who is trying to do everything they can not to be known as a friend of the Indians like President Kimball was?

Who has assigned mentally unstable, physically handicapped and other mediocre or below average full-time missionaries to missions with large population of Indians?

Who is trying to discredit or downplay the role of Lamanites in these last days and downplay their role in the building of New Jerusalem?

Who is telling church members to teach from the Book of Mormon and at the same time downplay the role of Lamanites in the Book of Mormon?

Who has come very close to denying that the Book of Mormon is about Indians or Lamanites?

Who is loving the Lamanites at a distance and would rather not rub shoulders with them?

Who is trying to take the place of Lamanites in their divine sacred roles and priesthood assignments in the Millennium?

Who is turning their backs on the children of Lehi and would rather not be "nursing fathers and mothers"?

Who is telling George P. Lee not to pray or talk about Lamanites or the poor?

What about the thousands you might have injured as you cut off Lamanite programs and as you downplayed the role of the Lamanites?

He also called out the way he had been isolated, limited in his assignments, and shunned by other Church leaders as a form of "discipline" for his persistence in teaching Lamanite-related theology:

Do you think these outdated man-made disciplinary practices and traditions encourages priesthood abuse, induces fear, and produces forced obedience?

Do you think these outdated disciplinary traditions and rules creates a sense of worship for those in power?

Do you think these archaic disciplinary rules and practices creates an atmosphere whereby love of power, love of status and love of money flourishes?

Do you think it possible that these types of practices and traditions encourages one to exercise control and unrighteous dominion upon the souls of the children of God?

Lee demonstrated his awareness of the rules of the silent agreement between Church members and the Church, that the innocence of the Church should not be compromised by public criticism:

I have never in the past publicly criticize[d] or ridicule[d] any of you. If I have any complaint against any of you, I will come directly to you as I had tried to do with this letter which is directed to you as a group. No matter what you may think or what you might have been told or heard, the fact remains that I have always sustained you, defended you and stood up for you while out in the field on assignments. . . . I have always cherished and held in high esteem all of my assignments and responsibilities and will hope and pray that the probation will be lifted soon and that I shall receive all of my assignments back, this time with no strings attached. I want to be treated fairly and as an equal with full fellowship among the Brethren and as an equal with full trust, respect, confidence and unconditional love.

Still, Lee compared the "arrogance" and insensitivity of white Church leaders to that of the Nephites, the protagonist civilization of the Book of Mormon, whose "pride" led to their destruction, and he connected the Church's hierarchical leadership style to white supremacy, writing, "We do not have the priesthood for self-aggrandizement or to be used to oppress anyone. There is no priesthood of God that authorizes any one man to oppress another or to intrude upon his rights in any way."

Conflict between Lee and other high-ranking leaders escalated, and the situation deteriorated to the point where Benson called an excommunication court for September 1, 1989. At his hearing, Lee stood before Benson members of the Church's First Presidency and the Quorum of the Twelve Apostles. He read a long, handwritten letter (subsequently released to the press) reiterating his objections to the white supremacy of the LDS hierarchy and the Church's abandonment of its focus on indigenous peoples. Lee advanced these from within the Book of Mormon theological framework he had developed in which Jews and "Lamanites" were true members of the "House of Israel" and others (including Europeans and European Americans, or whites) were "Gentiles," or "Foreigners" to the "House of Israel." According to his scriptural worldview, authority for preaching and administering the Gospel came to whites only for a specific historic season and purpose and only on the condition of their "righteousness." In diminishing the fact that indigenous peoples of the Americas were true members of the House of Israel and so destined leaders of God's work on earth and incorrectly claimed that role for themselves and others adopted into the tribe of "Ephraigm," white LDS Church leaders had demonstrated "pride" and "arrogance" that harmed people of color and "displaced" or "shoved" "true Israel out of his own home or house." Wrote Lee:

> It is getting to the point where every Gentile that is baptized is told and taught that he is literal seed of Ephraim unless he is a Jew, Indian or Black. This type of teaching encourages an attitude of superior race, white supremacy, racist attitude, pride, arrogance, love of power, and no sense of obligation to the poor, needy and afflicted. . . . You have come very close to denying that the Book of Mormon is about Lamanites.

> You have cut out Indian or Lamanite programs and are attempting to cut them out of the Book of Mormon. You are trying to discredit or downplay the role of Lamanites in these last days and downplay their role and importance in the building of the New Jerusalem. . . . You are Loving the Indians and other Lamanites at a distance and have no sense of responsibility to them because you displaced them and set yourself up as Ephrai[g]m more superior to the Lamanites and thus you are telling the Lamanites that you are No. 1 and they are second class. You are trying to take their place in their divine roles and assignments.

Lee uncompromisingly compared the Church's theological and programmatic displacement of indigenous peoples to colonization and genocide:

> You are slowly causing a silent subtle scriptural and spiritual slaughter of the Indians and other Lamanites. While physical extermination may have been one of Federal government's policies long ago but your current scriptural and spiritual extermination of Indians and other Lamanites is the greater sin and great shall be your condemnation for this. . . . In short, you are betraying and turning your backs on the very people on whom your own salvation hangs.

He concluded the letter by calling out the "pride, arrogance and un-righteous dominion and control which encourages priesthood abuse, induces fear and produces forced obedience"; the "love of power, status, position which creates a sense of worship for those in control and power"; and the "love of money" that means that "the well-to do . . . get all the important assignments and callings" while "neglecting the poor who need our help the most." The court ended with Lee's excommunication for "apostasy and other conduct un-becoming a member of the Church."[36] According to press reports, Lee was "astounded at the speed with which he was ousted. Within minutes, two officials came to his office and told him to turn over all church property, including a credit card and a signed pass with which faithful Mormons gain entry to their temples. 'I was stripped of every-thing,' said Lee. . . . 'It was just absolutely cold.' "[37]

News of Lee's excommunication hit hard on the Navajo reservation, and Salt Lake City dispatched top-ranking leaders to meet with local congregations. Just a few months after his excommunication, Lee ran a write-in campaign during the 1990 Navajo Nation presidential elec-tion, garnering 23% of the vote.[38] A few years later, Lee was charged with attempted molestation of an underage girl, to which he confessed in court. He died in 2010. Critics were quick to seize upon the mo-lestation as the "real" reason for his excommunication, but given the ubiquity of physical and sexual abuse of indigenous peoples in reserva-tion schools, boarding schools, churches, and foster programs and the LDS Church's institutional shortcomings in addressing sexual abuse in its own predominantly white ranks, it seems right to hold a space to honor both the experience of Lee's victim and Lee's own tragic living out of the multiple traumas he himself endured. Had he not broken the silent agreement to protect the LDS Church's racial innocence in matters of white supremacy, would his attempted molestation have been discovered, reported, prosecuted, and acted upon? If racial and class status (as we have shown) intersect to provide a degree of im-munity against excommunication, certainly they can provide a degree of immunity against criminal prosecution as well. George P. Lee ex-perienced none of that immunity. Despite his dedication and service, to white LDS Church leaders who could not brook his unapologetic criticism of white supremacy, he was readily expendable.

* * *

In looking more closely at the ways George Romney, Lowry Nelson, Stewart Udall, Byron Marchant, and George P. Lee voiced their objections to white supremacy in the LDS Church, it is possible to see the specific contours of the silent agreement between LDS Church leaders and members to maintain racial innocence. Members were entitled to maintain privately their own perspectives and opinions. Church members who were well placed or influential enough— typically white, elite males with multigenerational relationships to members of the Church hierarchy—could leverage their privilege to express their criticisms out loud, almost as a vestigial or residual right to participate in an older mode of being Mormon, a nineteenth- and early-twentieth century Mormonism more isolated from the outside world, with familial and social networks that made identity feel irrevocable (if not inescapable) and intertribal conflict feel more natural. But as the Church expanded and the familiarity of these ties was strained, as isolation ended and more members out-migrated into wider circles of influence, as more people of color and other bearers of "difference" joined the ranks, the silent agreement constricted around an "ideology of faithfulness." According to this ideology, as Hokulani Aikau explains, members were not to openly criticize LDS Church policies, practices, or operations. They were not, especially, to levy criticisms directly of or at high-ranking LDS Church leaders, especially in a venue or manner that demanded a direct and immediate response. To do so was to disrupt, perhaps fatally, the immunity of the hierarchy to debate and deliberation and its claim to stand outside history as purveyors and administrators of the original plan of God. By virtue of his elite status and secure footing outside the Church, supported by the privileges of his whiteness, and because he chose to play within these rules—even their loosest construction—Stewart Udall was able to voice a powerful critique of the costs of white supremacy to the LDS Church and its people. His words gave voice and hope to many others who were not in a similar position of privilege. But they did not constitute the kind of direct action that civil rights leaders had demonstrated was necessary to fully disrupt the institutional workings of white supremacy. Those who attempted direct action in words and deeds like Byron Marchant found themselves put outside of the Church and all the affordances of belonging. People of color who attempted direct action in the 1970s and 1980s found themselves most vulnerable of all. If the maintenance of racial innocence demanded a human scapegoat, that role would be assigned to George P. Lee and other people of color who could not silently abide white supremacy in their places of worship and thus lost access to the opportunities, experiences, and sense of safety and community that Mormonism promised. But the greatest costs of maintaining white supremacy, as Stewart Udall rightly observed, were to faith itself: "We are wrong and it is past the time when we should have seen the right. A failure to act here is sure to demean our faith, damage the minds and morals of our youth, and undermine the integrity of our Christian ethic."

NOTES

1. "George Romney and the Delbert Stapley Letter," *Thoughts on Things and Stuff,* June 14, 2015, http://thoughtsonthingsandstuff. com/george-romney-and-the-delbert-stapley-letter/, last accessed February 12, 2018.
2. "Romney Assails Racial Injustice," *New York Times,* February 20, 1967, 30, https://timesmachine.nytimes.com/timesmachine/1967/ 02/20/82593994.html?pageNumber=30, last accessed February 12, 2018.
3. Roger D. Launius and Linda Thatcher, *Differing Visions: Dissenters in Mormon History* (Urbana: University of Illinois Press, 1998), 12–14. See also Roger D. Launius, "'Many Mansions': The Dynamics of Dissent in the Nineteenth-Century Reorganized Church," *Journal of Mormon History* 17 (1991): 145–168; Maciej Potz, "The Politics of Schism: The Origins of Dissent in Mormonism," *Studia Religiologica* 3 (2016): 203–218; Danny L. Jorgenson, "Dissent and Schism in the Early Church: Explaining Mormon Fissiparousness," *Dialogue: A Journal of Mormon Thought* 28.3 (1995): 15–39; Marvin Hill, *Quest for Refuge: The Mormon Flight Grom American Pluralism* (Salt Lake City: Signature Books, 1989).
4. Gina Colvin and Joanna Brooks, "Introduction," in *Decolonizing Mormonism: Towards a Postcolonial Zion* (Salt Lake City: University of Utah Press, 2018), 1–23.
5. Aikau, 87. .
6. Special Collections & Archives, Merrill-Cazier Library, Utah State University.

7. Edward Geary, "Mormondom's Lost Generation: The Novelists of the 1940s," *BYU Studies* 18.1 (1978), https://scholarsarchive.byu.edu/byusq/vol18/iss1/7/, last accessed February 12, 2018.

8. Levi Peterson, "Juanita Brooks as a Mormon Dissenter," *John Whitmer Historical Association* 8 (1998): 29, https://www.jstor.org/stable/43200808?seq=1#page_scan_tab_contents, last accessed February 12, 2018.

9. Special Collections & Archives, Merrill-Cazier Library, Utah State University.

10. Edward Kimball, "The History of LDS Temple Admission Standards," *Journal of Mormon History* 24.1 (1998): 147, https://digitalcommons.usu.edu/cgi/viewcontent.cgi?referer=https://www.google.com/&httpsredir=1&article=1030&context=mormonhistory, last accessed February 12, 2018.

11. Juanita Brooks, correspondence to Lowry Nelson, January 25, 1949, Lowry Nelson Papers, Box 20, Folder 4, University of Utah Marriott Special Collections Library.

12. William Carr, correspondence to Lowry Nelson, March 26, 1948, Lowry Nelson Papers, Box 20, Folder 4, University of Utah Marriott Special Collections Library; Lowry Nelson to Lester Bush, October 13, 1972, Lowry Nelson Papers, Box 20, Folder 7, University of Utah Marriott Special Collections Library; Leonard Arrington correspondence to Lowry Nelson, July 28, 1952, Lowry Nelson Papers, Box 20, Folder 11, University of Utah Marriott Special Collections Library.

13. Lowry Nelson, "Letter to the Editor," *Dialogue: A Journal of Mormon Thought* 2.3 (Fall 1967): 7, https://www.dialoguejournal.com/wp-content/uploads/sbi/articles/Dialogue_Vo2No3_7.pdf, last accessed February 12, 2018.

14. Lowry Nelson to David O. McKay, March 20, 1952, Box 20, Folder 5, Lowry Nelson Papers, University of Utah Marriot Library Special Collections.

15. Var. correspondence, Lowry Nelson Papers, Box 20, Folders 2–15, Marriott Library Special Collections, University of Utah.

16. Lowry Nelson Papers, Box 20, Folder 3, University of Utah Marriott Library Special Collections, University of Utah.

17. Lowry Nelson, "Mormons and Blacks," *Christian Century,* October 16, 1974, 949–950. See also Samuel Taylor, "The Ordeal of Lowry Nelson," *Dialogue* 26.3 (Fall 1993): 97.

18. Peterson, 273.

19. Stewart Udall, "Letter to the Editors," *Dialogue: A Journal of Mormon Thought* 2.2 (Summer 1967): 5–7, https://www.dialoguejournal.com/wp-content/uploads/sbi/issues/V02N02.pdf, last accessed January 30, 2018.

20. F. Ross Peterson, "'Do Not Lecture the Brethren': Stewart L. Udall's Pro-Civil Rights Stance, 1967," *Journal of Mormon History* 25.1 (1999): 283.

21. Claude Eggertsen to Lowry Nelson, March 8, 1960, Lowry Nelson Papers, Box 20, Folder 6.

22. "Stewart Udall: Conscience of a Jack Mormon" archive, https://archive.org/stream/StewartUdallConscienceOfAJackMormon/StuartUdall-OpenLetterOnRaceAndConsequencesOfConscience#page/n52/mode/1up.

23. See Wallace Turner, "Udall Entreats Mormons on Race," *New York Times,* May 19, 1967, 1; the same article ran via the Associated Press in the following places: "Udall Asks LDS Review Doctrine on Negroes," *Salt Lake Tribune,* May 20, 1967, 1; "Udall Urges Mormons to End Negro Bias," *Los Angeles Times,* May 20, 1967; "Romney v. Udall on Negro Bias," *San Francisco Chronicle,* May 20, 1967; "A Demand That His Church Resolve Its Negro Issue Has Been Made by Stewart L. Udall, Secretary of the Interior, a Lifelong Mormon," *Southern Illinoisan,* May 23, 1967, 4; "Interior Secretary Stewart L. Udall, a Member of the Mormon Church, Has Urged His Faith to Renounce Its Discrimination Against Negroes 'Because We Are Wrong,'" *Nevada State Journal,* May 20, 1967, 1; "Stewart Udall, a Mormon, Demands That Church Clear Up Negro Issue," *San Bernardino County Sun,* May 25, 1967, 26; "Stewart Udall and the Mormon Church," *Arizona Daily Star,* May 20, 1967.

24. Daniel Herman, "Arizona's Secret History: When Powerful Mormons Went Separate Ways," http://www.common-place-archives.org/vol-12/no-03/herman/, last accessed February 12, 2018.

25. See Gary James Bergera and Ronald Priddis, *Brigham Young University: A House of Faith* (Salt Lake City: Signature Books, 1985), 299–301; Bringhurst, *Saints, Slaves, and Blacks,* 181–182. Jeffery O. Johnson, "Change and Growth: The Mormon Church and the 1960s," *Sunstone* 17 (June 1994): 28; Brian Walton, "A University's Dilemma: B.Y.U. and Blacks," *Dialogue* 6 (Spring 1971): 35.

26. Robert Baum, "Ordainer of Black Into Priesthood Excommunicated by LDS Church," *Salt Lake Tribune,* April 13, 1976, in Lowry Nelson Papers, Box 20, Folder 9.

27. "Obituary: Beatrice Peterson Marchant (1903–1996)," *Deseret News,* https://www.deseretnews.com/article/498229/DEATH--BEATRICE-PETERSON-MARCHANT-1903-TO-1996.html, last accessed February 12, 2008.

28. Michelle Marchant, "My Life Is a Gift, My Life Has a Plan," BYU Devotional Address, April 2, 2013, https://speeches.byu.edu/talks/michelle-marchant_my-life-is-a-gift-my-life-has-a-plan/, last accessed February 12, 2008.

29. Mark Barnes, "Byron's Song," *Ordain Women blog,* February 6, 2015, http://ordainwomen.org/byrons-song/, last accessed February 12, 2018.

30. Personal correspondence with author, April 3, 2018.

31. Mark Barnes, "Raised a Mormon Feminist," *Ordain Women blog,* October 13, 2013, http://ordainwomen.org/raised-a-mormon-feminist/, last accessed February 12, 2018.

32. Personal correspondence, April 3, 2018; see also Newell Bringhurst, *Saints, Slaves, and Blacks,* 188.

33. Bringhurst and Harris, 85.

34. Kimball, 40–41.

35. John-Charles Duffy, "The Use of 'Lamanite' in Official LDS Discourse," *Journal of Mormon History* 34.1 (2008): 139.

36. Associated Press, "Church Explains Excommunication to Navajos as Lee Seeks a Rebirth," September 10, 1989, https://www.deseretnews.com/article/62992/CHURCH-EXPLAINS-EXCOMMUNICATION-TO-NAVAJOS-AS-LEE-SEEKS-A-REBIRTH.html, last accessed February 12, 2018. See also coverage in the *Salt Lake Tribune,* September 10, 1989, 14B.

37. Complete text of Lee's letters and additional biographical information are available at Harrison Lapahie, "George P. Lee Archive, Including Transcriptions and Speeches," http://www.lapahie.com/George_Patrick_Lee.cfm. See also "The Lee Letters," *Sunstone Magazine* 72 (November 1989), https://www.sunstonemagazine.com/wp-content/uploads/sbi/issues/072.pdf, last accessed February 12, 2018.

38. Steve Pavlik, "Of Saints and Lamanites: An Analysis of Navajo Mormonism," *Wicazo Sa Review* 8.1 (1992): 28.

CHAPTER 6

THE PERSISTENCE
OF WHITE SUPREMACY
BEYOND DESEGREGATION

Systematic anti-Black racism did not end with the legal abolition of
chattel slavery in the United States. It simply changed shape: into
debt peonage, criminalization, mass incarceration, housing segregation, sexual predation, voter suppression, and discrimination of all
kinds. The same holds true for systematic anti-Black racism in white
American Christianity. Every denomination will have its own story
in this regard, whether its congregations have been segregated by theology, by church policy, or as an uncontested correlate of segregation
in everyday American life. I will focus on the Mormon story to analyze in detail how white supremacy persists in and through attempts
to reform it.

The best account we have of how the LDS Church's priesthood ban
came to an end on June 8, 1978, comes from Edward Kimball, son
of LDS Church President Spencer W. Kimball, the prophet to whom
the change was revealed. Writing in *BYU Studies* in 2008, Kimball
provides an intimate account of his father's decade-long struggle with
the issue, including fascinating details like the fact that his father
compiled a binder of clippings and independent scholarly writings
on the subject—details that give those of us in Mormon studies and
Mormonism's independent sector reason for hope. Among the other
factors that led President Kimball to earnestly pursue the question of
change, according to his son, were shifting views in favor of racial
equality in American society, growing interest in the Church in Africa,
the enormous challenge of applying a strict anti-Black priesthood ban

Mormonism and white supremacy. Joanna brooks, Oxford University Press (2020). © Oxford University Press.
DOI: 10.1093/oso/9780190081768.001.0001

in places like Brazil, and President Kimball's own humble tempera-ment.[1] His son writes:

> President Kimball felt that his predecessors had sought the Lord's will concerning the priesthood policy, and for whatever reason "the time had not come." But Spencer had to ask anew. He wanted urgently "to find out firsthand what the Lord thought about it." It was not enough just to wait until the Lord saw fit to take the initiative: the scripture admonished him to ask and to knock if he wanted to know for himself. He prayed, trying not to prejudge the answer: Should we maintain the long-standing policy, or has the time come for the change?[2]

The answer came on June 1, 1978, and was announced on June 8 in a letter from President Kimball and his two first counselors in the Church Presidency to Church leaders worldwide:

> Aware of the promises made by the prophets and presidents of the Church who have preceded us that at some time, in God's eternal plan, all of our brethren who are worthy may receive the priesthood, and witnessing the faithfulness of those from whom the priesthood has been withheld, we have pleaded long and earnestly in behalf of these, our faithful brethren, spending many hours in the Upper Room of the Temple supplicating the Lord for divine guidance.
>
> He has heard our prayers, and by revelation has confirmed that the long-promised day has come when every faithful, worthy man in the Church may receive the holy priesthood, with power to exercise its divine authority, and enjoy with his loved ones every blessing that flows therefrom, including the blessings of the temple. Accordingly, all worthy male members of the Church may be ordained to the priesthood without regard for race or color. Priesthood leaders are instructed to follow the policy of carefully interviewing all candidates for ordination to either the Aaronic or the Melchizedek Priesthood to ensure that they meet the established standards for worthiness.
>
> We declare with soberness that the Lord has now made known his will for the blessing of all his children throughout the earth who will

hearken to the voice of his authorized servants, and prepare themselves
to receive every blessing of the gospel.[3]

The announcement made newspaper headlines across the United
States. Many LDS Church members recall weeping when they heard
about the end of the ban on the radio. I was six years old in June 1978
and have no such recollection, but the impression I have cultivated over
forty years of hearing LDS people talk about the end of the ban was
that just about everyone felt it had become a burden and an embarrassment, and to have it lifted was a relief.

Kimball's announcement did not renounce or apologize for past
practice or call for collective repentance. It declared, simply, that
"the long-promised day" of equal access to priesthood and temple
ordinances had finally come. Systems of ideas, beliefs, and practices
privileging white over black that had sustained the ban for more
than a hundred years were not eradicated by President Kimball's
announcement. From the 1830s onward systematic racism had become deeply embedded in a host of legal, economic, social, political, and religious practices among the Mormon people and in LDS
institutions like Brigham Young University and Deseret Book. An
entire genre of doctrinal speculation justifying the ban as the consequence of spiritual deficiencies in the premortal souls of Black
folks manifest through their mortal incarnation as dark-skinned
descendants of Cain and Ham had not only been spread by word
of mouth among LDS people but also effectively canonized in
works of systematic theology like Bruce R. McConkie's *Mormon
Doctrine* (1958), a book that remained in print until 2010. When the
ban ended, these rationalizations remained in circulation and new
rationalizations emerged to preserve white innocence and defer the
work of repair and change.

Sociologist Armand Mauss writes about the Church's limited progress on racial reconciliation since 1978. He characterizes institutional
Mormonism's postban approach to anti-Black racism as "an organizational posture of benign and selective forgetfulness," so theorized by
its adherents:

If the church progresses in a continuous, linear path by divine guid-
ance, then contemporary realities and understandings replace those
from the past, which will eventually be forgotten. Obsolete ideas
and practices simply don't count any more, even if they originated as
divine revelations. Where discrepancies appear between the present
and the past, there is no point in reminding ourselves about the past.
Especially if an event in the past is embarrassing, then recalling it
and dwelling on it, even if only to repudiate it, merely confuses the
matter. Such negative thinking has no place in the Lord's kingdom.
If harm has resulted from earlier ways of thinking, then everyone involved should forgive everyone else and get on with constructing a
better future. Apologies or ringing declarations of disavowal should
not be necessary, since few peoples or individuals have histories free
of offense against others, and thus few are in a position to demand
apologies. With time, memories of these offenses will fade automatically, and we will all be better for it. Meanwhile, if we have not made
the requisite changes, let's not stir up useless and uncomfortable old
memories.[4]

Mauss is of course critical of this ideology especially as it isolates Black
Mormons and leaves them vulnerable to continuing racist treatment
and racist remarks in LDS settings and fails to address the concerns
of all Church members "disillusioned" by racism past and present. But
I would present two additional problems in this approach beyond its
pastoral failures. First, this approach is not simply passive "forgetfulness"; it constitutes an active erasure and rewriting of uncomfortable
aspects of Mormon history and endangers historical memory. Because
this erasure is "selective" and pertains only to matters that might
"embarrass" the Church, it cannot be considered benign. It continues
key practices of white supremacy in Mormonism by excluding Black
testimony, insisting on prophetic infallibility, repressing dissent, and
fostering silent agreements among Mormons and between Mormons
and the public to co-construct and preserve white innocence. Second,
by modeling this approach to complex moral problems, the Church
signals to members that "selective" "forgetting" of past wrongs is

enough to resolve them; that repentance need not involve the assumption of responsibility and reconciliation, let alone restitution or reparation; and that the discomfort that comes with individual and collective soul searching is "useless" and potentially harmful. It fosters a limited morality that prioritizes the comfort of the majority and institutional gains over truthfulness and humility.

While this approach is certainly not unique to Mormonism, within the LDS context, it does have deep historical footings. It represents the continuation of a historic Mormon rhetorical pattern used to protect unpopular LDS beliefs against outsiders that originated during the national controversy over polygamy, a practice I call "undergrounding." The nineteenth-century Mormon "underground" was a system of social networks that harbored LDS men and women evading prosecution or persecution for polygamy or unlawful cohabitation. It developed as a result of open political conflict between Mormons and host American society over family definition. On one side of this conflict, dominant American society criminalized polygamy to mark Mormons as aliens and deprive them of the rights of citizens; in defense of polygamy, Mormon communities constructed and maintained themselves as theocracies against US rule.[5] This nineteenth-century open conflict has exerted profound and lasting consequences on the way Mormons have participated in American public life. One of them has been the development of discursive strategies used by Mormons to maintain theocratic sovereignty in the face of outside pressure even after the abandonment of open polygamy. These strategies include nontransparency in public relations, cultivation of distinct "insider" and "outsider" narratives of belief and practice, and careful public speech to protect private knowledge. An ethos privileging opacity, institutional loyalty, hierarchy, and guardedness developed in LDS Church institutions (including Deseret Book and Brigham Young University) as Mormons attempted to preserve a residue of theocracy and difference even as they were assimilated into broader US society.[6] The private-public split resulted in a form of self-consciousness described by one Mormon studies scholar as a "divided sense of self" and related habits of double-coding in public speech, especially in situations where LDS people perceive a threat to their way of being.[7] Mormons sometimes joke about this practice as "lying for the Lord," but the fact that it has been used in campaigns to oppose women's rights and LGBTQ+ civil rights and that it is useful as well to the perpetuation of white supremacy makes it important to think critically about "undergrounding." In this chapter, I will show through rhetorical analysis how LDS Church institutions have wrestled with these communicative patterns—defensive postures of nontransparency in regard to the history of Mormon racism, cultivated "insider" and "outsider" narratives, and carefully managed speech to deflect public interest and defer substantial change—and how these patterns have contributed to the continuation of white supremacy in Mormonism.

* * *

Despite his hardline stances against the Equal Rights Amendment and harsh condemnations of homosexuality, Spencer W. Kimball's leadership in ending the temple and priesthood ban made this diminutive, warm, gravelly voiced (he was a throat cancer survivor) man beloved among the Mormon people. After his death in 1985, Kimball was succeeded by Ezra Taft Benson, an arch-conservative, staunch anti-Communist, and former secretary of agriculture under US President Dwight D. Eisenhower, whose major prophetic initiatives included renewing the Church's focus on the Book of Mormon and recalling Mormon women to forgo career development and pursue their role as "Mothers in Zion." His leadership also coincided with increased repression of Mormon feminists and intellectuals, culminating in six high-profile excommunication courts in September 1993.

Benson had a long history of extreme social conservatism—both religious and secular. In 1967, he had contributed a foreword (previously published by the segregationist Billy James Hargis in his *Christian Crusade* magazine) to the white supremacist tract *The Black Hammer: A Study of Black Power, Red Influence, and White Alternatives*,[8] a work that continues to be used by adherents of the

Christian identity movement today. (Its cover featured a violently racist cartooning of a Black man's head, inset within a sickle and hammer, decapitated and dripping blood into a puddle. Additional illustrations within the book include anti-Black racist cartoons drawn in the tradition of nineteenth-century minstrel show imagery.) That September, Benson delivered an address at a meeting at the Mormon Tabernacle lambasting the civil rights movement as a tool of "Communist deception," and repeated this assertion again over the pulpit at the October 1967 General Conference. LDS Church–owned Deseret Book published the talk in its entirety in booklet form in 1968. Benson had also seriously entertained the prospect of becoming George Wallace's presidential running mate in 1968. For his administration, addressing the lasting legacies of the priesthood and temple ban was not an administrative priority.

The tone at LDS Church headquarters changed when Gordon B. Hinckley became LDS Church president in 1995. Hinckley, who had spent many decades in Church public relations, sought to improve the public image of the Church, in part by making himself available to the media in a way prior LDS Church presidents had not. The eighty-five-year old Hinckley presented himself with energy, optimism, and confidence. From the moment he stepped to the podium at the March 1995 press conference where his presidency was announced and opened himself to questions from journalists—something no other twentieth-century Church president had done—he appeared to invite and embrace a new kind of openness, an image he carefully pursued by retaining a New York–based public relations firm to guide LDS Church messaging from the mid-1990s onward. Hinckley did not, however, fundamentally change the patterns of nontransparency, deflection, and guardedness that had for more than a century characterized Mormonism's management of its most sensitive issues.[9]

In April 1996, Hinckley agreed to a solo interview with Mike Wallace on CBS's 60 Minutes. No other LDS Church president had ever accepted such an invitation. As did Barbara Walters in 1978, Wallace asked about the Church's anti-Black racism. Hinckley leaned forward, smiled, and maintained steady eye contact and an apparently untroubled disposition:

MW: From 1830 to 1978 . . .

GH: Mmm hmm.

MW: Blacks could not become priests in the Mormon Church, right?

GH: That's correct.

MW: Why?

GH: Because . . . the leaders of the church at that time . . . interpreted that doctrine that way.

MW: Church policy had it that blacks had the mark of Cain. Brigham Young said, "Cain slew his brother and the Lord put a mark upon him, which is the flat nose and black skin."

GH: It's behind us. . . . Look, that's behind us. Don't worry about those little flicks of history.

MW: Skeptics will suggest, "Well, look, if we're going to expand, we can't keep the blacks out."

GH: Pure speculation.[10]

Hinckley did not present LDS Church history accurately: Black men were, in fact, ordained to the priesthood through the 1840s and held priesthood authority through the end of the nineteenth century. But Hinckley's strategic public relations approach prioritized ease and confidence over accuracy. It is not easy to address a complicated historical issue effectively in soundbites; Hinckley opted to contain and manage it. "It's behind us," he said, then took a breath, leaned in, and reasserted himself. "Look, that's behind us." A different approach might have acknowledged the shortcomings of prior Mormon leaders, the imprint of racism on American history in general and Mormon history in particular, its lasting impacts on institutions and individuals, and the moral importance of working now and in the present to do better. But for President Hinckley the focus was on establishing a new tone, a new public presence for the LDS Church. His priorities were institutional preservation and growth.

Where he did apply gentle pressure was in addressing to Wallace (and by inference the broader Mormon and non-Mormon audience) an instruction that sounded like encouragement: "Don't worry about those little flicks of history," Hinckley said, smiling. In so doing, he made small ("little") and insignificant ("flicks") the problem of anti-Black racism, minimizing as a past "worry" the impact of racism on Black lives in Mormonism and beyond and indicating no responsibility on the part of white Mormons (or others with similar histories of discrimination) for their past practices or of the impact those practices had on the Mormon faith and the spiritual lives of its members. The public relations priorities of the institution took precedent over pastoral concerns for the experience of Black Mormons and the moral responsibility of white Mormons. Significantly, in his conversation with Wallace, Hinckley did not endorse any of the various rationales past LDS Church leaders had put forward as doctrine. "The leaders of the Church at that time interpreted the doctrine in that way," he stated, again seeking to contain racism in a past historical moment. But this means that Hinckley opted not to openly reject past rationales or past interpretations as flawed, incorrect, or harmful. This is especially significant given that these rationales remained in print in books like *Mormon Doctrine* and on the shelves of Church-owned bookstores like Deseret Book for sale to the faithful.

He did not say "we were wrong." In fact, his entire mode of presentation—tone, facial expressions, tempo—telegraphed an undisturbed sense of "rightness." Nothing in his remarks unsettled the possessive investment in rightness that institutionalized Mormonism's possessive investment in whiteness. It left the entire infrastructure of anti-Black Mormon racism intact, maintaining rhetorical strategies of containment and deflection that had been used continuously by LDS Church leaders to maintain resistance to outside pressure for change. While his style of presentation may have differed from his predecessors', in his strategic deflection and evasion Hinckley worked deep in the tradition of LDS Church institutional rhetoric and thus communicated a sense of continuity and conservatism to LDS Church members.

As the twentieth anniversary of the 1978 revelation approached, grassroots efforts to address the persistence of anti-Black folklore met with some interest from general authorities like Marlin Jensen, one of the few liberal-leaning members of the LDS Church hierarchy, a member of its Public Affairs committee, and executive director of the Church History Library. David Jackson, an African American convert, together with a white fellow congregant named Dennis Gladwell and LDS sociologist Armand Mauss prepared briefs for Jensen outlining the problem and proposing pathways forward, including withdrawing controversial texts like *Mormon Doctrine* by Bruce R. McConkie and issuing public statements by the First Presidency specifically repudiating past racist teachings. Someone close to the discussion leaked it to the *Los Angeles Times*, which in May 1998 ran a story reporting that "key leaders" were "debating a proposal to repudiate historic church doctrines that were used to bolster claims of black inferiority." Within days of the *Los Angeles Times* story, the LDS Public Affairs department on behalf of President Hinckley and his counselors issued a categorical denial with the comment that "the 1978 official declaration continues to speak for itself." Once again, Hinckley resorted to the time-tested LDS institutional rhetorical strategy of nontransparency: circling the wagons and defensively shutting down communications in response to perceived pressure from the outside.[11]

This is not to say that Hinckley made no efforts to improve Mormon-Black relations. In 1998, he spoke by invitation at the national convention of the NAACP in Salt Lake City. Under his leadership, the Church launched an ambitious project to put its volunteers and its expertise in genealogy to work digitizing the records of the Freedman's Bank so that African American genealogists could have ready access to information about its almost five hundred thousand depositors, a task completed by 2001. Hinckley himself also sought to build a personal relationship with Pastor Cecil Murray of the Los Angeles African Methodist Episcopal (LA AME) Church and apologized personally to Murray for the Church's role in slavery—an LA AME Church founding member named Biddy Mason had made her way to California after being enslaved in Utah by a Mormon pioneer family. His discussions with Murray culminated in a statement Hinckley made over the pulpit at the Church's semiannual General Conference in April 2006:

> I have wondered why there is so much hatred in the world. . . . Racial strife still lifts its ugly head. I am advised that even right here among us there is some of this. I cannot understand how it can be. It seemed to me that we all rejoiced in the 1978 revelation given President Kimball. I was there in the temple at the time that that happened. There was no doubt in my mind or in the minds of my associates that what was revealed was the mind and the will of the Lord. . . . Now I am told that racial slurs and denigrating remarks are sometimes heard among us. I remind you that no man who makes disparaging remarks concerning those of another race can consider himself a true disciple of Christ.[12]

Black Mormon leaders received the statement with rejoicing. Because it was given during a sacred occasion, over the pulpit, by the "prophet, seer, and revelator" of the Church, it carried inarguable authority. It would encourage and support rank-and-file Church members seeking to uproot racism in their midst. But it framed racism as an individual moral problem. It did nothing to repudiate the Church's own collective historical practice of anti-Black discrimination, nor the system of ideas, beliefs, and practices that had sustained it for so long.

* * *

Observant LDS people take in messages from their leadership in a culturally specific way shaped by almost two centuries of intense differentiation from the mainstream and resistance to anti-Mormonism, the high demands of belonging to a religion headed by a living prophet, the LDS use of secrecy as an element of the sacred, and a cultivated tolerance for holding to beliefs radically at odds with mainstream norms. Church members know how to rank the value and reliability of the venues through which information comes. Church members are officially discouraged from using sources not published by the LDS Church as members develop Sunday school lessons and lay sermons ("talks") to give in Church meetings and pursue personal study.

Books, scholarly journals, magazines, and web resources not produced by the Church, even those produced by LDS Church members, can be stigmatized unless they are seamlessly orthodox in their presentation. Conferences and public events not hosted by the Church were strongly criticized in a 1991 statement by the Church's First Presidency directed specifically at "symposia," which concluded, "There are times when public discussion of sacred or personal matters is inappropriate." The "personal" matters, according to the statement, included Church problems and controversies. This stigma has eased considerably in some quarters with the rise of Mormon studies programs in non-LDS universities. But it is still popular belief that faculty at Church-owned Brigham Young University are not to publish in independent Mormon scholarly journals like *Dialogue* or appear on the program at conferences like the independent Sunstone Symposium, and scholars like myself and others who have published dissenting views on LGBTQ+ issues are not invited to speak at Brigham Young University campuses.[13] The LDS Church History Library even declined permission for me to publish something so benign as archival photographs of the Mormon Tabernacle Choir at Mount Rushmore in this book, having required as a condition of permissions a copy of the text in which the photographs would appear.

Church members also know how to rank the value and reliability of the individual who provides the information. What is said by the prophet, especially during the sessions of General Conference, is considered of the highest truth value. The prophet is understood by observant Mormons to speak for God to the Church. Lower-ranking general authorities—especially in the Quorum of the Seventy or regional representatives—can also speak truth, but it may be inflected with personal elements that make it less defining and reliable. What is spoken by general authorities in non-LDS settings also tends to rank lower in terms of value and reliability, especially if the content diverges a bit from orthodoxy.

The exception to this ranking schema is any information that comes from high-ranking Church authorities by insider connection or word of mouth. Early experiences of violent anti-Mormonism (including mob attacks on Mormon homes, assaults, sexual assaults, and murders of Mormon leaders and missionaries) and decades of hiding out from opponents of polygamy and the federal officers and armies who did their work instilled especially in multigenerational, highly observant Mormons a strong sense of the necessity of "undergrounding." This sense is reinforced to this day as polygamy is maintained in doctrine and polygamous sealings (marriages) effectual not during mortality but in the eternities are permitted in LDS temples despite the Church's formal abolition of public polygamy in 1890 and the repeated disavowal of polygamy in statements by Church leaders for the 130 years since. These factors have given "insider" knowledge high status both in terms of truth and in terms of perceived significance to the survival and success of the faith. Adept Mormons come to understand that there are some beliefs others might not accept or understand, and that it is believers' duty to quietly preserve them. This is bolstered by the value placed on secrecy in LDS temple worship, wherein the most observant members of the faith undertake rituals of personal devotion within LDS temples that they promise not to share with the uninitiated. What is said in public on many issues can be understood as a tactical concession to preserve the Church's theocratic sovereignty. These deeply embedded schemas of information set up a strong and self-perpetuating "insider/outsider" dynamic in Mormon communication. The internet has complicated this dynamic, especially as it has created new venues for the presentation of LDS Church content that do not bear the immediate impact and revelatory status of a live prophetic statement over the pulpit at General Conference. Increased activity by the LDS Church's Public Affairs division and seasonal discoordination between the LDS Church hierarchy and Public Affairs have also fueled speculation on which communications are tactical rather than revelatory. Progressive members hungry for change will scour press releases and internet content for any indication that feeds their hopes, while orthodox members will refuse any information that does not confirm an orthodox worldview unless it is delivered as revelation from the prophet himself.

This is the context in which some LDS Church authorities started to respond after 2000 to the problem of perpetuated anti-Black doctrinal folklore. White supremacist views of Blackness as a "curse" and the souls of Black folks as spiritually inferior had found their way into lesson manuals and ostensibly comprehensive accounts of systematic theology (like *Mormon Doctrine*) since the 1880s. High-ranking Church leaders had openly opposed the civil rights movement over the pulpit at General Conference. Cautions against interracial marriage had found their way into administrative handbooks and Church curricula for youth. When the Church lifted the anti-Black priesthood and temple ban, Apostle Bruce R. McConkie, one of the most vocal proponents of anti-Black doctrinal speculation, said "forget everything that I have said. . . . We spoke with a limited understanding" at a June 1978 address at Brigham Young University.[14] But McConkie's statement was never canonized. The prophet never said so much over the pulpit at General Conference. Nowhere in the Church's vast curriculum of lesson manuals and publications did the First Presidency say, "We were, collectively, wrong." There was no official rejection of the centuries of accumulated racist rationale. It was possible—indeed, probable—to grow up in LDS settings after 1978 and receive as gospel truth from one's parents and teachers the full complement of anti-Black folk doctrine. And this folk doctrine continued to shape the way many white LDS people conducted themselves in the Church and in the world. Well-placed Black Mormon leaders like the heads of the Church's Genesis group were in a position to convey the continuing impact of Mormonism's accumulated racist folk doctrine to general authorities who had the ears to hear. Public Affairs officials too became aware of the need for better information, especially with the dawning of the internet era as Church members could find their way to accounts of Mormon history that contradicted the official story and laid bare the Church's efforts to control its story.

No doubt these issues were on the mind of Elder Jeffrey Holland, a former president of Brigham Young University and member of its high-ranking Quorum of the Twelve Apostles known for his sensitivity on matters of consequence to the Church's progressives. Of all of the Quorum of the Twelve Apostles, Holland, who holds a PhD in American Studies from Yale University, was regarded as the one most attuned to the complex politics of telling the truth about Mormon history. This is fully reflected in his interview with (non-LDS) filmmaker Helen Whitney, who directed PBS's monumental, multipart documentary *The Mormons* (2006). Documentaries like *The Mormons*, the Church's own novel public relations efforts (such as the "I'm a Mormon" campaign) after 2007, and especially Mitt Romney's national political campaigns opened Mormons to unprecedented visibility and scrutiny. This heightened the tension around critical issues like race, as Holland's March 2006 exchange (subsequently web-published) with Whitney reflects:

HW: I've talked to many blacks and many whites as well about the lingering folklore [about why blacks couldn't have the priesthood]. These are faithful Mormons who are delighted about this revelation, and yet who feel something more should be said about the folklore and even possibly about the mysterious reasons for the ban itself, which was not a revelation; it was a practice. So, if you could, briefly address the concerns Mormons have about this folklore and what should be done.

JH: One clear-cut position is that the folklore must never be perpetuated. . . . I have to concede to my earlier colleagues. . . . They, I'm sure, in their own way, were doing the best they knew to give shape to [the policy], to give context for it, to give even history to it. All I can say is however well intended the explanations were, I think almost all of them were inadequate and/or wrong. . . . It probably would have been advantageous to say nothing, *to say we just don't know*, and, [as] with many religious matters, whatever was being done was done *on the basis of faith* at that time. But some explanations were given and had been given for a lot of years. . . . At the very least, there should be no effort to perpetuate those efforts to explain why that doctrine existed. I think, to the extent that I know anything about it, as one of the newer and younger ones to come along, . . . we simply do not know why that practice, that policy, that doctrine was in place.

HW: What is the folklore, quite specifically?

JH: Well, some of the folklore that you must be referring to are suggestions that there were decisions made in the pre-mortal councils where someone had not been as decisive in their loyalty to a Gospel plan or the procedures on earth or what was to unfold in mortality, and that therefore that opportunity and mortality was compromised. I really don't know a lot of the details of those, because fortunately I've been able to live in the period where we're not expressing or teaching them, but I think that's the one I grew up hearing the most, was that it was something to do with the pre-mortal councils. . . . But I think that's the part that must never be taught until anybody knows a lot more than I know. . . . We just don't know, in the historical context of the time, why it was practiced. . . . That's my principal [concern], is that we don't perpetuate explanations about things we don't know. . . . We don't pretend that something wasn't taught or practice wasn't pursued for whatever reason. But I think we can be unequivocal and we can be declarative in our current literature, in books that we reproduce, in teachings that go forward, whatever, that from this time forward, from 1978 forward, we can make sure that nothing of that is declared. That may be where we still need to make sure that we're absolutely dutiful, that we put [a] careful eye of scrutiny on anything from earlier writings and teachings, just [to] make sure that that's not perpetuated in the present. That's the least, I think, of our current responsibilities on that topic.[15]

Here, Holland ever so carefully walks the line, navigating the enormous pressure not to appear to undercut any previous LDS Church leader: "I have to concede to my earlier colleagues." He does not say that the ban itself was wrong, but he does observe that the various rationales offered for the ban were "inadequate" and "wrong." Holland had access to clear historical expositions by independent LDS historians of how the ban came into being. Still, he insists that "we just don't know" how or why it came into being. Thus, it would have been "advantageous" *to the Church*, he says, had no rationale been offered at any time, and no rationale should be "perpetuated" "going forward." He recommends it be taken on faith that previous LDS Church leaders acted "on the basis of faith" to institutionalize anti-Black segregation. The problem, unfortunately, is that the primary faith that undergirded the institutionalization of the anti-Black priesthood and temple ban was the faith shared by white Church leaders in the secular ideology of white supremacy, the priority of relationships among white people, and the infallibility of an all-white LDS Church leadership.

Perhaps the most significant fact of the interview is its tone, venue, and context. Holland's cautious and highly modulated approach, the way he speaks to Whitney, is not the way Church leaders speak over the pulpit at General Conference in polished, declarative, affirmative, authoritative statements. His remarks sound unofficial. They do not carry the weight of revelation and change. And because Holland is the quorum's known intellectual sympathizer and because he made these in a conversational exchange with a non-Mormon interviewer in an unofficial, non-LDS venue (especially one with an intellectual/progressive/liberal aura), his words did not reach or register with the vast majority of Church members worldwide. Only those specifically hunting for some evidence of change on this issue would have found in his words reason for hope. Nothing in his remarks, though significant in their confirmation that rationale should not be perpetuated, unsettled Mormonism's possessive investment in rightness.

The extent to which general anti-racist sentiment as expressed by President Hinckley in April 2006 and the cautionary "perpetuate nothing" approach Elder Holland endorsed in his March 2006 interview with Helen Whitney did not disrupt the perpetuation of racist folklore within Mormon settings became clear in early 2012 during the Mitt Romney campaign for the presidency. Though candidate Romney masterfully deflected questions linking him to Mormonism and the Church disciplined its messaging to create a respectable distance from the candidate, persistent media pressure succeeded in puncturing Mormonism's carefully managed boundary between insider and outsider narratives. On February 28, 2012, the *Washington Post* ran a Romney-related story exploring Mormonism's history with African Americans, including the history of the priesthood and temple ban and the activism of Black Mormons. Brigham Young University religion professor Randy Bott was interviewed in his office in the "Joseph Smith Building" on the Brigham Young University campus to explain "a possible theological underpinning of the ban":

> According to Mormon scriptures, the descendants of Cain, who killed his brother, Abel, "were black." One of Cain's descendants was Egyptus, a woman Mormons believe was the namesake of Egypt. She married Ham, whose descendants were themselves cursed and, in the view of many Mormons, barred from the priesthood by his father, Noah. Bott points to the Mormon holy text the Book of Abraham as suggesting that all of the descendants of Ham and Egyptus were thus black and barred from the priesthood. . . .
>
> "God has always been discriminatory" when it comes to whom he grants the authority of the priesthood, says Bott, the BYU theologian. He quotes Mormon scripture that states that the Lord gives to people "all that he seeth fit." Bott compares blacks with a young child prematurely asking for the keys to her father's car, and explains that similarly until 1978, the Lord determined that blacks were not yet ready for the priesthood. "What is discrimination?" Bott asks. "I think that is keeping something from somebody that would be a benefit for them, right? But what if it wouldn't have been a benefit to them?" Bott says that the denial of the priesthood to blacks on Earth—although not in the afterlife—protected them from the lowest rungs of hell reserved for people who abuse their priesthood powers. "You couldn't fall off the top of the ladder, because you weren't on the top of the ladder. So, in reality the blacks not having the priesthood was the greatest blessing God could give them."[16]

Bott was no extremist. A tenured faculty member at the flagship Church-sponsored university, Bott taught classes enrolling several hundred students each semester, from whom he received sterling evaluations. He taught courses designed to prepare prospective missionaries for service. His tenured position at Brigham Young University gave him access and authority to shape the views of tens of thousands of future LDS Church lay leaders and members, as did his service as a lay clerical leader. He used this authority to perpetuate speculation and racist folklore that had no theological or scholarly merit. There were faculty members on campus like Professor Eugene England in the Department of English who had written about the racism and embarrassment of the priesthood and temple ban in ways that were both searching and scholarly. *BYU Studies*, the university-sponsored scholarly journal, had published as recently as 2008 Edward Kimball's outstanding essay on the ban and its dismantling. Bott taught and spoke in willed ignorance and defiance of these—not just once, to the *Washington Post*, but semester after semester to Brigham Young University students. None of his colleagues in the Brigham Young University Religion Department exercised the essential scholarly responsibility of peer review to hold Professor Bott accountable.

When news of Bott's remarks broke, the LDS Church responded immediately with the following statement:

> The Church's position is clear—we believe all people are God's children and are equal in His eyes and in the Church. We do not tolerate racism in any form. For a time in the Church there was a restriction on the priesthood for male members of African descent. It is not known precisely why, how, or when this restriction began in the Church but what is clear is that it ended decades ago. Some have attempted to explain the reason for this restriction but these attempts should be viewed as speculation and opinion, not doctrine. The Church is not bound by speculation or opinions given with limited understanding. We condemn racism, including any and all past racism by individuals both inside and outside the Church.[17]

It was the first time since the end of the ban thirty-four years earlier that the Church had officially acknowledged and denounced the racist folklore the ban had engendered. It was also the first time the Church had acknowledged the historical periodicity of the ban: the "restriction" had not been given by God from time immemorial, as prior statements since 1949 had indicated; rather, "for a time in the Church there was a restriction," though, according to the statement, no one knew "why, how, or when this restriction began." Clearly, the "we don't know" approach to the issue articulated by Jeffrey Holland in 2006 had gained support among high-ranking Church leaders. But those who studied LDS history did in fact know that the ban began sometime between 1847 and 1852, that it originated with Brigham Young and was institutionalized over the course of one hundred years following, and that revelation had nothing to do with it. This much the Church's newsroom statement did not convey. Nor did any general authorities address the issue over the pulpit, nor was a corrective amendment inserted into LDS curricula. The newsroom statement was important, but it did not enact a course correction in a way that would register broadly. Only dedicated readers of the Church's press releases who were most hungry for signs of change were likely to notice.

* * *

Perhaps it was the embarrassment of 2012's Randy Bott debacle. Perhaps it was the intense media attention engendered by the Romney campaign and the "Mormon moment." Perhaps it was the Church's extraordinary rates of growth in some African nations. Perhaps it was faithful LDS Church members—Black and white—pressing for a clearer renunciation of the racist past. No one knows exactly what moved LDS Church leadership to publish beginning in 2013 a series of unattributed "Gospel Topics" essays on Mormonism's most complicated historical subjects, including a two-thousand-word essay on "Race and the Priesthood" that materialized silently on the LDS Church's website in December. The Church later posted a brief introductory essay for the series explaining that it had been motivated by the quantity of "information" on Mormonism newly available through digital media, including information from "questionable and often inaccurate sources," to "publish straightforward, in-depth essays" on critical issues in the Mormon faith. The essays, it was noted, had been "approved by the First Presidency and the Quorum of the Twelve"—a critical imprimatur. The information in the essays was for the most part not new: it had been sourced with the help of historians from professional scholarship, church histories, and scripture. What was novel was the Church's new effort to address such issues directly and officially and to provide detail revealing the humanity and complexity of Mormon history rather than holding to sweeping assertions of the timelessness of doctrine and the infallibility of LDS prophets.

Certainly, one of the factors in the development of the "Gospel Topics" essays was the digital-era LDS "faith crisis" phenomenon. The advent of digital media challenged the LDS Church's ability to define truth, manage insider and outsider narratives, and control an official story on Mormon history or doctrine. Before the rise of digital, aside from the highly educated and committed patrons of Mormonism's independent presses and periodicals like *Dialogue*, rank-and-file Church members relied almost entirely on LDS Church–approved lesson manuals, carefully vetted Church-published materials sold at Church-owned Deseret Books, and media channels owned by the Church's subsidiary Bonneville Communications. Information from other sources was viewed by many members as inherently suspect. These media habits were among the legacies of the polygamy crisis, which sharpened Mormons' habit of self-definition by differentiation against a hostile outside "world." In truth, some non-Mormon media about Mormons was hostile, especially literature developed by evangelical Christian anti-Mormon ministries specifically to exploit sensitive and controversial elements of the faith and its history. Other non-Mormon media just *felt* hostile because insular Mormon communities were not accustomed to the robustly interrogative quality of normal civil discourse. Mormons had our version of our story and it worked for us.

Until it didn't. Especially after the rise of Web 2.0 in the mid-2000s, every Mormon home gained search engine–driven, one-click access to a range of perspectives—from avowedly anti-Mormon and ex-Mormon to faithful but critical progressives to "TBM: true-believing

Mormon" apologists—on the most sensitive and controversial issues in Mormon life, from the origins and historicity of the Book of Mormon to Joseph Smith's polygamy (which had been largely excised from official church curriculum) to gender and racial inequality. Church members who had as nineteen- and twenty-year-old boys knocked on doors in impoverished neighborhoods around the world asking others to make enormous sacrifices to join and support the LDS Church on the strength of their testimonies in the literal truth of Mormon scriptures and the infallibility of Mormon leaders found themselves middle-aged men alone late at night peering into a computer screen at a far more complicated story. Podcasts like "Mormon Stories" and "Mormon Expression" gained tens of thousands of listeners as they provided new venues for LDS people who had once harbored their questions and doubts privately. The far-reaching impact of Web 2.0 among Mormon extended kinship networks only accelerated the growth of the Mormon "faith crisis" community, which gained a national profile in coverage by the *New York Times* and the *New Republic* in July 2013.[18] In October 2013, President Dieter Uchtdorf, a member of the Church's First Presidency and a leader recognized for his moderate-to-progressive sensibilities, acknowledged the "faith crisis" movement and called for greater understanding. Over the pulpit at General Conference, Uchtdorf said, "Some struggle with unanswered questions about things that have been done or said in the past. . . . To be perfectly frank, there have been times when members or leaders in the church have simply made mistakes. There may have been things said or done that were not in harmony with our values, principles, or doctrine." Viewed by LDS scholars as an important concession to the fallibility of past Church leaders, Uchtdorf's remarks were picked up by the national media.[19] It was no longer feasible to manage the Mormon past through selective remembering and forgetting and careful public speech. Digital-era Mormons needed frank, accurate, complete, and accessible information about challenging issues.

The gently plainspoken, positive tone modeled by President Uchtdorf carried through the "Gospel Topics" essays and other note-worthy changes as well. Significantly, the essays moved beyond the scripture-only proof texting that dominated Church materials from the 1940s through the 2000s to reference in footnotes scholarly histories that added value and insight. The "Race and the Priesthood" essay opens by stating the Church's theological commitment to the universal love of God and by describing how the Church's mode of organizing congregations fostered "racial integration," but then frankly acknowledges that the Church "from the mid-1800s until 1978" "did not ordain men of black African descent to its priesthood or allow black men or women to participate in temple endowment or sealing ordinances." In March 2013, the Church had updated headnotes in its official scriptures to reflect the fact that Joseph Smith ordained Black men to the priesthood.[20] But the essay was the first time an official LDS Church source had captured not only the historical periodicity of the ban but also the often overlooked fact that Mormon women of Black African descent had experienced exclusion as well.

The essay helpfully situates Mormonism's specific anti-Black racist history within the broader history of racism in the United States and American Christianity, including long-standing American Christian folk doctrines rationalizing the enslavement and oppression of Black people in connection with the biblical curses on Cain and Ham. These forces influenced debates about slavery in US territories during the 1850s, including debates in Utah territory:

> In two speeches delivered before the Utah territorial legislature in January and February 1852, Brigham Young announced a policy restricting men of black African descent from priesthood ordination. At the same time, President Young said that at some future day, black Church members would "have [all] the privilege and more" enjoyed by other members.

The essay remembers the persistence of Black Mormon pioneers Elijah Abel and Jane Manning James in maintaining their claim to full priesthood authority and temple access even as nineteenth-century Mormon institutions sought to deny them. It notes the innovation of the doctrinal speculation on priesthood and temple exclusion as a consequence of Black inferiority in the premortal existence and tracks limited efforts made by President David O. McKay to clarify the boundaries and edges of the Church's policy during the middle decades of the twentieth century. Significantly, the essay identifies the faith of Black Latter-day Saints in Brazil and West Africa as the primary force that "moved Church leaders" to ask God whether it was time for black Church members to "have all the privilege" as Brigham Young promised, and recounts the revelation as an event revered and welcomed with "joy" by LDS Church members around the globe. It closes by reiterating the essence of the Church's 2012 newsroom statement:

> Today, the Church disavows the theories advanced in the past that black skin is a sign of divine disfavor or curse, or that it reflects unrighteous actions in a premortal life; that mixed-race marriages are a sin; or that blacks or people of any other race or ethnicity are inferior in any way to anyone else. Church leaders today unequivocally condemn all racism, past and present, in any form.

It was the first time LDS Church leaders had with a unified voice and in an official format rejected all rationalizations for the ban. By making these statements, the Church gave members an official resource to cite to counter persistent racist folklore that could surface at home or at church.

Scholars and activists applauded the essay and asked for more. In a special issue of the *Journal of Mormon History* dedicated to celebrating and extending the essay's enterprise, Max Mueller lauded "the Church's most frank and comprehensive effort to confront the reality of its racist past" but worried that the essay had "not reached as far as perhaps the Church intended."[21] Black LDS activists suggested that the essay be cited "regularly at LDS General Conference," "translate[d] . . . into all the languages that the church uses to communicate with its global membership," and "read from the pulpit in every Mormon congregation and mission in the world."[22] Historian W. Paul Reeve related to the *Salt Lake Tribune* that because "the pieces were

PERSISTENCE OF WHITE SUPREMACY

not signed by LDS leaders, not prominently displayed online nor sent to bishops to be read over the pulpit to Mormon congregations," many members had not heard of them, and some Mormons "drew upon the essay in church meetings and were met by resistance from fellow Mormons who said the essays were not official and merely [church] Public Affairs pieces."[23] Reeve's experience documents the reality of the split between "insider" and "outsider" narratives internalized by LDS Church members, with the implication being that the Public Affairs office as bureaucratic functionaries might generate narratives to manage outsiders' impressions and inquiries but that these were not the same as essential truths revealed to LDS prophets and held sacred within the LDS community.

Others pressed for even deeper work to get at the systems of power and privilege that created and sustained the anti-Black exclusion policy. Wrote Gina Colvin in the *Journal of Mormon History*, "For me, the race essay was powerful and important in revising traditional narratives of black 'premortal undeservedness' to hold the priesthood but it didn't go far enough to turn those same academic tools on the LDS Church in order to question 'why' these narratives held, and what larger discourses of white supremacy Mormon institutional racism hangs from."[24] In Colvin's view, the story of the Church's priesthood and temple ban was in part a story about the Church's specific historic oppression of African American Mormons, but it was also a story about how and why Mormonism became a place where such oppressions could take hold and thrive. The work of identifying the mechanisms through which white supremacy infiltrated and dominated sacred spaces, the means by which it worked, would have to be done as well if there was to be hope not just of abolishing specific prejudices and harmful folk doctrines but of developing in their place entirely new habits of humility and accountability on race. Dismantling the possessive investment in whiteness and the possessive investment in rightness within Mormonism would take more than a retooling of historical narratives, although that was an essential and potentially impactful first step. It would take the cultivation of an entirely new approach to race that put no stock in maintaining Mormonism's racial innocence.

That approach has yet to materialize. The Church continues to support the Genesis group and lend support to projects developed by African American Mormon community leaders like Marvin Perkins, founder of the African American Outreach Program and creator of the "Blacks in the Scriptures" website, and "Sistas in Zion" authors and speakers Tamu Smith and Zandra Vranes. The Church-owned *Deseret News* published perspectives from Vranes after Charlottesville, and LDS Church facilities in Washington, DC, and suburban Salt Lake City hosted "Legacy of Black Pioneers" conferences in 2018 and 2019 organized, guided, and conducted by African American Mormon authors, speakers, and activists. The Church also produced in June 2018 the "Be One" event at its massive Conference Center in Salt Lake City, featuring music, spoken word, dance, and testimony by Black African and African American LDS people as well as high-ranking Church leaders including President Russell M. Nelson. Other academic and scholarly efforts and events on African American Mormon issues and race and racism in the Church have been organized and supported by Utah Valley University and the University of Utah.

But scholarship on anti-racism and ending white supremacy teaches us that if substantial lasting change is to take place, it must take place not only in the hearts of the Black Mormons who live the lasting impacts of the ban and exert enormous energy supporting each other and educating non-Black LDS Church members but also in the minds and hearts of all LDS people and in the institutional infrastructure of the LDS Church. The change must take place not only in the content of the official Mormon story but also in the way that story is absorbed and what it teaches. The official shift from a categorical defense of the ban as the will of God from time immemorial to an acknowledgment that the ban was a policy put in place by Brigham Young (under the influence of white American racism) represents an enormous step forward in the telling of the Mormon story. The larger lessons of what this shift suggests about the Mormon practice of continuing revelation, the infallibility of LDS Church leaders, the "rightness" of the LDS Church, and what collective repentance might look like have scarcely been considered. Moreover, an even fuller historical narrative of the ban would extend beyond its introduction by Brigham Young to consider the role that generations of white LDS Church leaders and members played in institutionalizing and sustaining the ban. Some LDS people bore false witness about Church history; opposed truths told by Black coreligionists; subscribed to the ugliest secular forms of white supremacy; imported them into Church manuals, lessons, and talks as doctrine; and used sacred spaces to hold forth against full civil equality for African Americans in the United States. These too are historical facts and are part of the Mormon story, and these too bear consequences for the souls of Mormons, white, Black, and brown. Abolishing legal slavery and publishing accurate histories of anti-Black racism were essential steps forward, but they did not dismantle systems of white supremacy in the United States. Abolishing the ban and publishing accurate histories of its institutionalization are essential steps forward, but they do not dismantle systems of white supremacy in Mormonism.

Few historically white American churches have institutionalized anti-racist curriculum that goes beyond the normative "teaching tolerance" approach to get at the systematic, pervasive, and deadly quality of white supremacy. White American Christianity has directed its energies at other endeavors, some equally laudable, but others designed primarily to convey and affirm white racial innocence. Because of its legibly human history and the extremity of its institutionalized ban on full Black participation, Mormonism has an opportunity to show moral leadership and support model endeavors in truth telling and reconciliation. But at least two obstacles stand between Mormonism and moral leadership in this area. First, the still embedded culture of "undergrounding" mitigates against a truth-telling and reconciliation approach. Second, there is the problem of priorities and resources. The Church has chosen not to invest the force of its moral energies in anti-racism. It has invested deeply in various political campaigns to oppose civil equality for LGBTQ+ people and, when the national campaign against gay marriage failed, in efforts to claim "religious freedom" protections for Mormonism's refusal (somewhat modified in April 2019) to welcome same-sex couples and their children. This fight and the political blowback it has entailed have reactivated the deeply embedded habits of "undergrounding" developed by Mormons during the polygamy crisis. Like many human beings, Mormons retrench under pressure.

There is an intersection between the Church's racial history and its opposition to LGBTQ+ equality. It has surfaced in the way the Church has used Black spokespeople and Black civil rights struggle histories in the service of its anti-gay rights agenda. During California's Proposition 8 campaign in 2008, when the Church used religious meetings and buildings to activate tens of thousands of Mormon volunteers and donors to end same-sex civil marriage, California African American Mormons served as the Church's public face at rallies and in the media. Black Mormon spokespeople perpetuated ugly secular homophobia and cited the memory of Dr. Martin Luther King Jr. and the Jesse Jackson ideal of a "Rainbow Coalition" in service of the cause. One Black Mormon spokesperson compared the street-level aggressions against "Yes on 8" to aggressions against Black civil rights.[25] (The aggressions went both ways, as media sources attest.) After the campaign, as the national tide was turning in favor of marriage equality, in 2009, Elder Dallin H. Oaks, a legal scholar and high-ranking member of the Quorum of the Twelve Apostles, delivered several public addresses in defense of "religious freedom" that compared pushback against "Yes on 8" demonstrators to "voter-intimidation of blacks in the South."[26] Given Mormonism's history of anti-Black racism and opposition to the civil rights movement, using Black stories in this way did not model thoughtful, accountable moral leadership.

To be sure, the Proposition 8 campaign came before the Church produced its 2012 Bott-gate statement and made the substantial, significant changes that culminated with the 2013 "Race and the Priesthood" essay. But the pattern of using Black stories in the service of a "religious freedom" defense against welcoming gays and their children has continued beyond those watershed events. In July 2017, Elder Quentin Cook, a member of the Quorum of the Twelve Apostles, delivered an address to a gathering of Black clergy members and theologians at the Seymour Institute Seminar on Religious Freedom hosted at Princeton

Theological Seminary. The Seymour Institute, named after William J. Seymour, a major figure in the history of American Pentecostalism who is credited with the beginnings of the famed Azusa Street Revivals in 1907, brings together Black clergy and theologians from a range of denominations to collaborate on conservative theological projects focusing on heterosexual marriage and normative gender roles. The institute is based at Ella Baker House in Boston and funded by the Witherspoon Institute, a conservative think tank that also funded the controversial "Regenerus Study" (2012), which alleged the insufficiency of LGBTQ+ parenting and was cited as evidence in unsuccessful legal cases against same-sex marriage. The majority African American program also featured William P. Mumma, president of the Becket Fund for Religious Liberty, known for litigation on behalf of plaintiffs seeking exemption on faith-based grounds from providing contraceptives through employer-paid health insurance. The Church of Jesus Christ of Latter-day Saints was the only major religious institution besides the Church of God in Christ (COGIC) to be represented on the program.[27]

The institute's description characterized the election of Donald J. Trump to the presidency as "a pause in the agenda that pitted liberal politics against people of faith and threatened our religious freedom. This presents an opening for Christians to advance the cause of Jesus. In contrast to a culture that has been increasingly hostile to the gospel, there is now an opportunity to present religious freedom in its true, life-giving light." The conference organizers sought opportunity to "rebrand religious freedom." Although Elder Cook opened his remarks by stating that the LDS Church does not engage in partisan politics, his participation in the event indicated that the Church had prioritized deep coalition-building work with conservative think tanks and their religious affiliates.

It is a tremendous responsibility to be one of the only white speakers on a program convened by Black leaders on issues of importance to the Black community. Respect for the hosts and host traditions obliges humility, deference, demonstrated knowledge of Black history including those who have made your own work possible, openness to feedback, acknowledgment of complexity, and recognition of white privilege—all of this in a way that does not decenter the occasion or consume energy required for the most important work at hand. To do anti-racist work in such a setting might involve acknowledging one's situatedness in history, including past histories of discrimination, and citing Black role models and authorities by name to show respect—all of this in a way that does not oblige the Black hosts or the host tradition to offer you special recognition or exculpation. It is a matter of unburdening everyone in the room of maintaining the white racial innocence that often serves its white bearers as a shield against accountability, responsibility, vulnerability, and hard work. Among the privileges of whiteness are exemption from racial discomfort and the feeling of being wrong. My experiences as a white scholar studying and writing about race and as a white university administrator working with faculty-related diversity programs—the many times when I have made mistakes as well as times I have learned and done better—have taught me that forgoing these privileges and one's presumption of innocence is necessary to attempting to work in solidarity with African American people.

Elder Cook's remarks hit many of these marks. He acknowledges the hospitality and leadership in its chosen endeavor of the Seymour Institute and cites writings by its African American directors. He also indicates respect for Martin Luther King Jr. and cites a sermon by Dr. King, as well as writings by William Wilberforce, whom he remembers as an eighteenth-century British "Christian evangelical" who advocated persistently for the end of the slave trade. Cook indicates that his fondness for Wilberforce and other figures of English history is stoked in part by the fact that the "sympathetic study and teaching of British history, as well as the history of western civilization, have been under attack for some time" and that these amount to an "attack" on "Christianity." His remarks betray a less-than-objective view of history scholarship and a disinclination to consider the perspectives of Christians (including LDS people) and other faithful peoples around the globe who have suffered loss of life, property, well-being, and sovereignty under British colonialism. Still, it is a view shared by Cook's African American host organization, and Cook seeks to build common ground.

On the commonly held idea that Christianity is under attack and that numerous liberal social movements put "religious freedom" on the defensive, Cook pivots to share the story of Latter-day Saint persecution. He is careful to stress that he is not making a comparison: "I wish to concur unequivocally with what Dr. Eugene Rivers and Dr. Kenneth Johnson wrote: 'The black American experience as a function of slavery is unique and without analogue in the history of the United States. . . . While other . . . groups have experienced discrimination and hardship, none of their experiences compare with the physical and cultural brutality of slavery.'" He then proceeds to tell a Mormon history of persecution. At some points of the story, Elder Cook does not accurately represent what professional LDS historians have documented about the unevenness of race relations in early LDS communities, and his attribution of anti-Mormon mob violence in Missouri to the Church's progressive stance on race omits many other more salient factors like the Church's practice of polygamy and fears of Mormon political takeover. Cook highlights the murder of seventeen Mormon men and boys at Haun's Mill, Missouri, and the extermination order issued by the state. He concludes this recounting by stating: "Let me say once again, I am not comparing Latter-day Saint trials with the horrendous slavery experience of African Americans. But it does allow us to see religious freedom through a somewhat similar lens"—a commitment shaped through the experience of minority persecution. He closes his address by outlining the elements of the Church's "Fairness for All" approach, which includes protections for individual believers, religious organizations, and LGBT people alike to live without fear of discrimination and ostracism and serve the needs of their respective communities, including the rights of those who oppose homosexuality on religious grounds not to accommodate LGBT clients or members.

Nowhere in the address does Cook mention the Church's own century-long ban on Black equality. Nowhere does he acknowledge the Church's own efforts to exclude Blacks from its programs and

universities, nor efforts to exclude Blacks from full and equal participation in civic life endorsed by LDS Church leaders. He completely
avoids the subject of Mormon anti-Black racism, though its anti-Black
racism is the second thing after polygamy most African Americans
associate with the LDS faith tradition. Claiming one's own history of
oppression and seeking to use shared oppression as the basis for a relationship to a community of color without taking responsibility for
one's own culpability in the oppression of that community of color is
a rhetorical act scholars have called "racing for innocence."[28] It uses
a history of persecution to excuse, distract, and step around the hard
work of setting relationships right, addressing uncomfortable histories,
and seeking reconciliation. By utilizing Mormon rhetorical habits of
undergrounding, including nontransparency about LDS history and
managing insider and outsider narratives through careful speech,
Cook preserves white racial innocence and with it white supremacy,
and he enlists his conservative Black hosts in a silent agreement to preserve white innocence as well. Moreover, his remarks signal to Cook's
secondary audience—the many LDS readers who would read them
because they were subsequently published on the Church's website—
that it was okay not to acknowledge racism in the Mormon past and
present. If a high-ranking Church leader could speak so confidently
to a gathering of African American clergy, certainly we were doing
all right.

Except we weren't. Just one month after Elder Cook's remarks, a
prominent extremist white supremacist blogger, who cited her LDS
faith as a rationale for her racism, made national news as a planned
headliner at the August 2017 Charlottesville white nationalist rally,
reminding Mormons that though the ban was gone and the history
was accurate, we still had a tremendous amount of work to do. As
Elise Boxer, an indigenous (Dakota/Chicana) scholar of Mormonism,
writes:

> Mormons have accessed and claimed whiteness at various times when
> what we need to be doing is discussing whiteness and Mormon history
> and thinking about the white colonial privilege to explore issues of race,

racism, and power in the Mormon Church and its history. The question is to challenge how Mormon history has been written and continues to be written by scholars in the field. If we remain so focused on Mormon religious persecution or aspects of history that interest only Mormons, we are limiting the field of Mormon studies. When we examine early Mormon history, if we move beyond religious persecution, we can then explore and talk about moments when Mormons access and reaffirm their whiteness.[29]

Boxer's remarks map out a path for Mormon studies in moving beyond adjudicating Mormon persecution and its minoritarian fascinations to take stock of the way LDS people and institutions have interacted with massive modern systems like colonialism and whiteness that have benefited white lives at the expense of black and brown ones. The work, of course, would not be limited to professional scholarship. It would have to be undertaken by rank-and-file LDS people, a self-searching, a coming to see our faith through the eyes of Mormons of color, as they have experienced it—in complicated ways that give reason for humility and reason for hope alike. Nor would this work be limited to Mormonism. Every predominantly white American Christianity has its own work to do in assessing how anti-Black racism has structured its history and how even when their facades have been dismantled, those structures persist into the present.

NOTES

1. See also Armand Mauss, *All Abraham's Children: Changing Mormon Conceptions of Race and Lineage* (Urbana: University of Illinois Press, 2005), 232–241.
2. Edward L. Kimball, "Spencer W. Kimball and the Revelation on Priesthood," *BYU Studies Quarterly* 47.2 (2008): 1, https://scholarsarchive.byu.edu/cgi/viewcontent.cgi?article=3908&amp=&context=byusq&amp=&sei-redir=1&referer=https%253A%252F%252Fscholar.google.com%252Fscholar%253Fhl%253Den%252

6as_sdt%253D0%252C5%2526q%253DKimball%252Bbyu%252B studies#search=%22Kimball%20byu%20studies%22, last accessed February 28, 2017.

3. "Official Declaration 2," *Doctrine and Covenants*, The Church of Jesus Christ of Latter-day Saints, https://www.lds.org/scriptures/dc-testament/od/2, last accessed February 28, 2018.

4. Armand L. Mauss, "Casting Off the Curse of Cain: The Extent and Limits of Progress since 1978," in *Black and Mormon*, ed. Newell Bringhurst and Darron T. Smith (Urbana: University of Illinois, 2004), 107.

5. Daymon Smith, *The Last Shall Be First and the First Shall Be Last: Discourse and Mormon History* (PhD dissertation, University of Pennsylvania, 2007), 30; Edwin Firmage and R. Collin Mangrum, *Zion in the Courts: A Legal History of the Church of Jesus Christ of Latter-day Saints, 1830–1900* (Urbana: University of Illinois Press, 2001), 137.

6. Daymon Smith argues that these practices of undergrounding were forced out with excommunication of LDS fundamentalists in the 1930s and virtually sealed out by the work of the LDS Church Correlation Committee in the middle twentieth century (369). See *The Last Shall Be First and the First Shall Be Last: Discourse and Mormon History* (Ph.D dissertation; Philadelphia: University of Pennsylvania, 2007). I would argue that correlation works in dialectical tension within and against older practices of undergrounding that index Mormon theocracy, difference, and status. See Joanna Brooks, "'On the Underground': What the Mormon 'Yes on 8' Campaign Reveals About Mormons in American Political Life," in *Mormonism and American Politics*, ed. Jana Riess and Randall Balmer (New York: Columbia University Press, 2015).

7. Boyd Petersen, "Hugh Nibley and the 'Inmigration' of Mormon Education" (unpublished ms., November 6, 2009).

8. Wes Andrews and Clyde Dalton, *The Black Hammer: A Study of Black Power, Red Influence and White Alternatives* (Oakland, CA: Desco Press, 1967). See also D. Michael Quinn, "Ezra Taft Benson and Mormon Political Conflicts," *Dialogue: A Journal of Mormon Thought* 26.2 (Summer 1992): 1–87.

9. Hinckley's long career and profound influence on Mormon public relations is discussed throughout J. B. Haws, *The Mormon Image in the American Mind* (Oxford: Oxford University Press, 2015).

10. "An Interview with Gordon B. Hinckley," *60 Minutes,* April 7, 1996, web-published January 31, 2008, https://www.cbsnews.com/news/an-interview-with-gordon-hinckley/, last accessed February 28, 2018.

11. Harris and Bringhurst, 129–130.

12. Gordon B. Hinckley, "The Need for Greater Kindness," April 2006, https://www.lds.org/general-conference/2006/04/the-need-for-greater-kindness?lang=eng, last accessed February 28, 2018.

13. The Church of Jesus Christ of Latter-day Saints, "Statement on Symposia," November 1991, https://www.lds.org/ensign/1991/11/news-of-the-church/statement-on-symposia?lang=eng, last accessed February 28, 2018.

14. Bruce R. McConkie, "All Are Alike Unto God," CES Religious Educators Symposium, August 18, 1978, https://speeches.byu.edu/talks/bruce-r-mcconkie_alike-unto-god-2/, last accessed February 28, 2018.

15. Helen Whitney, "Interview: Jeffrey Holland," *PBS American Experience/Frontline: The Mormons,* March 4, 2006, http://www.pbs.org/mormons/interviews/holland.html, last accessed February 28, 2018.

16. Jason Horowitz, "The Genesis of a Church's Stand on Race," *Washington Post,* February 28, 2012, https://www.washingtonpost.com/politics/the-genesis-of-a-churchs-stand-on-race/2012/02/22/gIQAQZXyfR_story.html?utm_term=.8192b720336e, last accessed February 28, 2018.

17. The Church of Jesus Christ of Latter-day Saints, "Church Statement Regarding 'Washington Post' Article on Race and the Church," February 29, 2012, https://www.mormonnewsroom.org/article/racial-remarks-in-washington-post-article, last accessed February 28, 2012. See also Joseph Walker, "LDS Church Condemns Past Racism Inside and Outside the Church," February 29, 2012, https://www.deseretnews.com/article/765555339/LDS-Church-condemns-past-racism-inside-and-outside-the-church.html.

18. Laurie Goodstein, "Some Mormons Search the Web and Find Doubt," *New York Times,* July 21, 2013, http://www.nytimes.com/2013/07/21/us/some-mormons-search-the-web-and-find-doubt.html?ref=todayspaper&_r=0&pagewanted=print, last accessed February 28, 2018; Isaac Chotiner, "Mormons Start Questioning Their History, Stumble on Racism," *New Republic,* July 22, 2013, https://newrepublic.com/article/113969/mormons-history-racism-and-religion, last accessed February 28, 2018.

19. Laurie Goodstein, "A Leader's Admission of 'Mistakes' Heartens Some Doubting Mormons," *New York Times*, October 8, 2013, http://www.nytimes.com/2013/10/09/us/a-leaders-admission-of-mistakes-heartens-some-doubting-mormons.html, last accessed February 28, 2018.

20. Peggy Fletcher Stack, "New Mormon Scriptures Tweak Race, Polygamy References," *Salt Lake Tribune*, March 19, 2013, http://archive.sltrib.com/article.php?id=55930173&itype=CMSID, last accessed February 28, 2018.

21. Max Mueller, "Introduction: Beyond 'Race and the Priesthood,'" *Journal of Mormon History* 41.3 (July 2015): 1–10, http://www.jstor.org.libproxy.sdsu.edu/stable/pdf/10.5406/jmormhist.41.3.1.pdf?refreqid=excelsior%3A135f37910dcffd48f0c38db674408d0f, last accessed February 28, 2018.

22. Peggy Fletcher Stack, "39 Years Later, Priesthood Ban Is History, but Racism Within Mormon Ranks Isn't, Black Members Say," *Salt Lake Tribune*, June 9, 2017, http://archive.sltrib.com/article.php?id=5371962&itype=CMSID, last accessed February 28, 2018.

23. Peggy Fletcher Stack, "New Mormon Mission: How to Teach Members the Messy Part of LDS History," *Salt Lake Tribune*, March 8, 2015, http://www.sltrib.com/home/2229999-155/new-mormon-mission- how-to-teach?fullpage=, last accessed March 1, 2018.

24. Gina Colvin, Elise Boxer, Laurie Maffly-Kipp, Melissa Inouye, and Janan Russell-Graham, "Roundtable Discussion: Challenging Mormon Race Scholarship," *Journal of Mormon History* 41.3 (July 2015): 258–281, http://www.jstor.org.libproxy.sdsu.edu/stable/pdf/10.5406/jmormhist.41.3.258.pdf, last accessed February 28, 2018.

25. "Proposition 8: Showdown," *The Economist*, October 30, 2008, https://www.economist.com/node/12522924; "Proposition 8 and

the School Debate," *Santa Clarita Valley Signal*, October 31, 2008, http://archive.signalscv.com/archives/5472/; "A Proposition 8 Roundtable With Sonja Eddings Brown, Marvin Perkins, and Jon Stewart," *Latter-day Chino*, November 2008, http://www.chinoblanco.com/2008/11/prop-8-rountable-with-sonja-eddings.html; "Marvin Perkins: We Are One," *Main Street Plaza*, February 4, 2011, https://mainstreetplaza.com/2011/02/04/marvin-perkins-one/, last accessed February 28, 2018.

26. The Church of Jesus Christ of Latter-day Saints, "Apostle Says Religious Freedom Is Being Threatened," October 13, 2009, https://www.mormonnewsroom.org/ldsnewsroom/eng/news-releases-stories/apostle-says-religious-freedom-is-being-threatened, last accessed February 28, 2018.

27. The Church of Jesus Christ of Latter-day Saints, "Apostle Quentin L. Cook Speaks on Religious Freedom at Princeton Theological Seminary," July 26, 2017, https://www.mormonnewsroom.org/article/transcript-%C2%A0elder-quentin-l-cook-speaks-on-religious-freedom-at-princeton-university, last accessed February 28, 2018. See also Seymour Institute, "The Black Church and Religious Freedom in the Age of Trump," https://www.seymourinstitute.com/summer-seminar-1.html, last accessed February 28, 2018.

28. See especially Jennifer Pierce, *Racing for Innocence: Whiteness, Gender, and the Backlash Against Affirmative Action* (Palo Alto: Stanford University Press, 2012).

29. Colvin et al., 264.

CHAPTER 7

DISMANTLING WHITE SUPREMACY AND RACIAL INNOCENCE

We must foster and encourage conversations about race that include the motivation to undo colonial regimes that are constructed in discourse.

—Gina Colvin, *Journal of Mormon History* (2015)[1]

As members of the church, we need to have the hard and uncomfortable conversation of racism. We need to keep having it to expel all the hot-air anger and have it until we're able to reach effective dialogue during which we are truly hearing one another, learning, and changing our generations-old myth-based paradigm—however subconscious it may be.

—Alice Faulkner Burch, Relief Society President, Genesis Group, address delivered to Mormon History Association (2016)[2]

Be studious, but not
anything we didn't give you to study,
and not history
or older doctrine
or what we said that we don't say we
said about stuff we don't really
want to think about. Be Good.

—Mormon feminist poet Heather Harris Bergevin, *Lawless Women* (2018)[3]

Systems as pervasive as white supremacy do not just transform quietly. They must be recognized, investigated, understood, and intentionally abandoned or dismantled, and their impacts to communities of color repaired. As the religion scholar Jennifer Harvey has argued, reconciliation is not enough. Predominantly white American Christian communities that wish to take moral responsibility for the advantage-taking that has yielded white privilege and Black suffering must engage with the concept of reparations. In the domain of the secular, reparations are typically conceived of through the

Mormonism and white supremacy. Joanna brooks, Oxford University Press (2020). © Oxford University Press.
DOI: 10.1093/oso/9780190081768.001.0001

intervention of the state: compensatory payments for unjustly expropriated labor, lost opportunities, and lost land; debt cancellation; and subsidized access to child care, health care, nonpredatory postal banking, and education. But how does a religious community—a predominantly white American Christian community—begin to conceive of reparations? African Americans have every incentive to gain access to the advantages of economic incentives. But do they want to go to church with white folks? Especially given the role of white churches in fostering white supremacy? Who could blame them if they didn't?

If we are to believe Stewart Udall, the main benefit of undertaking a serious attempt not only at reconciliation but also reparation accrues to whites themselves—and for religious whites to the integrity of the Christian testimony they profess. And this requires on the part of whites and predominantly white American Christian denominations a commitment to dismantling the deep institutional, social, economic, political, and cultural scaffolding that has supported segregation in American religious life. In this book, I have tried to identify and analyze the elements of this scaffolding in my own religious community— that is, the things the Mormon people have done and continue to do that perpetuate anti-Black white supremacy:

- Prioritizing relationships among whites in the Mormon community over responsibilities to the well-being of fellow Mormons who are Black
- Actively excluding Blacks from religious and political power, thus discouraging a Black presence in Mormonism and rendering Black experience abstract and unknowable
- Abandoning factual versions of Mormon history in favor of correlated narratives presenting Black exclusion as the will of God from time immemorial revealed to infallible Mormon prophets
- Entering into silent agreements within the membership and with the American public to coaffirm the innocence and moral goodness of the white majority
- Repressing internal critique and dissent

- Using rhetorical evasion and duplicity to manage the legacy of Mormon anti-Black racism without taking responsibility for it

These contribute not only to what scholars call a possessive investment in whiteness but also to a *possessive investment in rightness* that supports white racial innocence, the privilege that allows whites to feel morally superior while avoiding grappling with the profound moral questions of race and racism. As the chapter-opening quotes reflect, despite dedicated efforts by Black Mormon advocates, stifling silence and stasis around anti-Black racism and white supremacy hold in most Mormon contexts. Black members are not sure what white members think about them; white members either presume or pretend that "all is well in Zion," fear "doing it wrong," or fear that, without a clear statement from the top that the ban was wrong, they don't have the moral authority to say so themselves.

What keeps white Mormons from opening our mouths? When queried on this issue, many white Mormons will express a generalized fear of "getting in trouble" with Church authorities, incurring reaction from other whites, straining relationships, and losing status, credibility, or opportunities. Professor Darron T. Smith, a scholar of race in LDS life, observes:

> Rather than engage in any dialogue that highlights racial privileging / discrimination and hence promotes growth in personal and social understanding, white people consciously suppress conflict (passive aggressiveness), not only because they wish to avoid the discomfort of confrontation but also because this avoidance enables them to maintain white privilege. Unwittingly, the church then becomes a site where whiteness operates in opposition to people of color.

The choice to maintain one's place in a power structure that rewards silence and solidarity with other whites at the expense of truth is a choice to support white supremacy.

Other ways that white Mormons have allowed the "possessive investment in rightness" to block productive conversation around race include correcting people of color who present information, experience, or perspective in forums ranging from Sunday meetings to Facebook; holding to literal interpretations of Old Testament, Book of Mormon, and Pearl of Great Price scriptures on skin color and "racial identities"; and holding to uninformed and unnuanced celebration of LDS historical figures who openly espoused racist sentiments, held slaves, or opposed Black emancipation and equality, including Abraham Smoot, Eliza R. Snow, J. Reuben Clark, Ezra Taft Benson, and others. Underrepresentation of people of color in leadership roles also makes it impossible, Smith writes, to "move beyond the profound distortions brought on by the warp of privilege."[4]

Is it possible for Mormonism to take a more intentional approach toward addressing anti-Black racism and white supremacy? Recent Mormon history provides three models for social transformation. First, there is movement from the top: change effected "vertically" through statements and institutional changes made by LDS Church leaders. In June 2017, *Salt Lake Tribune* religion reporter Peggy Fletcher Stack published a list compiled by Black LDS Church members of additional changes the LDS Church could make to effect movement from the top, including using more Black Africans and African Americans in LDS Church media (including films shown within LDS temples), introducing Black LDS history into Church curricula (including missionary training), and directing that the "Race and the Priesthood" essay be studied in LDS congregations. Additional steps to address past wrongs committed by LDS people could plausibly follow the model of the Church's response after 2007 to the Mountain Meadows Massacre, which included collaborative efforts with descendants of massacre victims and local Paiute tribes blamed for the massacre, an explicit statement of responsibility and regret, and a physical memorialization of the wrongs at the massacre site, later designated a National Historic Landmark.[5] It is possible to imagine similar efforts including reparations to descendants of slaves owned and traded by LDS Church leaders and an incorporation of materials directly exploring the racist human origins of the ban and calling members to take responsibility for divesting from justifications for it in Church curricula and in General Conference talks. It is also possible to imagine a rigorous, scholarship-supported conversation about LDS Church–owned institutional commemorations of individuals like Abraham Smoot who owned slaves and decisively and intentionally obscured the truth to maintain the supremacy of white over Black in Mormonism and exclude generations of Black people from what LDS people would understand as the blessings of temple rite participation, including ritual "sealings" that would have secured Black family relationships in the eternities. With major buildings at Brigham Young University named after Smoot (administration building) and Joseph F. Smith (College of Family, Home, and Social Sciences), who also obscured the truth to secure Black priesthood exclusion, as well as other LDS Church leaders like J. Reuben Clark (law school), Harold B. Lee (library), David O. McKay (College of Education), and George Albert Smith (fieldhouse), who are on record as advocates of anti-Black racial segregation, and Ezra Taft Benson (chemistry building) and Ernest Wilkinson (student center), who opposed the civil rights movement or sought to evade responsibility for institutional segregation, LDS Church–owned institutions like Brigham Young University have an opportunity to enter into a national conversation about history, institutionalized racism, privilege, accountability, responsibility, and restitution. Several leading American universities including Brown, Georgetown, and Harvard have undertaken productive scrutiny of their institutions' formative historical intersections with slavery and white supremacy, and Brigham Young University has the opportunity to join their company.

Second, movement from the margins includes efforts by LDS scholars, activists, and non-LDS groups and individuals to bring about conditions that will persuade LDS Church leaders to pursue theological and institutional change. Past examples include spiritual and political efforts in the 1960s and 1970s by Genesis group founders Ruffin Bridgeforth, Darius Gray, and Eugene Orr; scholarship in the 1960s and 1970s by Armand Mauss and Lester Bush; subsequent writing by Gray, Margaret Young, Newell Bringhurst, Darron T. Smith, Janan Graham Russell, and others; and ongoing media advocacy and education efforts by Tamu Smith, Zandra Vranes, LaShawn Williams, Marvin Perkins, and many others. It is possible to imagine a stronger role for direct activism on the model of Ordain Women to pursue specific institutional changes around race, but this has not been the chosen approach.

Third, movement from the middle describes efforts by LDS Church members to organize to change perspectives and conduct among fellow Church members. Social media facilitates an unprecedented level of "horizontal" communication among Mormons, and recent years have seen groups like Feminist Mormon Housewives and Mormons Building Bridges, a grassroots network focused on promoting love and acceptance for LGBTQI+ people, work diligently and effectively through online content, public gatherings, and retreats that build capacity in grassroots changemakers. For movement from the middle to take shape around issues of racism, white LDS people will have to choose to see the possessive investment in whiteness and the possessive investment in rightness as corrosive to the tradition.

But perhaps the greatest work ahead is the dismantling of prophetic infallibility as an alibi for the Church's reversals on issues of critical importance. The possessive investment in rightness that was developed to shore up Mormonism's possessive investment in whiteness also served to manage its contradictory positions on issues like polygamy. It furnished the terms by which LDS Church leaders managed a series of accommodations that secured Mormonism's survival and white Mormons' access to the privileges of white American citizenship. It also utterly shaped twentieth- and twenty-first-century Mormonism. First, it has served as a tool for managing and transitioning from the incoherence and instability of early Mormon belief and practice to its modern institutional correlation. Second, it has helped Mormonism manage ongoing contradictions in its scripture, prophetic statements, and actions. Third, it has helped Mormonism maintain its internal differentiation, its coherence, its "optimum tension" (as Armand Mauss put it) with the white mainstream, while yet accessing white mainstream advantages.[6] But this has come at an expense. The possessive investment in whiteness and the possessive investment in rightness have put Mormons in opposition to efforts by minority peoples worldwide for dignity, autonomy, sovereignty, land, and well-being. They have allied the Mormon people with dominant power structures that allocate life chances by race. They have stood in the way of engagement, productive conflict, and truth seeking. They have put the LDS Church in the impossible position of defending the purity and literal veracity of our faith's entire nineteenth-century record, and it has cut off from communion with the Church those who could not do the same. Infallibility has served Mormon communities to foster continuity across discontinuity but to do so in a way that sacrifices those deemed expendable and suffocates those held in place. Most importantly, the possessive investment in whiteness and the possessive investment in rightness have corroded the theological integrity of Mormonism as a Christian-identified faith. The same can be said of any white American Christianity that has not undertaken its own historical soul-searching and committed collectively to reconciliation and reparation for the massive moral wrongs of anti-Black systematic racism in the United States. Because I love my faith community and believe we can do better, I offer our experience to others as a witness and a warning.

NOTES

1. Gina Colvin, Elise Boxer, Laurie Maffly-Kipp, Melissa Inouye, and Janan Graham Russell, "Roundtable Discussion: Challenging Mormon Race Scholarship," *Journal of Mormon History* 41.3 (July 2015): 258–281, http://www.jstor.org.libproxy.sdsu.edu/stable/pdf/10.5406/jmormhist.41.3.258.pdf, last accessed February 28, 2018.

2. Alice Faulker Burch, "Black Women in the LDS Church and the Role of the Genesis Group," lecture delivered at the Mormon Women's History Initiative Breakfast, Mormon History Association Conference, June 11, 2016, http://www.mormonwomenshistoryinitiative.org/mwhit-breakfast-2016.html, last accessed March 1, 2018.

3. Heather Harris Bergevin, *Lawless Women* (Salt Lake City, UT: BCC Press, 2018).

4. Darron Smith, "Unpacking Whiteness in Zion: Some Personal Reflections and General Observations," in *Black and Mormon*, ed. Newell Bringhurst and Darron Smith (Urbana: University of Illinois, 2004), 148–166. See also Darron Smith, "The Persistence of Racialized Discourse in Mormonism," *Sunstone* 126 (2003): 31–33.

5. See Peggy Fletcher Stack, "Mountain Meadows Now a National Historic Landmark," *Salt Lake Tribune*, July 5, 2011, http://archive. sltrib.com/article.php?id=52107971&itype=CMSID, last accessed November 1, 2017.

6. On optimum tension, see Armand Mauss, *The Angel and the Beehive: The Mormon Struggle With Assimilation* (Urbana: University of Illinois Press, 1994), 7–11. On the value of folk belief in inerrancy to retrenchment, see especially Mauss's "The Mormon Struggle With Assimilation and Identity: Trends and Developments Since Midcentury," *Dialogue: A Journal of Mormon Thought* 27.1 (1994): 129–149. See also John Turner, "'All the Truth Does Not Always Need to Be Told': The LDS Church, Mormon History, and Religious Authority," in *Out of Obscurity: Mormonism Since 1945,* ed. Patrick Mason and John Turner (New York: Oxford University Press, 2015), 318–340.

BIBLIOGRAPHY

"35 Memorable Photos From the Church News Archives." *Deseret News*. September 29, 2014. https://www.deseretnews.com/top/2740/2/Donny-Osmonds-wedding-35-memorable-photos-from-the-LDS-Church-News-archives.html.

Aikau, Hokulani K. *A Chosen People, a Promised Land: Mormonism and Race in Hawai'i*. Minneapolis: University of Minnesota Press, 2012.

Alexander, Thomas G. *Mormonism in Transition: A History of the Latter-Day Saints, 1890–1930*. Champaign-Urbana: University of Illinois Press, 1996.

"An Interview With Gordon B. Hinckley," *60 Minutes*. April 7, 1996; web-published January 31, 2008. https://www.cbsnews.com/news/an-interview-with-gordon-hinckley/. Last accessed February 28, 2018.

Andrews, Wes, and Clyde Dalton. *The Black Hammer: A Study of Black Power, Red Influence and White Alternatives*. Oakland, CA: Desco Press, 1967.

Applebaum, Barbara. *Being White, Being Good: White Complicity, White Moral Responsibility, and Social Justice Pedagogy.*Lanham, Maryland: Lexington Books, 2010.

Arrington, Leonard J. "Dialogue's Valuable Service for LDS Intellectuals." *Dialogue: A Journal of Mormon Thought* 21.2 (1988); 134–136.
. https://www.dialoguejournal.com/wp-content/uploads/sbi/articles/Dialogue_V21No2_136.pdf.

Arrington, Leonard J. *Great Basin Kingdom: An Economic History of the Latter-Day Saints, 1830–1900*. Champaign-Urbana: University of Illinois Press, 2005.

Arrington, Leonard J., and Davis Bitton. *The Mormon Experience: A History of the Latter-Day Saints*. Champaign-Urbana: University of Illinois Press, 1992.

Baldwin, James. "My Dungeon Shook: Letter to My Nephew on the One Hundredth Anniversary of the Emancipation." In *The Fire Next Time*. New York: Dial Press, 1963.

"The Barbara Walters Special: Donny and Marie Osmond." February 1978. Published February 14, 2012. https://www.youtube.com/watch?v=bPWIEfmPYxo.

Barnes, Mark. "Byron's Song." *Ordain Women blog.* February 6, 2015. http://ordainwomen.org/byrons-song/. Last accessed February 12, 2018.

Barnes, Mark. "Raised a Mormon Feminist." *Ordain Women blog.* October 13, 2013. http://ordainwomen.org/raised-a-mormon-feminist/. Last accessed February 12, 2018.

Beecher, Maureen Ursenbach. "The Eliza Enigma." *Dialogue* 11 (1978): 40–43. http://www.dialoguejournal.com/wp-content/uploads/sbi/articles/Dialogue_VIINo1_33.pdf.

Bergera, Gary James. *Conflict in the Quorum: Orson Pratt, Brigham Young, Joseph Smith.* Salt Lake City: Signature Books, 2002.

Bergera, Gary James. "The Orson Pratt—Brigham Young Controversies: Conflict Within the Quorums, 1853–1868." *Dialogue: A Journal of Mormon Thought* 13.2 (1980): 7–49.

Bergera, Gary James, and Ronald Priddis. *Brigham Young University: A House of Faith.* Salt Lake City: Signature Books, 1985.

Berlin, C. Elliott. "Abraham Owen Smoot: Pioneer Mormon Leader." MA Thesis, Brigham Young University, 1955. http://scholarsarchive.byu.edu/cgi/viewcontent.cgi?article=5522&context=etd.

Bernstein, Robin. *Racial Innocence: Performing American Childhood and Race From Slavery to Civil Rights.* New York: New York University Press, 2011.

Bloom, Harold. *The American Religion: The Emergence of the Post-Christian Nation.* New York: Simon & Schuster, 1992.

Bringhurst, Newell G. "Forgotten Mormon Perspectives: Slavery, Race, and the Black Man as Issues Among Non-Utah Latter-day Saints, 1844–1873." *Michigan History* 61 (1977): 352–370.

Bringhurst, Newell G. "Joseph Smith's Ambiguous Legacy: Gender, Race, and Ethnicity as Dynamics for Schism Within Mormonism After 1844: 2006 Presidential Address to the John Whitmer Historical Association." *John Whitmer Historical Association Journal* 27 (2007): 1–47.

Bringhurst, Newell G. "The 'Missouri Thesis' Revisited: Early Mormonism, Slavery, and the Status of Black People." In *Black and Mormon*, ed. Newell Bringhurst and Darron Smith, 13–33. Urbana-Champaign: University of Illinois, 2004.

Bringhurst, Newell G. "The Mormons and Slavery: A Closer Look." *Pacific Historical Review* 50.3 (1981): 329–338. www.jstor.org/stable/3639603.

Bringhurst, Newell G. *Saints, Slaves, and Blacks: The Changing Place of Black People Within Mormonism.* Greenwood Press; Westport, CT; Rutgers UP: New Brunswick, NJ., 1981.

Brodkin, Karen. *How Jews Became White Folks and What That Says About Race in America.* New Brunswick, NJ: Rutgers University Press, 1998.

Brooke, James. "Memories of Lynching Divide a Town." *New York Times.* April 4, 1998. http://www.nytimes.com/1998/04/04/us/memories-of-lynching-divide-a-town.html.

Brooks, Joanna. "'On the Underground': What the Mormon 'Yes on 8' Campaign Reveals About Mormons in American Political Life." In *Mormonism and American Politics,* ed. Jana Riess and Randall Balmer, 192–209. New York: Columbia University Press, 2015.

Burch, Alice Faulker. "Black Women in the LDS Church and the Role of the Genesis Group." Lecture delivered at the Mormon Women's History Initiative Breakfast, Mormon History Association Conference. June 11, 2016. Http://www.mormonwomenshistoryinitiative.org/mwhit-breakfast-2016.html. Last accessed March 1, 2018.

Burlein, A. *Lift High the Cross: Where White Supremacy and the Christian Right Converge.* Durham, NC: Duke University Press, 2002.

Bush, Lester. "A Commentary on Stephen G. Taggart's Mormonism's Negro Policy: Social and Historical Origins." *Utah Historical Quarterly* 35 (1967): 67.

Bush, Lester. "Mormonism's Negro Doctrine: An Historical Overview." *Dialogue: A Journal of Mormon Thought* 8 (Spring 1973): 11–68. https://www.dialoguejournal.com/2012/mormonisms-negro-doctrine-an-historical-overview/.

Cacho, Lisa Marie. "The Presumption of White Innocence." *American Quarterly* 66.4 (2014): 1085–1090.

Carter, Kate B. *The Story of the Negro Pioneer.* Salt Lake City: Daughters of the Utah Pioneers, 1965.

Chotiner, Isaac. "Mormons Start Questioning Their History, Stumble on Racism." *New Republic.* July 22, 2013. https://newrepublic.com/article/113969/mormons-history-racism-and-religion. Last accessed February 28, 2018.

Christensen, James B. "Negro Slavery in the Utah Territory." *Phylon Quarterly* 18.3 (1957): 298–305.

The Church of Jesus Christ of Latter-day Saints. "Apostle Quentin L. Cook speaks on religious freedom at Princeton Theological Seminary." July 26, 2017. https://www.mormonnewsroom.org/article/transcript-%C2%Aoelder-quentin-l-cook-speaks-on-religious-freedom-at-princeton-university.

The Church of Jesus Christ of Latter-day Saints. "Apostle Says Religious Freedom is Being Threatened." October 13, 2009. https://www.mormonnewsroom.org/ldsnewsroom/eng/news-releases-stories/apostle-says-religious-freedom-is-being-threatened.

The Church of Jesus Christ of Latter-day Saints. Church History Department Pitman Shorthand Transcriptions, 2013–2017. "The Lost Sermons" publishing project files, 1852–1867.

The Church of Jesus Christ of Latter-day Saints. "Church Statement Regarding 'Washington Post' Article on Race and the Church." February 29, 2012. https://www.mormonnewsroom.org/article/racial-remarks-in-washington-post-article.

The Church of Jesus Christ of Latter-day Saints. "Statement on Symposia." November 1991. https://www.lds.org/ensign/1991/11/news-of-the-church/statement-on-symposia?lang=eng.

Cihak, Herbert. "Bryan, Populism, and Utah." MA Thesis, Brigham Young University, August 1975. https://scholarsarchive.byu.edu/cgi/viewcontent.cgi?referer=https://www.google.com/&httpsredir=1&article=5601&context=etd.

Cleveland, Henry. "Alexander H. Stephens, in Public and Private: With Letters and Speeches, Before, During, and Since the War." 1886. http://teachingamericanhistory.org/library/document/cornerstone-speech/.

Coleman, Ronald. "The African-American Pioneer Experience in Utah." Lecture delivered August 30, 2017, Wellsville Historical Society. https://www.youtube.com/watch?v=frD1lLeo75A.

Coleman, Ronald G. "Blacks in Utah history: An Unknown Legacy." Peoples of Utah 9.1 (1981): 115–140.

Colvin, Gina, Elise Boxer, Laurie Maffly-Kipp, Melissa Inouye, and Janan Russell-Graham. "Roundtable Discussion: Challenging Mormon Race Scholarship." Journal of Mormon History 41.3 (July 2015): 258–281. http://www.jstor.org.libproxy.sdsu.edu/stable/pdf/10.5406/jmormhist.41.3.258.pdf.

Colvin, Gina, and Joanna Brooks, eds. Decolonizing Mormonism: Approaching a Postcolonial Zion. Salt Lake City: University of Utah Press, 2018.

Cone, James. The Cross and the Lynching Tree. Maryknoll, NY: Orbis Books, 2011.

Cone, James. "Theology's Great Sin: Silence in the Face of White Supremacy." Black Theology 2.2 (2004): 139–152.

Dailey, J. "Sex, Segregation, and the Sacred After Brown." Journal of American History 91(1): 119–144.

Davidson, Sara. "Feeding on Dreams in a Bubble Gum Culture." *Atlantic Monthly*, October 1973: 72.

Delgado, Richard, and Jean Stefancic. *Critical White Studies: Looking Behind the Mirror.* Philadelphia: Temple University Press, 1997.

Derr, Jill Mulvay, and Karen Lynn Davidson. *Eliza R. Snow: The Complete Poetry.* Salt Lake City: BYU Press, 2009.

Dochuk, Darren. *From the Bible Belt to the Sun Belt: Plain-Folk Religion, Grassroots Politics, and the Rise of Evangelical Conservatism.* New York: Norton, 2012.

Doctrine and Covenants. The Church of Jesus Christ of Latter-day Saints. https://www.lds.org/scriptures/dc-testament/od/2. Last accessed February 28, 2018.

DuBois, W. E. B. *Darkwater: Voices From Within the Veil.* New York: Harcourt, Brace, Jovanovich, 1920.

duCille, Anne. "The Occult of True Black Womanhood: Critical Demeanor and Black Feminist Studies." In *The Second Signs Reader: Feminist Scholarship, 1983–1996,* ed. Ruth Ellen Joeres and Barbara Laslett, 70–108. Chicago: University of Chicago Press, 1996.

Duffy, John-Charles. "The Use of 'Lamanite' in Official LDS Discourse." *Journal of Mormon History* 34.1 (2008): 118–167.

Dupont, Carolyn Renee. *Mississippi Praying: Southern White Evangelicals and the Civil Rights Movement.* New York: New York University Press, 2015.

"Duritha Trail Lewis." Our Family Heritage. July 3, 2011. http://ourfamilyheritage.blogspot.com/2011/07/duritha-trail-lewis.html.

Embry, Jessie L. "LDS Ethnic Wards and Branches in the United States: The Advantages and Disadvantages of Language Congregations." *Deseret Language and Linguistic Society Symposium* 26 (2000): 6.

Emerson, Michael, and Christian Smith. *Divided by Faith: Evangelical Religion and the Problem of Race in America.* New York: Oxford University Press, 2000.

Erbaugh, Elizabeth B. "Women's Community Organizing and Identity Transformation." *Race, Gender & Class* 32.1 (2002): 8–32.

Esplin, Ronald K. "Brigham Young and Priesthood Denial to the Blacks: An Alternate View." *BYU Studies* 19.3 (1979): 394–402.

Fellows, Mary Louise, and Sherene Razack. "The Race to Innocence: Confronting Hierarchical Relations Among Women." *Journal of Gender Race & Justice* 1 (1997): 335.

Findlay, J. F. "Religion and Politics in the Sixties: The Churches and the Civil Rights Act of 1964." *Journal of American History* 77.1 (1990): 66–92.

Firmage, Edwin, and R. Collin Mangrum. *Zion in the Courts: A Legal History of the Church of Jesus Christ of Latter-day Saints, 1830–1900*. Urbana: University of Illinois Press, 2001.

Fishkin, Shelley Fisher. "Interrogating 'Whiteness,' Complicating 'Blackness': Remapping American Culture." *American Quarterly* 47.3 (September 1995): 428–466.

Flake, Kathleen. *The Politics of American Religious Identity: The Seating of Senator Reed Smoot, Mormon Apostle*. Chapel Hill: University of North Carolina Press, 2005.

Fluhman, J. Spencer. *"A Peculiar People": Anti-Mormonism and the Making of Religion in Nineteenth-Century America*. Chapel Hill: University of North Carolina Press Books, 2012.

Foster, Lawrence. "From Frontier Activism to Neo-Victorian Domesticity: Mormon Women in the Nineteenth and Twentieth Centuries." *Journal of Mormon History* 6 (1979): 3–21.

Geary, Edward. "Mormondom's Lost Generation: The Novelists of the 1940s." *BYU Studies* 18.1 (1978). https://scholarsarchive.byu.edu/byusq/vol18/iss1/7.

"George Romney and the Delbert Stapley Letter." *Thoughts on Things and Stuff*. June 14, 2015. http://thoughtsonthingsandstuff.com/george-romney-and-the-delbert-stapley-letter/. Last accessed February 12, 2018.

Gilmore, Ruth Wilson. "Race and Globalization." In *Geographies of Global Change*, 2nd ed., ed. P. J. Taylor, R. L. Johnstone, and M. J. Watts, 261. Oxford: Blackwell, 2002.

Givens, Terryl. *By the Hand of Mormon: The American Scripture That Launched a New World Religion*. New York: Oxford University Press, 2002.

Givens, Terryl. *The Viper on the Hearth: Mormons, Myths, and the Construction of Heresy*. New York: Oxford University Press, 2013.

Givens, Terryl. *Wrestling the Angel: The Foundations of Mormon Thought: Cosmos, God, Humanity*. Vol. 1. Oxford: Oxford University Press, 2014.

Goodstein, Laurie. "A Leader's Admission of 'Mistakes' Heartens Some Doubting Mormons." *New York Times*. October 8, 2013. http://www.nytimes.com/2013/10/09/us/a-leaders-admission-of-mistakes-heartens-some-doubting-mormons.html.

Goodstein, Laurie. "Some Mormons Search the Web and Find Doubt." *New York Times*. July 21, 2013. http://www.nytimes.com/2013/07/21/us/some-mormons-search-the-web-and-find-doubt.html?ref=todayspaper&_r=0&pagewanted=print.

Gotanda, Neil. "Reflections on Korematsu, Brown and White Innocence." *Temple Political & Civil Rights Law Review* 13 (2003): 663.

Griffin, Gail B. "Speaking of Whiteness: Disrupting White Innocence." *Journal of the Midwest Modern Language Association* 31.3 (1998): 3–14.

Grover, Mark L. "The Mormon Priesthood Revelation and the Sao Paulo, Brazil Temple." *Dialogue: A Journal of Mormon Thought* 23.1 (1990): 39–53. http://www.dialoguejournal.com/wp-content/uploads/sbi/articles/Dialogue_V17N03_25.pdf.

Guitterrez, K. D. "White Innocence: A Framework and Methodology for Rethinking Educational Discourse and Inquiry." *International Journal of Learning* 12.10 (2005): 223–229.

Hague, Dyson. "The Doctrinal Value of the First Chapter of Genesis." In *The Fundamentals*, vol. 1, ed. R. A. Torrey, A. C. Dixon, et al. Chicago, IL: Testimony Publishing Company, 1910. https://archive.org/details/fundamentalstest17chic.

Hardy, B. Carmon. "Lords of Creation: Polygamy, the Abrahamic Household, and Mormon Patriarchy." *Journal of Mormon History* 20.1 (1994): 119–152.

Harrill, J. Albert. "The Use of the New Testament in the American Slave Controversy: A Case History in the Hermeneutical Tension Between Biblical Criticism and Christian Moral Debate." *Religion and American Culture: A Journal of Interpretation* 10.2 (Summer 2000): 149–186.

Harris, F. C. "Something Within: Religion as a Mobilizer of African-American Political Activism." *Journal of Politics* 56.1 (1994): 42–68.

Harris, Matthew L., and Newell G. Bringhurst. *The Mormon Church and Blacks: A Documentary History.* Champaign-Urbana: University of Illinois Press, 2015.

Hartley, William G. "From Men to Boys: LDS Aaronic Priesthood Offices, 1829–1996." *Journal of Mormon History* 22.1 (1996): 80–136.

Hartley, William. "The Priesthood Reform Movement, 1908–1922." *BYU Studies* 13.2 (1973): 137–156.

Harvey, Jennifer. *Dear White Christians: For Those Still Longing for Racial Reconciliation.* Grand Rapids, MI: William B. Eerdmans, 2014.

Hawkins, J. Russell, and Phillip Luke Sinitiere. *Christians and the Color Line: Race and Religion After Divided by Faith.* New York: Oxford University Press, 2013.

Haws, J. B. *The Mormon Image in the American Mind.* Oxford: Oxford University Press, 2015.

Haynes, Stephen. *The Last Segregated Hour: The Memphis Kneel-Ins and the Campaign for Southern Church Desegregation.* New York: Oxford University Press, 2012.

Haynes, Stephen R. *Noah's Curse: The Biblical Justification of American Slavery.* New York: Oxford University Press, 2002.

Herman, Daniel. "Arizona's Secret History: When Powerful Mormons Went Separate Ways." *Commonplace* 12.3 (2012). http://www.common-place-archives.org/vol-12/no-03/herman/.

Hickman, Martin B. "The Political Legacy of Joseph Smith." *Dialogue: A Journal of Mormon Thought* 3.3 (1968): 23.

Hicks, Michael. *The Mormon Tabernacle Choir: A Biography.* Urbana: University of Illinois Press, 2015.

Hill, Marvin. *Quest for Refuge: The Mormon Flight From American Pluralism.* Salt Lake City: Signature Books, 1989.

Hinckley, Gordon B. "The Need for Greater Kindness." April 2006. https://www.lds.org/general-conference/2006/04/the-need-for-greater-kindness?lang=eng.

hooks, bell. *Feminist Theory: From Margin to Center.* 1985. Rpt. Boston: South End Press, 2000.

Horowitz, Jason. "The Genesis of a Church's Stand on Race." *Washington Post.* February 28, 2012. https://www.washingtonpost.com/politics/the-genesis-of-a-churchs-stand-on-race/2012/02/22/gIQAQZXyfR_story.html?utm_term=.8192b720336e.

Horton, James Oliver. "Generations of Protest: Black Families and Social Reform in Ante-Bellum Boston." *New England Quarterly* 49.2 (1976): 242–256.

Houck, D. W., and D. E. Dixon. *Rhetoric, Religion and the Civil Rights Movement, 1954–1965.* Waco, TX: Baylor University Press, 2006.

Hunt, Cecil J. "The Color of Perspective: Affirmative Action and the Constitutional Rhetoric of White Innocence." *Michigan Journal of Race and the Law* 11 (2005): 477.

Hyde, Orson. "Slavery Among the Saints." *Latter-day Saints' Millennial Star* 13 (April 15, 1851). http://contentdm.lib.byu.edu/cdm/ref/collection/MStar/id/2335.

Ignatiev, Noel. *How the Irish became White.* New York: Verso, 1995.

Ioanide, Paula. "The Alchemy of Race and Affect: 'White Innocence' and Public Secrets in the Post–Civil Rights Era." *Kalfou* 1.1 (2014): 151–168.

James, Jane Manning. "The Autobiography of Jane Manning James: Seven Decades of Faith and Devotion." In *LDS Church History,* ed. James Goldberg. December 2013. https://history.lds.org/article/jane-manning-james-life-sketch?lang=eng.

Johnson, Jeffery O. "Change and Growth: The Mormon Church and the 1960s." *Sunstone* 17 (June 1994): 28.

Johnson, Kirk. "Mormons on a Mission." *New York Times,* August 20, 2010. http://www.nytimes.com/2010/08/22/arts/music/22choir.html?pagewanted=all.

Johnson, Lyndon B. "Annual Message to Congress on the State of the Union, January 4, 1965." The American Presidency Project. http://www.presidency. ucsb.edu/ws/index.php?pid=26907.

Johnson, Sylvester. *The Myth of Ham in Nineteenth-Century American Christianity*. New York: Palgrave Macmillan, 2004.

Jones, Christopher C. "'We Latter-day Saints Are Methodists': The Influence of Methodism on Early Mormon Religiosity." MA Thesis, Brigham Young University, 2009.

Jorgenson, Danny L. "Dissent and Schism in the Early Church: Explaining Mormon Fissiparousness." *Dialogue: A Journal of Mormon Thought* 28.3 (1995): 15–39.

Keating, AnaLouise. "Interrogating 'Whiteness,' (De)Constructing 'Race.'" *College English* 57 (1995): 901–918.

Kimball, Edward. "The History of LDS Temple Admission Standards." *Journal of Mormon History* 24.1 (1998). https://digitalcommons.usu.edu/cgi/ viewcontent.cgi?referer=https://www.google.com/&httpsredir=1&article=103 0&context=mormonhistory.

Kimball, Edward. "Spencer W. Kimball and the Revelation on Priesthood." *BYU Studies* 47.2 (2008): 5–78.

King, Martin Luther, Jr. Interview on "Meet the Press." April 17, 1960. https:// www.youtube.com/watch?v=1q881g1L_d8.

Klemsrud, Judy. "Strengthening Family Solidarity With a Home Evening Program." *New York Times*. June 4, 1973, 46. http://www.nytimes.com/ 1973/06/04/archives/strengthening-family-solidarity-with-a-home-evening-program.html.

Kuhl, Michelle. *Lynching Beyond Dixie: American Mob Violence Outside the South*. Logan: Utah State University Press, 2015.

Lacy, Michael G. "White Innocence Heroes: Recovery, Reversals, Paternalism, and David Duke." *Journal of International and Intercultural Communication* 3.3 (2010): 206–227.

Lacy, Michael G. "White Innocence Myths in Citizen Discourse, the Progressive Era (1974–1988)." *Howard Journal of Communications* 21.1 (2010): 20–39.

Lapahie, Harrison. "George P. Lee Archive, Including Transcriptions and Speeches." http://www.lapahie.com/George_Patrick_Lee.cfm.

Launius, Roger D. "'Many Mansions': The Dynamics of Dissent in the Nineteenth-Century Reorganized Church." *Journal of Mormon History* 17 (1991): 145–168.

Launius, Roger D., and Linda Thatcher. *Differing Visions: Dissenters in Mormon History*. Urbana: University of Illinois Press, 1998.

Lee, George P. *Silent Courage: An Indian Story: The Autobiography of George P. Lee, a Navajo.* Salt Lake City: Shadow Mountain, 1987.

Lensmire, Timothy J. "Ambivalent White Racial Identities: Fear and an Elusive Innocence." *Race, Ethnicity, and Education* 13.2 (2010): 159–172.

Lipsitz, George. *The Possessive Investment in Whiteness: How White People Profit From Identity Politics.* Philadelphia: Temple University Press, 2006.

Longazel, Jamie G. "Rhetorical Barriers to Mobilizing for Immigrant Rights: White Innocence and Latina/O Abstraction." *Law & Social Inquiry* 39.2 (2014): 580–600.

Lythgoe, Dennis L. "Negro Slavery and Mormon Doctrine." *Western Humanities Review* 21.4 (1967): 327.

Lythgoe, Dennis Leo. "Negro Slavery in Utah." MA Thesis, Department of History, University of Utah, 1966.

Mackey, Eva. "As Good as It Gets?: Apology, Colonialism and White Innocence." *Bulletin (Olive Pink Society)* 11.1–2 (1999): 34.

Madsen, Brigham D. "B. H. Roberts's Studies of the Book of Mormon." *Dialogue: A Journal of Mormon Thought* 26 (Fall 1993): 77–86.

Madsen, Brigham D. "Reflections on LDS Disbelief in the Book of Mormon as History." *Dialogue: A Journal of Mormon Thought* 30 (Fall 1997): 87–97.

Maffly, Brian. "Utah's Dixie Was Steeped in Slave Culture, Historians Say." *Salt Lake Tribune.* December 10, 2012. http://archive.sltrib.com/article.php?id=55 424505&itype=CMSID.

Makgoeng, April. "God Made Adam White: Constructions of Race in the Juvenile Instructor, 1866–1906." MA Thesis, Claremont Graduate University, 2017.

"The Lee Letters." *Sunstone Magazine* 72 (November 1989). https://www. sunstonemagazine.com/wp-content/uploads/sbi/issues/072.pdf.

Marchant, Michelle. "My Life Is a Gift, My Life Has a Plan." BYU Devotional Address. April 2, 2013. https://speeches.byu.edu/talks/michelle-marchant_ my-life-is-a-gift-my-life-has-a-plan/.

"Marvin Perkins: We Are One." *Main Street Plaza.* February 4, 2011. https:// mainstreetplaza.com/2011/02/04/marvin-perkins-one/.

Marx, G. T. "Religion: Opiate or Inspiration of Civil Rights Militancy Among Negroes?" *American Sociological Review* 32.1 (1967): 64–72.

Mary Ann (pseudonym). "Wife With a Purpose: Mormonism's Alt-Right Representative." *Wheat and Tares blog.* August 15, 2017. https://wheatandtares. org/2017/08/15/wife-with-a-purpose-mormonisms-alt-right-representative/.

Mason, Patrick. *The Mormon Menace: Violence and Anti-Mormonism in the Postbellum South.* New York: Oxford University Press, 2011.

Mauss, Armand L. *All Abraham's Children: Changing Mormon Conceptions of Race and Lineage*. Urbana: University of Illinois Press, 2005.

Mauss, Armand L. *The Angel and the Beehive: The Mormon Struggle With Assimilation*. Champaign-Urbana: University of Illinois Press, 1994.

Mauss, Armand L. "Casting Off the Curse of Cain: The Extent and Limits of Progress Since 1978." In *Black and Mormon*, ed. Newell Bringhurst and Darron T. Smith, 82–115. Urbana: University of Illinois, 2004.

Mauss, Armand L. "In Search of Ephraim: Traditional Mormon Conceptions of Lineage and Race." *Journal of Mormon History* 25.1 (1999): 131–173.

Mauss, Armand L. "The Mormon Struggle With Assimilation and Identity: Trends and Developments Since Midcentury." *Dialogue: A Journal of Mormon Thought* 27.1 (1994): 129–149.

Mauss, Armand L. "Mormonism's Worldwide Aspirations and Its Changing Conceptions of Race and Lineage." *Dialogue: A Journal of Mormon Thought* 34.3–4 (2001): 103–133.

Mauss, Armand L. "Refuge and Retrenchment: The Mormon Quest for Identity." In *Contemporary Mormonism: Social Science Perspectives*, eds. Marie Cornwall, Tim Heaton, and Lawrence A. Young, 24–42. Urbana: University of Illinois Press, 1994.

McConkie, Bruce R. "All Are Alike Unto God." CES Religious Educators Symposium. August 18, 1978. https://speeches.byu.edu/talks/bruce-r-mcconkie_alike-unto-god-2.

McRae, Elizabeth Gillespie. *Mothers of Massive Resistance: White Women and the Politics of White Supremacy*. New York: Oxford University Press, 2018.

Morgan, John. "The Southern States Mission . . . Discourse by Elder John Morgan, Delivered in the Assembly Hall, Salt Lake City, Sunday Afternoon, December 18, 1881." *Journal of Discourses* 23.6 (1883). http://scriptures.byu.edu/jod/jodhtml.php?vol=23&disc=06.

Morris, A. "The Black Church in the Civil Rights Movement: The SCLC as the Decentralized, Radical Arm of the Black Church." In *Disruptive Religion: The Force of Faith in Social Movement Activism,* ed. Christian Smith, 29–46. New York: Routledge, 1996.

Morrison, Toni. *Playing in the Dark: Whiteness and the Literary Imagination*. New York: Vintage, 1992.

Mouritsen, Dale C. "The Relationship of the Priesthood Correlation Program to the Latter-Day Saint Concept of Zion." MA Thesis, Brigham Young University, 1968.

Mueller, Max. "Introduction: Beyond 'Race and the Priesthood.'" *Journal of Mormon History* 41.3 (July 2015): 1–10. http://www.jstor.org.libproxy.sdsu. edu/stable/pdf/10.5406/jmormhist.41.3.1.pdf?refreqid=excelsior%3A135f3791 odcffd48f0c38db674408d0f.

Mueller, Max Perry. *Race and the Making of the Mormon People.* Chapel Hill: University of North Carolina Press, 2017.

Nelson, Lowry. Letter to the Editor. *Dialogue: A Journal of Mormon Thought* 2.3 (Fall 1967): 7. https://www.dialoguejournal.com/wp-content/uploads/sbi/ articles/Dialogue_Vo2No3_7.pdf.

Nelson, Lowry. "Mormons and Blacks." *Christian Century.* October 16, 1974, 949–950.

Nelson, Lowry. Papers. University of Utah Marriot Library Special Collections.

Newell, Linda King, and Valeen Tippetts Avery. "Jane Manning James." *Ensign.* August 1979. https://www.lds.org/ensign/1979/08/jane-manning-james-black-saint-1847-pioneer?lang=eng#note19-.

Newell, Quincy D. *Your Sister in the Gospel: The Life of Jane Manning James, a Nineteenth-Century Black Mormon.* New York: Oxford University Press, 2019.

Nolan, Tom. "The Family Plan of the Latter-day Osmonds." *Rolling Stone.* March 11, 1976, 46–52.

Noll, Mark. *Between Faith and Criticism: Evangelicals, Scholarship, and the Bible in America.* Vancouver: Regent College Publishing, 2002.

O'Donovan, Connell. "The Mormon Priesthood Ban and Elder Q. Walker Lewis: 'An Example for His More Whiter Brethren to Follow.'" *John Whitmer Historical Association Journal* 26 (2006): 48–100.

Orozco, Richard, and Jesus Jaime Diaz. "'Suited to Their Needs': White Innocence as a Vestige of Segregation." *Multicultural Perspectives* 18.3 (2016): 127–133.

Osmond, Donny. "My Beliefs: Questions and Answers." https://donny.com/my_beliefs/do-you-honestly-think-black-people-worldwide-dont-deserve-public-apology/.

Papanikolas, Helen. *The Peoples of Utah.* Salt Lake City: Utah State Historical Society, 1976.

Pavlik, Steve. "Of Saints and Lamanites: An Analysis of Navajo Mormonism." *Wicazo Sa Review* 8.1 (1992): 21–30.

Perlich, Pamela. "Utah Minorities: The Story Told by 150 Years of Census Data." Bureau of Economic and Business Research, Eccles School of Business, University of Utah. October 2002. http://gardner.utah.edu/bebr/Documents/ studies/Utah_Minorities.pdf.

Petersen, Boyd. "Hugh Nibley and the 'Inmigration' of Mormon Education." Unpublished ms. November 6, 2009.

Peterson, F. Ross. "'Do Not Lecture the Brethren': Stewart L. Udall's Pro-Civil Rights Stance, 1967." *Journal of Mormon History* 25.1 (1999): 272–287.

Peterson, Levi. "Juanita Brooks as a Mormon Dissenter." *John Whitmer Historical Association* 8 (1998): 29. https://www.jstor.org/stable/43200808?seq=1#page_scan_tab_contents.

Pew Research Center. "Religious Landscape Study: Racial and Ethnic Composition." 2014. http://www.pewforum.org/religious-landscape-study/racial-and-ethnic-composition.

Phelps, William W. "Free People of Color." *Evening and Morning Star* 2.14 (1833): 217–218.

Picower, Bree. "The Unexamined Whiteness of Teaching: How White Teachers Maintain and Enact Dominant Racial Ideologies." *Race, Ethnicity, and Education* 12.2 (2009): 197–215.

Pierce, Jennifer L. "'Racing for Innocence': Whiteness, Corporate Culture, and the Backlash Against Affirmative Action." *Qualitative Sociology* 26.1 (2003): 53–70.

Poll, Richard D., and Martin Hickman. "Joseph Smith's Presidential Platform." *Dialogue: A Journal of Mormon Thought* 3.3 (1968): 19–23.

Potz, Maciej. "The Politics of Schism: The Origins of Dissent in Mormonism." *Studia Religiologica* 3 (2016): 203–218.

"Proposition 8 and the School Debate." *Santa Clarita Valley Signal.* October 31. 2008. http://archive.signalscv.com/archives/5472/.

"A Proposition 8 Roundtable With Sonja Eddings Brown, Marvin Perkins, and Jon Stewart." *Latter-day Chino.* November 2008. http://www.chinoblanco.com/2008/11/prop-8-rountable-with-sonja-eddings.html.

"Proposition 8: Showdown." *The Economist.* October 30, 2008. https://www.economist.com/node/12522924.

Quinn, D. Michael. "Ezra Taft Benson and Mormon Political Conflicts." *Dialogue: A Journal of Mormon Thought* 26.2 (Summer 1992): 1–87.

Quinn, D. Michael. *The Mormon Hierarchy: Extensions of Power.* Salt Lake City: Signature Books, 1997.

Reed, Roy. "Wallace Seeks Mormon Votes. Draws Big Tabernacle Crowd." *New York Times.* October 13, 1968. https://timesmachine.nytimes.com/timesmachine/1968/10/13/317688762.html.

Reeve, W. Paul. "Guest Post: Newly Discovered Document Provides Dramatic Details About Elijah Able and the Priesthood." *Keepapitchinin.* January 18, 2019. http://www.keepapitchinin.org/2019/01/18/guest-post-newly-discovered-document-provides-dramatic-details-about-elijah-able-and-the-priesthood/.

Reeve, W. Paul. *Religion of a Different Color: Race and the Mormon Struggle for Whiteness*. New York: Oxford University Press, 2015.

Rich, Christopher B., Jr. "The True Policy for Utah: Servitude, Slavery, and 'an Act in Relation to Service.'" *Utah Historical Quarterly* 80 (2012): 54–74.

Ricks, Nathaniel R. "A Peculiar Place for the Peculiar Institution: Slavery and Sovereignty in Early Territorial Utah." MA Thesis, Brigham Young University, 2007.

Roberts, B. H. *A Comprehensive History of the Church*. Vol. 4. Salt Lake City: Church of Jesus Christ of Latter-day Saints, 1930.

Rodriguez, Dalia. "Investing in White innocence: Colorblind Racism, White Privilege, and the New White Racist Fantasy." In *Teaching Race in the Twenty-First Century*, ed. Lisa Guerrero, 123–134. New York: Palgrave Macmillan, 2008.

"Romney Assails Racial Injustice." *New York Times*. February 20, 1967, 30. https://timesmachine.nytimes.com/timesmachine/1967/02/20/82593994.html?pageNumber=30.

Ross, R. E. *Witnessing and Testifying: Black Women, Religion, and Civil Rights.* New York: Fortress Press, 2003.

Ross, Thomas. "Innocence and Affirmative Action." *Vanderbilt Law Review* 43.297 (1990a): 297.

Ross, Thomas. "The Rhetorical Tapestry of Race: White Innocence and Black Abstraction." *William and Mary Law Review* 32 (1990): 1.

Ross, Thomas. "White Innocence, Black Abstraction." In *Critical White Studies: Looking Behind the Mirror*, eds. Richard Delgado and Jean Stefancic, 263–266. Philadelphia: Temple UP, 1997.

Rove, Karl. *Courage and Consequence: My Life as a Conservative in the Fight*. New York: Threshold Books, 2010.

Seymour Institute. "The Black Church and Religious Freedom in the Age of Trump." https://www.seymourinstitute.com/summer-seminar-1.html.

Shipps, Jan. "Making Saints: In the Early Days and the Latter Days." In *Contemporary Mormonism: Social Science Perspectives*, eds. Marie Cornwall, Tim Heaton, and Lawrence A. Young, 64–83. Urbana: University of Illinois Press, 1994.

Shipps, Jan. *Sojourner in the Promised Land: Forty Years Among the Mormons*. Urbana: University of Illinois Press, 2000.

Smith, Darron. "The Persistence of Racialized Discourse in Mormonism." *Sunstone* 126 (2003): 31–33.

Smith, Darron. "Unpacking Whiteness in Zion: Some Personal Reflections and General Observations." In *Black and Mormon*, ed. Newell Bringhurst and Darron Smith, 148–166. Urbana: University of Illinois, 2004.

Smith, Daymon. *The Last Shall Be First and the First Shall Be Last: Discourse and Mormon History*. PhD Dissertation, University of Pennsylvania, 2007.

Smith, Joseph F. "The Negro and the Priesthood." *Improvement Era*. April 1924. https://archive.org/stream/improvementera2706unse#page/564/mode/2up.

Smith, William Benjamin. *The Color Line: A Plea for the Unborn*. New York: McClure and Phillips, 1905. https://ia800504.us.archive.org/7/items/colorlinebriefinoosmit/colorlinebriefinoosmit.pdf.

Snow, Eliza R. "The New Year 1852." *Deseret News*. January 10, 1852, 1.

Stack, Peggy Fletcher. "39 Years Later, Priesthood Ban Is History, but Racism Within Mormon Ranks Isn't, Black Members Say." *Salt Lake Tribune*. June 9, 2017. http://archive.sltrib.com/article.php?id=5371962&itype=CMSID.

Stack, Peggy Fletcher. "Mountain Meadows Now a National Historic Landmark." *Salt Lake Tribune*. July 5, 2011. http://archive.sltrib.com/article.php?id=52107971&itype=CMSID.

Stack, Peggy Fletcher. "New Mormon Mission: How to Teach Members the Messy Part of LDS History." *Salt Lake Tribune*. March 8, 2015. http://www.sltrib.com/home/2229999-155/new-mormon-mission- how-to-teach?fullpage=.

Stack, Peggy Fletcher. "New Mormon Scriptures Tweak Race, Polygamy References." *Salt Lake Tribune*. March 19, 2013. http://archive.sltrib.com/article.php?id=55930173&itype=CMSID.

Stapley, Jonathan. *The Power of Godliness: Mormon Liturgy and Cosmology*. New York: Oxford University Press, 2018.

Stathis, Stephen W., and Dennis L. Lythgoe. "Mormonism in the 1970s: Popular Perception." *Dialogue: A Journal of Mormon Thought* 10.3 (1977): 95–113.

Stauffer, John, and Benjamin Soskis. *The Battle Hymn of the Republic: A Biography of the Song That Marches On*. New York: Oxford University Press, 2013.

Stephens, Calvin Robert. "The Life and Contributions of Zebedee Coltrin." MA Thesis, Brigham Young University, 1974.

"Stewart Udall: Conscience of a Jack Mormon." https://archive.org/stream/StewartUdallConscienceOfAJackMormon/StuartUdall-OpenLetterOnRaceAndConsequencesOfConscience#page/n52/mode/1up.

Sullivan, Kathleen M. "Sins of Discrimination: Last Term's Affirmative Action Cases." *Harvard Law Review* 100 (1986): 78.

Taylor, Samuel. "The Ordeal of Lowry Nelson." *Dialogue* 26.3 (2012): 91–99.

Third District Court, Salt Lake County Probate Case Files, No. 39, "in the Matter of David Lewis." 1855. http://images.archives.utah.gov/cdm/ref/collection/p17010coll30/id/590.

Trainor, Jennifer Seibel. "'My Ancestors Didn't Own Slaves': Understanding White Talk About Race." *Research in the Teaching of English* 40.2 (2005): 140–167.

Turner, John. "'All the Truth Does Not Always Need to Be Told': The LDS Church, Mormon History, and Religious Authority." In *Out of Obscurity: Mormonism Since 1945*, ed. John Turner and Patrick Mason, 318–340. New York: Oxford University Press, 2015.

Turner, John. *Brigham Young: Pioneer Prophet*. Cambridge, MA: Harvard Belknap, 2012.

Turner, Wallace. "Mormon Liberals Expect No Change." *New York Times*. January 25, 1970. http://www.nytimes.com/1970/01/25/archives/mormon-liberals-expect-no-change-smith-mckays-successor-backs.html.

Udall, Stewart. Letter to the Editor. *Dialogue: A Journal of Mormon Thought* 2 (Summer 1967): 5–7. https://www.dialoguejournal.com/wp-content/uploads/sbi/issues/V02N02.pdf.

Walker, Joseph. "LDS Church Condemns Past Racism Inside and Outside the Church." *Deseret News*. February 29, 2012. https://www.deseretnews.com/article/765555339/LDS-Church-condemns-past-racism-inside-and-outside-the-church.html.

Walquist, Tammy. "Utah Lynching May Have Been Last." *Deseret Morning News*. June 19, 2005. https://www.deseretnews.com/article/600142549/Utah-lynching-may-have-been-last.html.

Walton, Brian. "A University's Dilemma: B.Y.U. and Blacks." *Dialogue* 6 (Spring 1971): 35.

Wekker, Gloria. *White Innocence: Paradoxes of Colonialism and Race*. Durham, NC: Duke University Press, 2016.

Whitney, Helen. "Interview: Jeffrey Holland." *PBS American Experience/Frontline: The Mormons*. March 4, 2006. http://www.pbs.org/mormons/interviews/holland.html.

Widtsoe, James. *Rational Theology*. 1937. https://archive.org/details/rationaltheologywidtsoe.

Wilkinson, Ernest L., ed. *Brigham Young University: The First One Hundred Years*. Provo: Brigham Young University Press, 1976.

Williams, Don B. *Slavery in Utah Territory: 1847–1865*. Salt Lake City, UT: Mt. Zion Books, 2004.

Williams, J. E. *African American Religion and the Civil Rights Movement in Arkansas*. Oxford: University Press of Mississippi, 2003.

Woodworth, Jed L. "Refusing to Die: Financial Crisis at Brigham Young Academy, 1877–1897." *BYU Studies Quarterly* 38.1 (1999): 9.

Yorgason, Ethan R. *Transformation of the Mormon Culture Region*. Champaign-Urbana: University of Illinois Press, 2003.

Young, Brigham. Addresses. Box 48, LDS Church Historical Department, Salt Lake City, Utah. https://archive.org/details/CR100317B0001F0017.

Young, Margaret Blair. "A Few Words From Orson Pratt." *Patheos*. June 11, 2014. http://www.patheos.com/blogs/welcometable/2014/06/a-few-words-from-orson-pratt/.

Young, Margaret Blair, and Darius Gray. *Bound for Canaan*. Revised and expanded. Salt Lake City: Zarahemla Books, 2013.

Young, Margaret Blair, and Darius Aidan Gray. "Mormons and Race." In *The Oxford Handbook of Mormonism*, eds. Philip Barlow and Terryl Givens. 363. New York: Oxford University Press, 2015.

INDEX

For the benefit of digital users, indexed terms that span two pages (e.g., 52–53) may, on occasion, appear on only one of those pages.